s in Legal History

ed by The University of North Carolina Press
ciation with the American Society for Legal History

R

ard White

RIAL BOARD

Cushing   George L. Haskins
ce M. Friedman   J. Willard Hurst
M. Gray   S. F. C. Milsom
Andrew Green   L. Kinvin Wroth
landlin

Custo
Kinshi
and G
to Sai

Stud

Publ
in as

EDIT

G. E

EDIT

John

Lawr

Charl

Thom

Oscar

Custom, Kinship, and Gifts to Saints

The *Laudatio Parentum* in Western France, 1050–1150

Stephen D. White

The University of North Carolina Press

Chapel Hill & London

Both the initial research and the publication of this work were made possible in part through a grant from the National Endowment for the Humanities, a federal agency whose mission is to award grants to support education, scholarship, media programming, libraries, and museums, in order to bring the results of cultural activities to a broad, general public.

The paper in this book meets the guidelines for permanence and durability of the Committee on Production Guidelines for Book Longevity of the Council on Library Resources.

92 91 90 89 88   5 4 3 2 1

Library of Congress Cataloging-in-Publication Data

White, Stephen D., 1945–
  Custom, kinship, and gifts to saints: the laudatio parentum
in western France, 1050–1150 / by Stephen D. White.
      p. cm.—(Studies in legal history)
  Bibliography: p.
  Includes index.
  ISBN 0-8078-1779-1 (alk. paper)
    1. Transfer (Law)—France—History. 2. Kinship (Law)—France—
History. 3. Law, Medieval—History. 4. Kinship—France—History.
I. Title. II. Series.
KJV1238.W48 1988
346.4404'36—dc19   87-30028
[344.406436]   CIP

TO KATE

Contents

Figures

Tables

Preface

WHEN I FIRST decided to examine the history of
the *laudatio parentum*, I planned on writing a brief, narrowly focused study that would be securely located in the field of medieval
legal history. Gradually, however, I realized that I could make better sense of this subject by broadening and reconceptualizing my
approach to it. Without abandoning my original intention to focus
primarily on the legal or normative aspects of the *laudatio*, I tried
to consider its history in relation to several other topics in the
history of medieval kinship and monasticism.

At the same time, as I became dissatisfied with my own ideas
about what earlier medieval law or custom consisted of, what "the
medieval family" was, what medieval people were doing when
they made or participated in gifts, and what constitutes a satisfactory way of explaining a medieval custom or social practice, I
turned for help to various writings of social theory and to anthropological studies of law, kinship, and gift-exchange because I was
convinced that historians, as various scholars have recently
shown, can learn a great deal from anthropology, even though
they can hardly expect to master the intricacies of this field.

Finally, while retaining considerable scepticism about the meaning and even the meaningfulness of certain kinds of tables designed to represent the statistical prevalence of medieval practices
such as the *laudatio*, I decided to construct and present some tables of my own—partly because I myself sometimes found them
meaningful, interesting, or at least suggestive and partly because I
wanted to allow readers to decide for themselves what meaning, if
any, to give them and to judge how effectively I had dealt with
certain problems that are partly statistical in character.

If the resulting book seems longer and more analytically complex than one might expect, this is mainly because I follow many
other historians in treating the *laudatio* as an important practice
that is itself worthy of close study. In addition, I believe that a
detailed discussion of this practice provides a useful framework
for considering more general problems in medieval history, notably the role of law or custom in societies that lacked many of the

features of more familiar legal cultures. Even though it is dangerous simply to assume that obscure rituals and puzzling customs provide important evidence about an entire society, I think that this assumption is justified in the case of the *laudatio*.

Because the history of the *laudatio parentum* in many parts of France has been treated in detail by earlier writers, I have seen no need to retrace their steps, but have concentrated instead on several thousand charters from several religious communities in the Touraine, the Vendômois, Anjou, and Maine during a period running from the mid-eleventh to the mid-twelfth century. Although I hope that my conclusions based on these materials will prove illuminating, I trust that future writers will extend, modify, and correct my arguments by studying evidence I have not considered. In particular, I hope that conclusions drawn from the study of monastic charters can be developed and criticized by historians working on other kinds of evidence. Possessing some of the trappings of a monograph, the book is an analytical essay, in which notes and bibliographical references have been kept to a minimum.

The book is meant to be read as a consecutive, integrated argument, in which many topics first discussed and documented in earlier chapters are considered in later ones from a different perspective. Chapters 5 and 6, especially, draw very heavily on material presented in earlier parts of the book. Although I have therefore included a fair number of cross-references, I have tried to avoid wearying readers with too many of them and have often proceeded on the assumption that once arguments or data have first been introduced, they will be familiar to readers and need not necessarily be documented when they reappear later on.

In referring to many individuals who play a part in the history of the *laudatio parentum*, my main concern has been to ensure that readers will be able to locate them in medieval sources, if they wish. In giving the first element of a medieval name, I have therefore followed the practice, in almost all cases, of using one of the Latin forms employed by a medieval scribe. I have translated the second element of a name only when I felt certain about the translation of a toponym or when I could not resist translating colorful and fully comprehensible cognomens. Translations from the Vulgate have been taken from the Douay/Rheims version.

Acknowledgments

I WISH TO THANK two teachers of mine, Giles Constable and Samuel E. Thorne, for introducing me to many of the issues considered in this book and for encouraging me to do further work on the *laudatio parentum*. Special thanks are due as well to Fredric L. Cheyette, who taught me a great deal about the subjects treated in this book, and to Caroline Walker Bynum and Patrick J. Geary, both of whom provided valuable comments on earlier drafts. I am also deeply indebted to Paul R. Hyams and William Ian Miller, who have generously shared with me their own ideas about medieval legal and social history and constructively criticized my own efforts to keep up with them. Although my footnotes mark many specific places where I have drawn on the writings of Georges Duby, they cannot indicate the full extent of my debt to him and his work. I have also learned a great deal from correspondence and conversations with Henry D. Abelove, Elizabeth A. R. Brown, Samuel K. Cohn, Natalie Z. Davis, Kate Gilbert, Thomas A. Green, Clark Maines, Richard T. Vann, G. Edward White, Lucia Perry White, and Morton G. White, several of whom also took great pains in reading and commenting on earlier drafts of this book. None of these people bears any responsibility for errors that I have doubtless made in trying to develop my argument. My thanks to Megan McLaughlin, who kindly allowed me to read and quote from her recent thesis on prayers for the dead.

Research on this book was generously supported by grants from the American Bar Foundation; the American Council of Learned Societies; the Institute for Advanced Study, Princeton, New Jersey; the National Endowment for the Humanities; and Wesleyan University.

Frances Warren provided invaluable assistance in laying out the statistical tables and in preparing the entire manuscript for publication. Lewis Bateman and Ron Maner of the University of North Carolina Press gave me expert editorial help.

Note on Abbreviations

The following abbreviations for kinship terms are used in the text, notes, and appendix:

B   Brother
D   Daughter
F   Father
H   Husband
M   Mother
S   Son
W   Wife
Z   Sister

Other kinds of kin are designated by combinations of these abbreviations, so that, for example, WBDH stands for Wife's Brother's Daughter's Husband.

Custom, Kinship, and Gifts to Saints

And I say to you: "Make unto you friends of the mammon of iniquity, that when you shall fail, they may receive you into everlasting dwellings." Luke 16:9

"I have been swallowing too much of that word, Pardner. I am no pardner of yours."

"Since when was you no pardner of mine, Gaffer Hexam, Esquire?"

"Since you was accused of robbing a man. Accused of robbing a live man!" said Gaffer, with great indignation.

"And what if I had been accused of robbing a dead man, Gaffer?"

"You COULDN'T do it."

"Couldn't you, Gaffer?"

"No. Has a dead man any use for money? Is it possible for a dead man to have money? What world does a dead man belong to? T'other world. What world does money belong to? This world. How can money be a corpse's? Can a corpse own it, want it, spend it, claim it, miss it? Don't try to go confounding the rights and wrongs of things in that way. But it's worthy of the sneaking spirit that robs a live man."

—Charles Dickens, *Our Mutual Friend*

Chapter 1

The *Laudatio Parentum*

WHEN A KNIGHT of Chaumont named Guazo came into the chapterhouse of the abbey of Marmoutier near Tours during the sixth decade of the eleventh century and gave to the brothers of this monastery some land that he held at La Borde, he did not act alone. He made his gift with the approval of his wife, Alpacia, and his two sons, Rotbertus and Isembardus. Similarly, when another knight called Gervasius gave various properties at Bury to the same monastery in 1080, he, too, acted along with a small group of his relatives. His wife, Osebia, consented to his gift, as did his six sons: Lancelinus, Guillelmus, Rodulfus, Bernerius, Guildinus, and Matheus. During the same period, the practice of making gifts of landed property with the approval of relatives was observed not only by knights, but also by people of even higher social status. Between 1032 and 1047 the extensive gifts of land that Salomon, lord of Lavardin, and his wife, Adela, made when they founded a priory of Marmoutier at Lavardin were approved by their two daughters, Matildis and Avelina. And when, in the 1030s, Count Odo II of Blois gave Marmoutier the right to gather dead wood in his forest at Chaumont, he acted at the request of his wife, Ermengardis, and with the approval of his sons, Theobaldus and Stephanus.[1]

In making gifts of land with the approval of relatives, rather than acting unilaterally, these benefactors of Marmoutier were conforming to an established pattern of behavior found throughout France during the eleventh and twelfth centuries. Although different scribes at different French religious communities used many different words and phrases to indicate that a gift to an abbey had been approved by the donor's relatives, modern scholars have routinely used, for the sake of convenience, a single phrase—the *laudatio parentum*—to refer to the act by which a person's relatives (*parentes*) gave their approval (*laudatio*) to his or her conveyances of landed property.[2] The practice of alienating land with the approval of relatives is not frequently recorded in French documents until about 1000, and after 1200 it began to die out. But during the intervening two centuries the prevalence of the *laudatio parentum* is revealed in thousands of charters recording transactions that are referred to in this book as "gifts to saints."

These transactions, in which a lay landholder, usually of noble or at least free status, gave landed property of one kind or another to a Christian saint and to a particular religious community dedicated to that saint did not constitute the only type of conveyance ever made between 1000 and 1200. Some French landholders no doubt granted dowries and fiefs and may occasionally have made other sorts of alienations to lay people or to religious establishments. But because gifts to saints were the land transfers most likely to be recorded systematically during much of the central Middle Ages, they provide the main evidence that historians can now use for reconstructing both the ways in which lay landholders transferred real property and the terms on which they held their land.[3] Moreover, because charters drawn up in Latin by monastic scribes in scores of abbeys and priories throughout France often indicate what sorts of relatives approved these transactions, these texts can give modern historians rare glimpses of how, on certain occasions, medieval people acted together with their relatives as members of kinship groups, whose size, composition, and structure are hardly ever revealed so clearly in other contemporary texts. After intensively studying monastic charters, historians have repeatedly concluded that at least between c. 1000 and c. 1200 it was common, or customary, or perhaps even legally obligatory for people who transferred land to do so with the approval of relatives. Evidently, it was in some sense the norm, if not the rule, in France at this time for land transfers to be made with the *laudatio parentum*.

As we shall soon see, the precise significance of this finding remains enigmatic. But the importance of the *laudatio parentum* itself and the value of studying it closely have been regularly recognized by scholars investigating medieval French land tenure, kinship, and social development. The *laudatio* in France has never before been the subject of a book-length study. But ever since the late nineteenth century, it has been analyzed in numerous scholarly works, including general histories of French law,[4] specialized studies on various aspects of medieval French legal history,[5] and analyses of social life in various regions within northern France.[6] The *laudatio* has also been discussed in recent studies of medieval French kinship, marriage, and female status,[7] as well as in broad works of synthesis on medieval European society.[8] Moreover, because practices similar to the *laudatio parentum* are found in other parts of the medieval world[9] and in various non-European societies as well,[10] studies of this French practice also have the potential to be used in comparative discussions of land tenure and kinship.[11]

In spite of the manifest importance of the *laudatio parentum*, however, and in spite of the close scrutiny that many medievalists have already given it, the most basic questions about it remain unanswered. After almost a century of research, it is still unclear whether the *laudatio* was really essential to the legal validity of eleventh- and twelfth-century land transfers, what sorts of kinship groups normally gave it and would have been expected to give it, and even why the *laudatio parentum* was given at all. Uncertainties about how to answer these fundamental questions have obstructed the formulation of full explanations for the initial appearance and growing prevalence of the *laudatio*, for its subsequent decline and ultimate disappearance, and for changes that evidently occurred between 1000 and 1200 in the composition of the kinship groups that normally gave it. As a result, while scholars continue to treat the *laudatio* as an important practice, the significance of its history remains elusive.

Because the *laudatio parentum* ultimately needs to be examined closely in each of the many different regions where it is found, the present work can provide no definitive analysis of this practice. But it proposes new approaches and new answers to several puzzling questions that are central to previous discussions of the *laudatio* and are linked to broader problems in medieval legal and social history. The most important of these questions are whether any legal rule required conveyances of landed property to be made with the *laudatio parentum*; how the kin groups that gave the *laudatio* can best be characterized and what they reveal about medieval French kinship in general; why conveyances were so commonly approved by relatives during the eleventh and twelfth centuries; and why the *laudatio* ultimately fell into disuse during the thirteenth century.

While building on earlier scholarship, the book differs in several respects from previous studies of the *laudatio parentum*. It examines closely several methodological questions that inevitably arise in analyses of the *laudatio* but that previous writers have not directly confronted. Furthermore, whereas earlier writers have studied the *laudatio* either in particular regions such as the Mâconnais or Picardy or else generally throughout northern France,[12] the present work adopts a slightly different focus. Instead of dealing comprehensively with all surviving documents from a particular geographical area, it shows how the history of the *laudatio parentum* is revealed in several thousand eleventh- and twelfth-century charters recording transactions involving five Benedictine abbeys in western France and does not treat documents from other western French abbeys.

Finally, the decision to use gifts to a small set of abbeys as the basis for an analysis of the *laudatio parentum* is integrally related to a more basic difference between this study and previous ones. Of central importance to this study is the fact that most recorded land transfers carried out with the approval of relatives were integrally related to complex social transactions involving lay people and religious communities. The *laudatio* is not treated simply as a conveyancing practice or familial act. Instead, it is seen as an integral part of transactions very similar to the ones that the English anthropologist E. E. Evans-Pritchard, following the French ethnologist Marcel Mauss, has called "total social movements or activities." These activities are "at the same time economic, juridical, moral, aesthetic, religious, mythological and socio-morphological phenomena."[13] In this study, gifts to saints are also seen to resemble what Max Weber called "status contracts," which he distinguished from modern contracts because they resulted in permanent changes in the social statuses of the contracting parties.[14] By themselves, anthropological or sociological analyses of gift-exchange in European or non-European societies provide no simple solutions to the problems that have arisen in previous studies of the *laudatio parentum*. But the work of Mauss and his successors nevertheless provides a useful framework for discussing the *lauda-*

tio.[15] It helps us to see that because transactions carried out with the *laudatio parentum* had important religious and social dimensions, they differed fundamentally from the donations and sales of later French law and cannot be fully understood if they are viewed from a purely legal or economic perspective.[16]

In the late nineteenth and early twentieth centuries, the religious and social dimensions of gifts made with the approval of a donor's relatives were not closely examined by the historians of medieval French law who initiated the systematic study of the *laudatio parentum*. To them, the *laudatio* was important primarily for what it seemed to reveal about the history of French real property law.[17] Both older and more recent legal historians recognized that at least in recorded cases, the recipients of lands conveyed with the approval of relatives were normally monastic communities.[18] But instead of treating transactions carried out in this way as exchanges that were integrally associated with the historically specific beliefs and practices of a distinctive culture, legal scholars fitted these transactions into two categories current in later French law, treating some of them as donations or alienations "à titre gratuit" and others as sales or alienations "à titre onéreux."[19] In the writings of legal historians, the *laudatio* therefore appears as a conveyancing practice associated with standard types of conveyances that had supposedly existed, in one form or another, throughout much of recorded French legal history.[20]

In this way, legal historians succeeded in neatly incorporating the study of the *laudatio parentum* into the history of French land law. By creating an artificial but still heuristically useful framework within which that history could be traced, primarily through an examination of conveyancing practices, these scholars were able to use analyses of the *laudatio parentum* as a means of addressing, for the period in which this practice flourished, a question that has sometimes generated intense interest and controversy in discussions of the land-holding systems found in many precapitalist or noncapitalist societies, both in western Europe and elsewhere: Was landed property held and controlled by individuals or by sets of joint-tenants whose individual proprietary interests could normally be distinguished from one another? Or was land held by families or other groups endowed with a well-established corporate identity, so that in these societies, communal, rather than individual, ownership was the norm?[21] In considering this question, earlier writers on the *laudatio* sometimes posited the existence of two related conflicts within eleventh- and twelfth-century French society: a political and economic conflict between the "individual" medieval landholder and his or her "family," and an ideological conflict between the "Romanist" principle of proprietary "individualism" and the "Germanic" principle of proprietary "communitarianism" or "family solidarity."[22] By charting the progress of these two struggles, students of the *laudatio* hoped to discover whether individual or communal ownership prevailed during the eleventh and twelfth centuries.

At the same time, by studying the *laudatio parentum* in conjunction with earlier and later practices governing lay alienations of real property, legal historians also found an oblique way of treating a related and equally controversial problem in the history of European law: Could the history of real property law from the time of the Germanic settlements down through the late Middle Ages and beyond be represented as a slow, continuous process through which a communitarian system of property-holding by kin groups or families gradually evolved into more individualistic forms of land tenure? That is, in the struggle supposedly underway between proprietary individualism and the economic solidarity of the family, did the former slowly but inexorably gain at the latter's expense? Or did the history of this struggle follow a more circuitous path?[23] In addressing this question, legal scholars considered the *laudatio* in relation to other customs governing the alienation of land during the medieval and early modern periods. In particular, they tried to relate the *laudatio* to two later customs known as the *retrait lignager* and the *réserve coutumière*, which served, in some degree, to maintain the interests of a landholder's kin in his or her property.[24]

Whereas legal historians have analyzed the *laudatio parentum* primarily for the purpose of illuminating the history of French land law, the social historians who have dominated discussions of the *laudatio* in recent times have been more interested first in determining what this practice can reveal about medieval kinship and then in linking the history of medieval kinship to other important social developments. Georges Duby, in particular, has integrated his analyses of the *laudatio* into a powerful and deeply re-searched interpretation of social, economic, political, and ideological change during the eleventh and twelfth centuries.[25] By representing the *laudatio* as a momentary but relatively well-docu-mented manifestation of the social ties that bound monastic bene-factors and their kin into "families" or kinship groups, social his-torians have used studies of this practice to address broad questions raised in different contexts by many other writers on kinship and family life: What were the basic structures of kinship in medieval society? What form did the most prevalent kinship groups take? How large were these groups? What was the place of married and unmarried women or younger and older children? To what extent were the members of these groups bound together by sentiments of "family solidarity" and by customs, such as the *lau-datio*, that may have served both to express and to reinforce such sentiments?[26] In addition, social historians who have analyzed the *laudatio* over several centuries have been able to address a ques-tion parallel to the one that legal historians had raised about the development of French property law: Can the historical develop-ment of the French family—or at least the French upper-class family—be accurately represented as a unilinear process, in which large clans were slowly but inexorably transformed into smaller and smaller kinship groups, until the modern "conjugal" family appeared? Or should this simple theory, as many recent scholars have suggested, be rejected in favor of a more complex develop-mental schema?[27]

Because some historians believe that the relatives who ap-proved a man's conveyances (and who are collectively referred to hereafter as the *consenting kin group* or *consenting group*) can, for some purposes, be equated with that man's "family," they have used statistical analyses of the changing composition of these groups to plot out diachronic shifts in French family structure.[28] According to Marc Bloch, for example, the tendency of consenting groups to become smaller and less structurally complex during the late twelfth and early thirteenth centuries probably indicates that the medieval family was then undergoing "a sort of contraction."[29] In a more subtle and complex way, Duby has used statistical stud-ies of the *laudatio* and associated practices to corroborate his gen-eral thesis that upper-class kinship organization changed dramatically during the eleventh and twelfth centuries, as the loosely structured cognatic kin groups into which earlier medieval nobles had often organized themselves were transformed into the agnatic *lignages* or *Geschlechten* that constituted the predominant form of upper-class family in the High Middle Ages.[30] Furthermore, after determining how often women or conjugal pairs participated in gifts to religious houses between 1000 and 1300, Robert Fossier has framed general hypotheses both about female status during different segments of this larger period and about the degree to which actual family practice conformed to medieval ecclesiastical doctrines holding that a married couple should be considered the core of every family.[31]

In addition to using studies of the *laudatio* to chart changes in medieval kinship organization, social historians have also tried to identify the main social functions of this practice. Viewing the prevalence of the *laudatio* as a clear sign of the "economic solidarity" that generally prevailed within eleventh- and twelfth-century upper-class families, Bloch suggested that the practice of making gifts of land only with the consent of kin may have impeded the development of a land market and that by checking the erosion or fragmentation of large estates, it helped greater and lesser nobles to maintain their preeminence in a world in which power was inextricably linked to the possession of land and to the control of people living on the land.[32] This idea has been developed by others, notably Duby, who has associated the *laudatio* with other familial practices, such as primogeniture and restrictions on the marriage of children, by which the heads of noble *lignages* tried to prevent family estates from being divided or slowly dissipated.[33]

Even broader significance has been attached to the *laudatio* by scholars who regard its prevalence as a sign of a crucially important, if intangible and elusive, feature of medieval family life and of medieval society generally. In their view, the percentage of charters recording the *laudatio* during a given period is a meaningful index of "family solidarity," whereas the percentage of documents not mentioning the *laudatio* is an index of "individualism." If "family solidarity" and "individualism" are treated as mutually antithetical principles, then increases over time in the first figure can be taken to reflect the development of greater familial cohesiveness, whereas declines can be regarded as signs of a trend toward individualism and toward the weakening of ties between kin.[34] It is therefore evident that lying behind social analyses of the *laudatio* are assumptions similar to the ones previously articulated by legal historians about the fundamental opposition between individual and family interests in landed property.[35] Social historians, however, have developed this old idea by using statistical indicators that are meant to provide more sensitive readings of fluctuations over time in individualism and family solidarity. Having used analyses of the *laudatio parentum* to identify and measure diachronic shifts in family structure and in family solidarity, they have then related these changes to other important developments, such as the growth of institutionalized governmental power and a correlative decline in social "disorder," expansions in commerce, population increases, changes in methods of agricultural exploitation, the growing influence of church teachings about marriage and family life, and the establishment of a feudal or seigneurial regime.[36] In these ways, analyses of the *laudatio* have been linked to social models designed to reveal the driving forces of medieval social development.

Despite the accumulation of a large body of scholarship on the *laudatio parentum*, there is still no consensus about how the history of this practice can best be interpreted. Whereas some writers claim that a relatively clear-cut legal rule or custom required that land be conveyed with the approval of relatives,[37] others at least allow for the possibility that the *laudatio* was merely a precautionary practice used to stabilize land transfers that individuals could legally make on their own.[38] Even if we assume that alienations were supposed to be made with the *laudatio parentum*, it is not clear what sorts of *parentes* were supposed to give this necessary approval or what principles governed the formation of consenting kin groups. Did a consenting group consist of all the donor's living relatives? If so, on what basis were these people recognized as kin? Did a consenting group include only the donor's coresidential kin, his blood relatives, or the members of another kind of well-defined kin group?[39] Or were these groups constituted on a less obvious basis or even in ways that were determined simply by chance or whim or by the success of efforts to secure the approval of as many kin as possible?[40] Even more perplexing is the question of why relatives approved conveyances of landed property at all. Although some scholars insist on linking the *laudatio* with a system of communal family landholding,[41] others have associated it with more individualistic forms of land tenure.[42]

Because scholars have had so much difficulty in establishing why the *laudatio* was so often given, who gave it or was supposed to give it, and whether it had to be given at all, they have not been able to determine conclusively why this custom came into being, what its growing prevalence reveals about the societies where it is found, or why it ultimately disappeared. Nor have they been fully equipped to explain precisely why the *laudatio* was evidently more common in some regions or periods than in others or why consenting familial groups varied so much in size and structure. Attempts to correlate the rise and fall of the *laudatio* with other social trends must therefore remain inconclusive.

There is no simple way of explaining why discussions of the *laudatio parentum* have reached this apparent impasse. Historians have come to different conclusions about how to interpret the *laudatio*, not only because they have studied different regions of France[43] and have employed different research strategies,[44] but also because the available evidence is ambiguous and therefore open to divergent interpretations. Modern theories depend almost as much on the vagaries of medieval scribes and the assumptions of modern scholars about medieval life as they do upon empirical findings. Medieval sources are defective in ways that impose narrow constraints on what historians can ever know with any certainty about the ceremonies at which the *laudatio* was given.

Almost everything to be learned about these ceremonies comes from monastic charters, which never provide much detail about how gifts to saints were made and rarely locate these transactions temporally in relation to earlier and later events. Instead of representing gifts to saints as phases in ongoing processes of social interaction and exchange, charters generally portray them as isolated legal acts. Frequently terse, awkwardly written, full of ambiguities on important points, and bound by rigid formulae, charters always omit crucial facts about the words, objects, and gestures that were used when laymen gave land to saints and monks. When documents include such details, they may be recording exceptional rather than normal practice. Or else they may only be telling us what the scribe thought should have been done.[45]

Under these circumstances, writers on the *laudatio parentum* cannot match the detailed descriptions of rituals presented by anthropologists who have actually witnessed the ceremonies that interest them.[46] In addition, charters rarely explain the significance of the rituals through which gifts to saints were made, and when they do so—usually in formulaic preambles—they may be presenting only a stereotyped view of transactions that other contemporaries interpreted differently.[47] These sources, moreover, say very little about lay, as opposed to monastic, understandings of gifts to saints. At best, Latin charters represent lay interpretations of these transactions only through a multilayered screen of linguistic and cultural translation.[48] At worst, charters tell us nothing whatever about lay attitudes and present only retrospective and self-interested views of gift-giving ceremonies, produced by scribes who had not necessarily witnessed the events that they recorded, whose main concern was to defend the property interests of their own abbey, and who therefore made extensive use of traditional formulae that now render many charters almost totally opaque to modern readers.[49] Under these circumstances, the inevitable gap between written record and lived experience may turn out to be a chasm. The gap between medieval charter evidence and modern historical interpretation is even wider, because the scribes who produced charters knew nothing of concepts such as "family solidarity" or "real property law" that figure so prominently in modern discussions of the *laudatio*.

Because medieval sources provide no clear, conclusive answers to central questions about the *laudatio parentum*, historians are relatively free to interpret this practice in ways that are inevitably both speculative and projective. When they try to interpret the *laudatio* and explain its history, they must rely heavily on historical imagination, on their sense of how medieval French society was organized and how it changed, and on the unarticulated social theories that inform even the most innocent-looking monuments of empirical medieval scholarship.[50] However solid the evidentiary foundations of modern work on the *laudatio* may seem, the available data actually provide only a few well-fixed points for a picture that scholars can complete only by establishing the nature of transactions carried out with the *laudatio* and by theorizing about the motives and values of medieval people, about the structure of medieval society, and about the processes through which medieval society and culture changed.

Therefore, to explain the existence of divergent interpretations of the *laudatio parentum*, we should not limit our attention to such narrow questions of research strategy as which region to study, how to identify the appropriate geographical, temporal, or social units of analysis, or how to code, count, and classify particular instances in which the *laudatio* was or was not given. Like all discussions of significant features of medieval life, analyses of the *laudatio* depend heavily on the identification and interpretation of recurrent patterns of medieval social life. As a result, we cannot simply cite regional variation in the evidence as the sole explanation for the different conceptions held by scholars. It is, indeed, quite likely that between 1000 and 1200, each small region within medieval western Europe may have had its own distinctive customs and *mentalités*, which presumably changed significantly over this period. Nonetheless, a justifiable concern with the particularity and malleability of local customs and beliefs should not drive historians to the hyperparticularist or hypernominalist conclusion that every medieval social act was virtually unique, that every region was utterly distinctive, and that the search for patterns in medieval social life is, by definition, epistemologically unsound. Even after making due allowance for regional differences, we can still see that debates on the *laudatio parentum* ultimately turn on how historians construe a practice that is generally similar throughout France and in other parts of medieval Europe.

No matter what region writers on the *laudatio* study and how they organize their evidence, they must establish the nature of the transactions carried out with the *laudatio* and decide whether to equate them with modern conveyances or to regard them as complex social exchanges. They must also address basic questions about the character of medieval French custom, kinship, land tenure, and gift-exchange, while also asking how best to identify, measure, and explain major social developments in eleventh- and twelfth-century France. Historians cannot determine whether the *laudatio parentum* was essential to the legal validity of gifts to mon-

asteries without answering several questions generally left to jurists, anthropologists, or social theorists: How can we tell whether
people living in a remote culture—or even a familiar one—are following rules or norms? When the existence of rules or norms is
inferred largely from evidence about behavior or practice, how can
we be sure how those rules were conceptualized or verbalized by
the people whose behavior is being studied? How, in general, are
legal rules to be identified and distinguished from moral and religious norms, customs, or mere behavioral patterns? And is it always useful and appropriate to distinguish legal rules from other
sorts of norms, especially when studying societies differing mark-
edly from our own? Finally, should the rules of behavior that historians reconstruct after the fact from observed behavior be used
to explain that behavior, when there is no evidence that the actors
in question were following rules at all?[51] In the present context,
these questions are particularly important to answer because monastic charters reveal much more about medieval behavior than
they do about legal rules or norms, because participants in gifts to
saints may have been discharging what we would now regard as
religious, as distinct from legal, duties, and because the communities in which the *laudatio parentum* is found lacked some of the
main defining characteristics of modern legal systems.[52]

When we shift our attention to the kin groups that participated
in gifts to saints in order to explain how they were formed, we
encounter other methodological problems sometimes treated in
anthropological studies of kinship.[53] Although we can usually
identify the types of relatives belonging to any particular consenting kin group, it is far more difficult to determine why a relative of
a given type gave the *laudatio* or to decide what studies of consenting groups can reveal about more general features of medieval
French family life. Were there rigid, well-understood rules or customs prescribing precisely which kin should join in gifts to saints?
Or was participation determined in flexible or even random ways?
If such rules existed and were consistently applied, did they
specify precisely the types of kin who were obliged to give the
laudatio? Or did they only indicate which kin were eligible to do
so? Did the rules govern only this one activity? Or were they continuously operative in several spheres of life, so that consenting
groups possessed an enduring corporate identity? If such rules

did not exist or were only applied to groups engaged in this one activity, what general conclusions about medieval family life can emerge from studies of kin groups that assembled only for the purpose of giving the *laudatio parentum*? Consideration of these questions leads us on to problems closely related to the ones raised above about the nature of earlier medieval custom. Did northern French communities have a clearly articulated kinship system that legalistically dictated the ways in which groups of relatives were formed? Or was kinship a more malleable cultural category that individuals and groups could manipulate and re-shape themselves, as they joined together, pursuing different strategies in different ways for different purposes?[54]

The most troubling methodological questions about the *laudatio parentum* arise when we ask why familial participation in gifts to saints was so common for several centuries. This question is itself ambiguous. Historians can try to answer it by considering the mo-tives, intentions, and purposes of participants in gifts to saints and the meaning that these people attributed to gift-giving cere-monies. On the other hand, scholars may choose to explain the prevalence of the *laudatio* by identifying the social function of this practice or constructing a theory of medieval real property law from which a legal or normative rationale for the *laudatio parentum* can be logically deduced. As a result, different historians examin-ing the same data can easily propose different solutions to the problem of why the *laudatio* was such a common practice.[55] These explanations, moreover, are also potentially controversial because they inevitably touch on a question to which great historical, ideo-logical, and political importance is often attached: Was communal ownership of land the norm in western Europe during much of the Middle Ages? To some writers on the history of land tenure, "communal ownership" seems a peculiar and almost unnatural institution that could hardly have prevailed anywhere, even in so-called "tribal societies." To others, however, it is virtually axiomatic that historically, individual private ownership of real property arose in Europe out of communitarian systems. Even when focus-ing narrowly on a specific practice such as the *laudatio parentum*, historians may sometimes have found it hard to free themselves completely from the constraints of this continuing controversy.[56]

The problem of explaining the prevalence of the *laudatio paren-*

tum is also difficult to solve because historians and other scholars have not determined whether such concepts as "sale," "alienation," "price," or "ownership"—as used in legal and economic analyses of exchanges in capitalist societies—are adequate tools for the task of analyzing exchanges in precapitalist economies. In the absence of any coherent and generally accepted theory that both describes and explains the ways in which land, property, and subject peoples in medieval France were exchanged or distributed, historians are in a relatively unfavorable position to understand a practice such as the *laudatio* that was inextricably associated with exchanges that can either be equated with the sales or free gifts of modern law or else likened to the exchanges of gifts studied by anthropological specialists on tribal and other noncapitalist societies.[57]

When historians try to trace and explain the long-term history of the *laudatio parentum*, they encounter additional obstacles. Increases or declines in the occurrence of this practice can be interpreted in very different ways, depending upon the historian's assumptions about the nature of the *laudatio*; the same is true of changes over time in the frequency with which certain kinds of kin groups or certain kinds of relatives approved gifts to saints.[58] Moreover, when historians claim that the decline of the *laudatio parentum* or changes over time in the composition of consenting familial groups resulted from other social changes, they are committing themselves to particular theories of medieval social development. Such efforts can lead to very different conclusions, depending on how we interpret the *laudatio parentum* and relate it to other aspects of medieval life. Clearly, changes in the most prevalent methods of making gifts to saints coincided in time with major shifts in political organization, with an increase in total population, with the development of new legal structures, and with important modifications in religious practices and attitudes.[59] But the question of how the history of the *laudatio parentum* was linked with these complex processes is bound to be both problematic and controversial.

This brief critique of previous scholarship indicates that a clearer understanding of the *laudatio parentum* cannot be achieved simply by gathering more evidence. Instead, historians need to reexamine and revise various basic assumptions underlying most previous discussions of the *laudatio*. In order to show that the relatives who gave the *laudatio* were not merely approving land transfers, but participating in elaborate social transactions, chapter 2 presents a preliminary picture of gifts to saints and focuses closely on the social and religious dimensions of these exchanges. Because gifts to saints, like Mauss's "total prestations" or Weber's "status contracts," were meant to effect permanent changes in human society and in the world of the supernatural, they involved far more than mere transfers of material resources. Building on this premise, each subsequent chapter begins by posing central questions that have arisen in previous discussions of the *laudatio*. Chapter 3 begins by considering arguments about whether a legal rule required that transfers of land be made with the approval of relatives. But because we are dealing with societies in which legal rules were not clearly distinguished from other sorts of norms, this initial inquiry gives way to an effort to establish "the normative status" of the *laudatio parentum*. After first analyzing the varying composition of the kin groups that approved gifts to saints in our sample and then proposing partial explanations for these variations, chapter 4 then demonstrates that because the composition of consenting groups was not regularly shaped by consistently applied rules of recruitment, findings about what sorts of relatives approved gifts to saints should not be used as direct evidence about the size and structure of the so-called medieval "family." Nevertheless, studies of the *laudatio* can still be used to illuminate medieval French kinship, provided that we abandon the view that a juridical system of kinship strictly governed the composition of kinship groups and proceed instead on the assumption that kinship was a fluid concept that could be construed and employed in many different ways.

Chapter 5 considers why gifts to saints were so commonly made with the *laudatio parentum* and why this method of gift-giving was apparently considered proper. It begins by reviewing various legal explanations for the prevalence of this practice. Within limits, several of these theories are illuminating. But because they treat gifts made with the *laudatio* as mere land transfers, they cannot fully account for the participation of kin in what were actually complex social transactions. To complement and supplement legal approaches to this problem, chapter 5 therefore proposes some other ways of accounting for the prominent role that kin often played in making gifts to saints. Chapter 6 then presents a critique of previous efforts to use studies of the *laudatio parentum* to chart the history of the medieval family, or to represent the history of this practice as the story of a struggle between "individualism" and "family solidarity." The chapter concludes by proposing several ways of explaining the manifold changes that lie behind the quantitative history of the the *laudatio parentum*.

Because the purpose of this extended argument is not to relate the history of the *laudatio parentum* to the social history of a single region, but rather to discuss several general questions about this practice, a wide range of charter evidence, drawn from many parts of France, could have been used to support the conclusions proposed here. But in order to achieve a more focused discussion and to facilitate certain types of analysis, a relatively small set of documents has been selected for study. This book is based on charters that record eleventh- and twelfth-century transactions between lay people and five different northern French abbeys: Saint Aubin of Angers,[60] Marmoutier,[61] Saint Mary of Noyers,[62] La Trinité of Vendôme,[63] and Saint Vincent of Le Mans.[64] These texts are unusually plentiful for the period from c. 1050 to c. 1150, when the *laudatio* flourished,[65] and thus they are remarkably rich in the kinds of details that are vital to an understanding of the problems treated here. Although each of the five monasteries had its own distinctive character and history, they still had much in common. Saint Aubin, Saint Vincent, and Marmoutier, which had all been founded in the early Middle Ages, were effectively refounded in the late tenth or early eleventh centuries, when La Trinité and Noyers were established.[66] All five abbeys were Benedictine houses that grew richer and more powerful during the eleventh and earlier twelfth century but then entered a period of stabilization, if not actual decline. In addition, the monks of each abbey practiced the same sort of religious life and were recruited from the same restricted circle of upper-class landholders. Although each of these monasteries occupied its own geographical niche in western or west-central France, the various territories in which they held their lands were linked together in certain respects. Dur-

ing much of our period, Anjou, Maine, the Touraine, and the Vendômois were all ruled by counts of Anjou;[67] and by the thirteenth
century, if not earlier, these same regions, along with Perche and
the Dunois, were governed by similar inheritance customs.[68]

The records of the five abbeys, unfortunately, are especially rich
only for the later eleventh and earlier twelfth centuries. But for
reasons that may not be totally accidental, this is precisely the era
when, in these regions, the *laudatio parentum* was especially common. As a result, the charters of these five houses provide a usable core of detailed evidence for the study of the *laudatio*, whose
long-term history will be discussed in chapter 6, primarily through
references to modern studies. Moreover, because the records kept
at these particular abbeys or at their dependent priories are remarkably circumstantial and because they often record gifts that
different members of the same kinship groups made to a single
abbey over a long span of years, they are especially valuable for a
study that treats the *laudatio parentum* as an integral part of larger
and more complex social transactions and that represents these
transactions not as discrete events, but as ongoing processes of
exchange.

Chapter 2

Gifts to Saints and the *Laudatio Parentum*

ON HUNDREDS OF different occasions during the eleventh and twelfth centuries, many of the richer, more powerful landholders of Anjou, Maine, the Touraine, the Vendômois, and other neighboring *pays* followed a custom commonly observed in other parts of medieval western Europe, as they made perpetual gifts of various kinds to Saint Aubin of Angers, Saint Vincent of Le Mans, Saint Mary of Noyers, La Trinité of Vendôme, and Saint Martin near Tours.[1] While some of these gifts probably took the form of precious objects that would ornament monastic buildings or play a role in monastic rituals,[2] the most enduring and valuable of these prestations, as well as the ones best known to us now, transferred rights over land and other productive resources to God, to a dead saint such as Martin or Mary, and to the living monks who temporarily represented that saint on earth at places such as Marmoutier or Noyers.[3] From the later tenth century down into the twelfth century, numerous monastic benefactors gave away to one or another of these five Benedictine abbeys certain specifically designated rights over arable lands, meadows, vineyards, fishponds, waste grounds, forests, bakehouses, mills, churches, tithes, serfs, and other sources of wealth, power, and prestige.[4] At the same time, the more politically powerful of these donors sometimes surrendered diverse powers, generally known as "customs," that they would otherwise have used to extract wealth from the inhabitants of monastic estates.[5]

If we leave aside exemptions from these seigneurial exactions and outright grants of unfree people and all their posterity,[6] we can say that gifts to saints normally consisted of landed wealth, provided that we also remember that a medieval gift of what is now called landed property was a complex act that presupposed the existence of a distinctive social order. When a monastic community was granted rights of control over certain forms of landed wealth during the eleventh and twelfth centuries, the monks representing that community assumed particular social roles that often entailed the exercise of power over some people and at least nominal dependence upon others. Between c. 980 and c. 1150 it was gifts of land and of power over people that ultimately provided most of the material support necessary to sustain the remarkable growth in wealth, power, and reputation of Benedictine monasteries, such as Saint Vincent, Marmoutier, Saint Aubin, La Trinité, and Noyers. At the same time, the ceremonies at which these gifts were made provided occasions for the establishment or reaffirmation of complex and enduring social relationships linking monastic communities to their neighbors.

Originally founded in 572 and dedicated to the sainted martyrs Vincent and Lawrence, the abbey commonly known as Saint Vincent of Le Mans had probably been abandoned by its monks in the late ninth century, after which time only canons seem to have lived there.[7] But during the late tenth and early eleventh centuries, the restoration of this monastery was begun by Avesgaudus, bishop of Le Mans (996–1032), who endowed it with lands in the northern part of his diocese and had a new abbey church built.[8] Shortly thereafter, the bishop's kinsman and eventual successor Gervasius du Château-du-Loir, who had taken over the see of Le Mans in 1034, replaced the canons with monks. The new bishop's nephew, also named Avesgaudus, was appointed to rule as the first regular abbot in many years.[9] From around 1060 down to about 1120, the monastic community at Saint Vincent grew rapidly, as prominent lords and knights from the region endowed this foundation with substantial gifts of landed property and as the abbey gradually acquired control from its various patrons over at least fifty churches.[10] Among the abbey's more notable benefactors were the bishops of Le Mans, the viscounts of Maine, the lords of Bellême, and the clients of these magnates.[11] Most of the properties acquired from such donors lay to the north and northeast of Le Mans in a triangular area bounded on the south by the Huisne and on the west by the Sarthe. But the monks also re-

ceived gifts of both land and churches to the east and south, between the Huisne and the Loir, as well as in Lower Maine, Normandy, and even Wales.[12] Although the period between 1230 and
1250 has been identified as the high point in the history of this
monastery,[13] the most important and valuable donations that the
monks of Saint Vincent received were made in the antecedent period running from about 1040 to 1140.[14] Subsequently, descendants of some of the abbey's earlier benefactors and others who
had no prior connection with Saint Vincent conveyed lands and
associated rights to the saint's monks at Le Mans. But these later
gifts were generally less valuable than the older ones, and some of
them were outright sales.[15]

A similar chronological pattern of initial growth followed by stabilization or actual decline can be seen in the history of gifts to
Marmoutier.[16] Although the origins of this extraordinarily important and powerful abbey, located near Tours on the right bank of
the Loire, can be traced back to the time of Saint Martin in the
early third century,[17] the monastery assumed a new form in the
980s. At that time it was rebuilt with the support of Count Odo I
of Blois; it was also detached from the chapter of Saint Martin of
Tours and reformed under Cluniac influence, without, however,
becoming formally affiliated with Cluny.[18] At Marmoutier, whose
landed wealth grew rapidly during the eleventh and twelfth centuries,[19] the replacement of canons by monks and the appoint-
ment of a regular abbot occurred more than a generation before
similar changes were carried out at Saint Vincent of Le Mans. But
the periods of the greatest growth in the landed holdings of the
two monasteries coincided closely with one another.

It was the abbacies of Albertus (1032–64) and Bartholomeus
(1064–83) that saw the foundation of most of the thirty-nine
priories that the abbey of Saint Martin eventually established in
Maine, Perche, the Dunois, the Vendômois, and the Blésois.[20]
Conveyances to Marmoutier from these five regions are especially
well documented and can be usefully studied in conjunction with
gifts to Saint Vincent and our other abbeys. But it is important to
bear in mind that the holdings of Marmoutier also extended into
Anjou, the Touraine, Poitou, and Normandy and into regions outside northwestern France.[21] Throughout these territories, the
monks of Saint Martin acquired powerful benefactors. In the

Vendômois, for example, Marmoutier received important gifts from the provosts of the castle of Vendôme, the lords of Lavardin, and Fulcherius Dives, whose many descendants played important roles in the histories of Marmoutier and La Trinité.[22] Gifts to Saint Martin continued to be made during the very late eleventh and the early twelfth centuries; and in subsequent centuries, the abbey maintained what one historian has called its ecclesiastical "empire."[23] In the mid-twelfth century, however, the rate of giving slowed down appreciably, just as it did at Saint Vincent and at many other Benedictine abbeys.[24] Nevertheless, during the period of its greatest expansion, Marmoutier gained property and influence within a vast territory, so that its lands and churches extended into many of the areas in which Saint Vincent of Le Mans, La Trinité of Vendôme, Saint Aubin of Angers, and Saint Mary of Noyers held property.[25]

A particularly close connection existed between Marmoutier and La Trinité.[26] Both monasteries held extensive properties in the Vendômois, and monks of Saint Martin had some influence on the spiritual life led at the younger abbey. Founded sometime between 1032 and 1038 by Geoffrey Martel, then count of Vendôme (1031–1060) and later count of Anjou (1040–1060), and by Geoffrey's wife, Agnes of Burgundy, the monastery of La Trinité was strategically located on the Loir near the castle of Vendôme. By the time of its formal dedication and consecration in 1040, the monastery had been endowed by its various patrons with churches and extensive landed properties in the Vendômois, as well as in several other regions, notably Maine and Saintonge.[27] Aside from Geoffrey and Agnes, the more important benefactors of La Trinité during its earlier years included the lords of relatively nearby castles, such as Lavardin, Montoire, Fréteval, Montdoubleau and Beaugency; the provosts of the castle of Vendôme itself; powerful knights, like Burchard de Caresmot, Ingebaldus Brito, and Odo Rufus; and Gervasius du Château-du-Loir, bishop of Le Mans.[28] Also found among the abbey's patrons at this time were people of lower status. But by the end of the century, nobles were virtually the only people to patronize La Trinité, and this trend evidently continued during the twelfth century.[29] It also appears that in the last quarter of the eleventh century, the number of conveyances made to La Trinité began to decline, so that here, as at Saint Vincent and Marmoutier, the period of major expansion in the abbey's properties and wealth had clearly ended by the mid-twelfth century, if not earlier.[30] According to a recent historian of the abbey,

> The geographic area from which the abbey drew its greatest support was an elongated rectangle enclosing the two parallel valleys of the Loire and its smaller northern tributary, the Loir. . . . The castles of Fréteval, Lisle, Lavardin, Montoire and la Chartre, lying along the Loir as it runs southwest, all housed patrons of the abbey, as did those of Montdoubleau and Château-la-Vallière on the tributaries of the Loir. Along the Loire and its tributary the Brenne were the seats of the lords of Beaugency, Blois, Amboise, and Château-Renault; the three castellans of Craon, Rançon and Château-Gontier joined the barons of these castles as patrons of somewhat lesser degree.[31]

Thus, the regions in which La Trinité had properties and patrons overlapped in several places with the territories into which the power of Marmoutier extended. It is not surprising to find, therefore, that the monks of Holy Trinity had a complex and often conflict-ridden relationship with the great monastery of Saint Martin near Tours[32] and that many important benefactors of the former also patronized the latter.[33]

Because the properties of both Marmoutier and La Trinité extended to the west of these abbeys, down the Loire and the Loir, the history of both houses intersected at various points with the history of Saint Aubin of Angers.[34] Located at the very center of Angevin power, the religious community of Saint Aubin had a history quite similar to that of the three abbeys just discussed. Like Marmoutier and Saint Vincent's, Saint Aubin was founded, according to tradition, in the very early medieval period. But after a period of decline, it gained new prestige when it was effectively refounded in the late tenth century by a prominent nobleman, in this case the count of Anjou.[35] Like La Trinité, the abbey of Saint Aubin enjoyed the special patronage of the counts of Anjou, who retained close religious and political ties with it throughout the period.[36] Finally, like all three of the monasteries already discussed, the community of Saint Aubin gradually acquired numerous lordly and knightly patrons from several different regions, so that its sphere of influence radiated out in several directions from Angers, where the main abbey was situated.[37] Throughout these regions, the monks of Saint Aubin were patronized by lords and knights, a substantial number of whom were the followers of Saint Aubin's principal patrons, the counts of Anjou.[38] During the twelfth century, however, lavish patronage of this abbey either ceased or else slowed, so that the effects of decline were felt here, just as they were at Saint Vincent, Marmoutier, and La Trinité.[39]

Although the Benedictine community at Saint Mary of Noyers was less renowned than the four other establishments and although it lay on the margins of Angevin power, its history conforms closely to the patterns already noted.[40] By the last third of the eleventh century, if not a little earlier, this monastery had established itself as an important religious center. Founded by a local noble in around 1031, the new abbey of Noyers had a favorable location in the lower Touraine, fairly close to Poitou, and it soon extended its influence within the Touraine and into the Châtelleraudais.[41] Situated on the right bank of the Vienne, just a bit south of the castle of Nouâtre, Noyers was only a few kilometers from the juncture of the Vienne and the river Creuse; and it lay close to several main roads in the region and to several good landing places on the Creuse and the Vienne.[42] Soon after the monastery's foundation, the monks of Saint Mary began acquiring substantial holdings in outlying areas. At least by the time of abbots Rainerius (1072–c. 1080) and Stephanus (c. 1080–1111), Noyers had become a major center.[43]

While some of its lands lay quite far to the west, at Messemé in the Loudunois, and as far north as Saint-Patrice on the Loire and Tours itself, most of its lands, mills, churches, and other properties lay within a territory whose shape seems to have been partially determined by the courses of the Vienne and the Creuse and by the location of the region's main fortifications. This territory can be schematically represented as extending outwards from Noyers and from the nearby castle of Nouâtre towards six other castles, two of which were also on the Vienne: to the northwest, L'Isle-Bouchard, situated in the Vienne about thirteen kilometers downstream; to the southeast, about thirty kilometers up the Vienne, Châtellerault; Sainte Maure, around ten kilometers from Noyers to the north and east, on the way to Tours; Marmande, twelve kilo-

meters due south on a small stream feeding into the Vienne, op-
posite Buxière; Faye-la-Vineuse, eighteen kilometers to the south-
west, between the Veude and the Male and not too far from Marmande; and Champigny-sur-Veude, around eighteen kilometers
away.[44] During the abbacies of Evrardus (1031), Andreas (1032),
Gaufridus (1062–72),[45] Rainerius, and Stephanus, the community
of Noyers developed close, if not invariably amicable, ties with the
lords of the strongholds just listed and with the lesser lords and
knights of the region. Although the monks of Saint Mary were
only occasionally patronized by great lords from outside the region, notably the counts of Anjou, their house did not remain
unaffected by long-term trends that shaped the development of
Benedictine foundations to the north and northwest.[46] In particular, they, too, were affected by the monastic decline of the twelfth
century, so that after 1150, if not a little earlier, the era of expansion in their house's properties was almost certainly over.[47]

As the preceding discussion indicates, the monasteries of Saint
Vincent, Marmoutier, La Trinité, Saint Aubin, and Noyers were all
closely associated with the ruling elites of western and west-central France. From time to time, bishops, canons, and priests,[48] as
well as townspeople, craftsmen, and even peasants made gifts to
these religious communities.[49] But by far the most numerous and
most generous patrons of these five religious houses were lay
lords and knights. The dependence of monks on these members
of secular society took a clear and openly acknowledged form. As
members of communities whose members were expected to reproduce themselves while they themselves remained unmarried and
celibate, monks depended on lay society to provide them with a
steady stream of new brothers drawn mainly from the families of
lords and knights (*milites*).[50] In addition, although they abstained
from most forms of productive labor, swore to individual poverty,
and carried on religious rituals with great frequency, strict regularity, and high ceremony, monks could support themselves by
acting collectively as landlords. Land, along with the labor to work
it and various forms of feudal rent could be provided to them by
lords and knights holding larger or smaller estates and maintaining increasingly tight control over peasants.[51] Thus, the "empire"
of Marmoutier and the smaller but still extensive holdings of the

other four monasteries were gradually built up mainly through gifts of counts, viscounts, castellans, other magnates, and simple knights[52] and, to a lesser extent, through gifts made by the wives, widows, and heiresses of these men.[53]

The complex transactions, of which gifts to saints constituted only the most prominent element, could assume different forms and presumably varied somewhat from region to region and from monastery to monastery. But in Benedictine abbeys of western France, they normally conformed to a fairly well-defined model. The saintly beneficiaries, as represented on earth by an undying community of celibate monks, were to hold the gifts for ever and ever, and in return for perpetual gifts to the saint, lay benefactors received or expected to receive various countergifts consisting of certain tangible and more intangible benefits.[54]

The monks of our five abbeys dispensed several coveted privileges that were not just given freely to anyone who wanted them. To begin with, there were anniversary masses to be faithfully celebrated on the day of the donor's death or the deaths of others—usually kin—whom he specifically designated[55] and whose names, along with his, were written down in the abbey's martyrology.[56] It was also sometimes specified that their anniversaries should be celebrated in the same way as those of the abbey's own monks.[57] In certain cases, anniversary masses were to be supplemented by other commemorative rituals, such as feasts or the distribution of alms to the poor.[58] In addition, monks often promised to chant special masses with particular frequency immediately after the donor or his designates had died, when their souls were thought to have special need of monastic intercession.[59] The monks also gave certain benefactors the privilege of confraternity—often called "the society and benefit" of the abbey—so that a donor and those whom he designated became closely associated, as monks at other abbeys often were, with the monastic community's prayers and acts of ritual charity.[60]

In many instances, monastic benefactors were given burial rights for themselves and for others so that the corpses of these people could be placed in a monastic cemetery or cloister, where they would sometimes lie next to their relatives and where they would be relatively close to the abbey's relics, proximity to which was highly prized.[61] Monks even promised to build and maintain tombs for some of their benefactors.[62] Many lay donors were also accorded places in a monastic community that they themselves or relatives of theirs could immediately or later occupy, as child oblates, as full-fledged choir monks, or as monks *ad succurrendum*, who entered abbeys when approaching death so that they could die in monastic habits.[63] Some lay benefactors also received more opulent hospitality than ordinary guests were accorded.[64] Finally, in return for gifts made to abbeys, monks often gave their benefactors clothing, jewelry, animals, small measures of grain or wine, material goods of other kinds, and money ranging in value from a single penny to ten or fifteen pounds.[65]

The transactions in which lay people received these privileges from monks in return for gifts of land cannot be accurately interpreted through the use of concepts developed for the purpose of analyzing modern law or economics.[66] Gifts to saints resemble donations because they were nominally made freely and spontaneously, with no expectation of recompense. But they differ fundamentally from truly free gifts because they were always supposed to be balanced by countergifts. Insofar as they were made in return for something else, gifts to saints therefore resembled modern sales. But even when donors received money as well as prayers and other spiritual privileges in return for landed property, they were engaging in a distinctive kind of exchange unknown to modern law. For reasons that will be more fully explored below,[67] the things that landholders exchanged with monks cannot be considered commodities to which prices were assigned and which would be bought or permanently alienated in an impersonal market. The spiritual benefits, the lands, and even the money that passed between donors and monks each had a social identity and could not be completely alienated forever by the people who exchanged them, and the countergifts made to monastic benefactors differed from prices paid for commodities to which a specific monetary value could be assigned. The parties to exchanges of this kind, moreover, were not strangers, fully independent of one another, who merely met in "the market." They had preexisting relationships to each other. In addition, by giving a gift to a saint, a lay benefactor established with his monastic beneficiaries an ongoing social relationship that was supposed to last forever and to link him indirectly to one of the saints and to God. Accordingly,

gifts to saints were not instantaneously consummated.[68] Furthermore, relationships established through gifts to saints presupposed the existence of specific attitudes toward death and the
posthumous attainment of salvation. Finally, these transactions
could only have been carried out in a society in which relationships of a particular kind were regularly established between religious communities, on the one hand, and upper-class kinship
groups, on the other.

On an ideological level, there was only a tenuous and delicately
ambiguous connection between the gifts that a landholder made
to a saint and the gifts that he received in return from the saint's
monastic representatives. Although every gift to a saint was supposed to be balanced by a countergift, it was vitally important that
exchanges between landholders and monks not be construed as
sales. In practice, however, gifts to saints could be put to different
uses and were open to self-interested manipulation and divergent
interpretations that began to trouble monastic reformers of the late
eleventh and twelfth centuries. On the one hand, a monastic
benefactor could try to use his gift as a political instrument to
compel his beneficiaries to give him the countergift he desired: he
could try to buy spiritual privileges. On the other hand, monks
could use their power of endowing their benefactors with special
religious status to induce a landholder to endow their abbey with
his lands: they could sell spiritual privileges. As a result, certain
writers from this period periodically raised questions about the
true nature of gifts to saints, which were inherently ambiguous.
Was a monastic benefactor simply buying favor from a monastic
community and doing so with the help of the relatives who approved his gift? And was his gift therefore a simoniacal act? Were
monks selling for worldly wealth what should be properly treated
as priceless religious benefits?[69] Although these questions may
have troubled monks at our five abbeys and some of their benefactors as well, they did not arise in such an acute form as to undermine the practice of giving gifts to saints or to induce participants
to clarify the nature of transactions that could not have been clari-
fied without simultaneously being transformed and deprived of
their established meaning.

According to the formulaic records produced by monastic
scribes, monastic benefactors made these gifts of property and of

power over people for the sake of their own souls and the souls of their relatives and friends.[70] According to monastic charters, donors were motivated by conventional sentiments inspired by Christian teachings. They were supposedly weighed down with remorse for their sins. They feared both the approach of death and the prospect of posthumous punishment.[71] Nevertheless, the people supposedly moved by these commonplace but intensely felt anxieties had also been taught that if they acted properly, their position would not be completely hopeless. For God was at least potentially merciful and might choose to admit them to heaven. Donors, therefore, were supposedly ready to heed biblical injunctions to give alms and, more particularly, to exchange transitory earthly wealth for the hope of eternal benefits in heaven.[72] According to monastic records, they were especially mindful of one biblical command that identifies the ostensible rationale for their gifts to saints: "Make unto you friends of the mammon of iniquity, that when you shall fail, they may receive you into everlasting dwellings."[73]

Although the biblical texts did not clearly indicate to whom gifts of alms were to be given, the religious ideology of the period resolved this potentially troubling question by postulating that saints and monks should be the principal recipients of these benefactions.[74] Gifts to saints, who were God's friends[75] and would intercede with him for the givers, were to be made through the mediation of monks, without whose intercession friendship with God or God's saints could not reliably be established. As a result, monastic benefactors were often represented as hoping that if they granted a portion of their ephemeral earthly inheritance to one of God's close, sainted friends, the saint and his monastic dependents on earth would then recognize these lay people as friends or even as kin of a sort and intercede on their behalf with God. God would then forgive them their sins and ultimately give them an enduring inheritance in the kingdom of heaven. There, the saint would admit his friends to an exalted community where they would hold heavenly inheritances in perpetuity.[76] Thus, from one perspective, the lay benefactors of a monastic community can be seen as the clients of the saint to whom the community was dedicated and whose network of patronage radiated outward from the places where his monks celebrated his cult.[77]

At the same time, by handing over a portion of their earthly wealth and power to the saint's terrestrial representatives, lay benefactors also expected to acquire the manifold, if ill-defined, advantages of being closely linked to a religious community with influence on earth as well as in heaven.[78] Secular princes, such as the counts of Anjou, used the foundation of an abbey such as La Trinité as a means of enhancing their own prestige in the secular world and as a way of establishing, consolidating, and extending their own political power.[79] Lesser men, such as the lords of Faye-la-Vineuse or Marmande, made influential friends when they patronized a monastery such as Noyers.[80] In addition, the monastery to which lay gifts were made often seems to have been a sort of secondary household and burial ground for upper-class kin groups. Some members of these groups lived for years as brothers of the communities their kin had endowed,[81] while others were brought there only after death for interment.[82] Some arrived shortly before death in order to die as monks,[83] and some visited the abbey regularly in order to be present for important church festivals and to visit the tombs of their kin.[84] Finally, it is important to note that in a society where nobles maintained their prestige and their contacts with others through lavish generosity, surpluses of land could be exchanged for what one scholar calls "symbolic capital," which could normally be reconverted into more tangible forms of power.[85]

The benefits accruing to monks from exchanges with lay benefactors were equally varied, complex, and ambiguous. In a sense, gifts to saints merely provided the members of religious communities such as Saint Aubin or Marmoutier with the material support that they and others thought they needed and were entitled to have, so that day and night, they could properly perform their continual task of interceding with God and with God's friends, the saints, on behalf of the living and dead for whom they regularly prayed.[86] At the same time, in acquiring wealth, influential benefactors, and recruits from powerful families, monks gained political influence and spiritual prestige that helped them both to influence the religious and secular life of the regional communities in which abbeys were located and to extend even further the patrimony of their own patron saint.[87] Finally, because gifts to saints provided monks not only with movable goods, but also with land

and lordship, monastic beneficiaries gained power over other people, whose labor, as some monks and other churchmen freely acknowledged, sustained the monks in their own religious activities, just as it had sustained the political pursuits of upper-class monastic benefactors.[88] Monks collected rents and tithes, managed landed property, and exploited the labor of their serfs and other tenants, while also assuming limited jurisdictional powers.[89] They often became involved in lengthy lawsuits with lay landlords and with other religious foundations and were deeply implicated in the ongoing political struggles of their own regions.[90]

Gifts to saints were therefore associated with larger political processes through which both lay lords and monks struggled for hegemony in a highly unstable political world that contemporaries believed to be part of a comparably unstable cosmological order.[91] The practice of giving gifts to saints thus presupposed the existence of a particular social order, within which monks, warriors, and peasants played radically different roles, as well as a complementary Christian cosmology, which had its own distinctive way of representing the relationships between supernatural beings, the living, and the dead.[92]

Given the transcendent, as well as the practical, import of gifts to saints, it is not surprising to find that the times for making them were not chosen randomly and that, like marriages and other important social transactions, exchanges between lay people and monks were normally carried out slowly and ceremoniously in several distinct stages, each of which had its own special geographical setting. In unusual cases, a sudden surge of anxiety about sin, illness, or death drove lay people to make gifts to monasteries from their deathbeds, on the battlefield, or after they had committed some terrible sin.[93] Normally, however, a gift to an abbey was not carried out suddenly, through an instantaneously efficacious act. Instead, it was effected through a lengthy, measured process that entailed negotiations between and within the groups involved as well as a series of mutually corroborating ceremonies.[94] Initial agreements between lay people and monks were often worked out in the homes of the former,[95] in houses owned by the latter,[96] or else in the domiciles of third parties who may have been linked to both monks and benefactors.[97] Here, the gift or the decision to make it was sometimes memorialized, as monks and lay people shared a ceremonial meal[98] or joined in other commemorative rituals.[99] Later on in the process, the scene shifted to a monastic building, usually the chapterhouse.[100] There, a staff, a knife, a glove, a hammer, a book, or some other object suddenly charged with symbolic meaning[101] was passed by hand from the abbot or prior to the lay donor, so as to represent the process by which spiritual benefits were exchanged for land.[102] In addition, when donors were granted "the society and benefit" of the monastery and thereby became participants in a religious community's prayers and good deeds, kisses were exchanged between lay and monastic participants. When the donor was female, however, she kissed a lay surrogate.[103] Finally, the parties processed to the monastic church, where the donor, on bended knee, would make his gift all over again by placing on the high altar either the same object that had been passed back and forth in the chapter or else some other object newly incorporated into the system of symbolic exchange.[104] With this last act—which was sometimes performed just after Mass in the presence of many[105]—the exchange ceremony came to a halt, having now effected a permanent change in the relationships between the participants.[106] But because the same exchange would probably be confirmed or reenacted on later occasions,[107] the exact moment of its completion cannot be specified. The parties supposedly believed that the transaction would truly end only on Judgment Day.[108]

Other ritual acts were also associated with gifts to saints. Before or after a gift had been placed on the altar, the benefactor's name, sometimes along with the names of his relatives and friends, would be noted down, so that these people would be prayed for on the anniversaries of their deaths. The act of recording the names was sometimes delayed, but certain donors insisted that it be performed on the spot, for illiterate as they generally were, they recognized its significance.[109] At every stage of the transaction, formal words were also spoken by the leading participants,[110] and when a ceremony involved children who were too young either to pronounce or remember the proper words or to be held accountable for their speech, they still played their ceremonial part, when a penny or two was placed in their cribs, when they supposedly approved a gift by touching a charter recording it, or when their mother or nurse consented for them and received small token gifts.[111]

Although the transaction normally began when a lay benefactor made a gift to monks, who then reciprocated by making counter-gifts to the donor, the straightforward sequence of gift followed by countergift was not always rigidly followed. For one thing, the gift may sometimes have been made several times over, at different times and in different places,[112] and when the gift was reaffirmed, further gifts to the same abbey were also likely to be made.[113] Moreover, the normal sequence of gift and countergift could be inverted. Sometimes, the monks spontaneously granted burial rights or privileges of confraternity to lay people, and only then would the latter make their gifts to a saint, lest they appear to be receiving a kind of charity properly accepted only by lower-class people.[114] In these ways, the temporal outlines of gifts to saints became blurred, so that even participants may have been uncertain about when, precisely, one exchange ended and another began.

There was no confusion, however, about when such exchanges should be made or reaffirmed. Temporally, gifts or confirmations of gifts tended to be clustered around critical moments in the main donor's life-cycle or in the developmental cycle of a kin group to which he belonged. In addition, the timing of some transactions may have been linked to the liturgical calendar.[115] Lay people often gave property to a monastic community when they were sick and thought they were dying.[116] At such times, they left their own households to become monks and were permitted to don and die in monastic habits.[117] Many other people participated in gifts to saints just after the death of a close relative or close friend.[118] Others still made their gifts when it was time for a child of theirs to enter an abbey as a novice.[119] Men often confirmed the gifts of their fathers shortly after their fathers' deaths.[120] Even when a gift was not timed so as to coincide with an important moment of social transition, the participants in the exchange must have had such moments in mind, because in one way or another, every such gift was associated with one or more deaths—the donor's eventual death, the deaths of his ancestors, or the deaths of his wife, his children, his collateral kin, or his lord.[121] These transactions can therefore be associated with Christian practices and beliefs that were organized, at least for the laity, around a few crises, notably death, when people gathered to participate in special ceremonies.[122]

The privilege of full participation in exchange rituals was not accorded to most inhabitants of the regions where the transactions were carried out. Aside from monastic servants, who sometimes witnessed gifts to their own abbey, and the peasants who became serfs of an abbey when they gave themselves and all their posterity to saints,[123] lower-class people rarely participated actively or figured prominently in gifts to saints. Occasionally, they made small gifts of land to abbeys,[124] but when the rituals served, as they often did, to transfer or divide power over serfs or *colliberti*,[125] these people were treated as objects of exchange, rather than as participants in exchange rituals. By contrast, lords and knights participated actively in gifts to saints and normally acted, not as isolated individuals, but as members of groups that included their kin, lords, or dependents.

Here, at last, we come back to the *laudatio parentum*. At the abbey church and in the chapterhouse, the lord abbot or prior was invariably accompanied by other senior monks and was sometimes joined by the entire chapter and by other members of the patron saint's *familia*.[126] Also present in the church, represented by relics and images, was the patron saint himself.[127] On the other side, in both chapterhouse and church, the lay benefactor was usually accompanied by relatives, who often approved or joined in his gift to the saint.[128] Wives, sons, daughters, male and female siblings, and other kin appeared at the abbey to join in gifts after traveling from their regular dwelling places to do so. Even when relatives did not initially participate in their kinsman's gift to an abbey, they often approved it at least once on some later occasion, before or after their kinsman's death.[129] Also present at the abbey at certain ceremonies were the main donor's lords or followers, who were sometimes joined in turn by their own kin. When these associates of the donor did not initially appear at the abbey to approve his gift, they frequently gave their consent later on, at home, in the house of a third party, or at the monastery itself.[130] Finally, in certain instances, dead bodies of the donor's relatives sometimes lay buried close to the places where exchange ceremonies were carried out,[131] and their tombs occasionally served as sites for making or confirming gifts.[132] How the monks and lay people placed themselves in the chapterhouse or church, we cannot tell. But certain conventions had presumably been established about the positioning of participants and about their movements from position to position as they performed different segments of the ceremony. The monks, the main donor and his associates, and the witnesses were all joining in an established ritual, which was performed at least several times a year at each of our five abbeys or their priories and which, like other religious and secular rituals, presumably conformed to prescribed patterns of speech, gesture, and movement.

When the terms of a gift were first worked out, sometimes in a house lying far from the religious community in question, witnesses were present to see, hear, and remember what happened.[133] Because upper-class people were expected to die in the presence of others, witnesses were on hand even for the gifts that dying men made after first confessing their sins,[134] and when there was no opportunity for a monk to attend at the dying man's bedside, the prospective donor would charge his son or other associate to make a gift for him.[135] In the chapterhouse and in the abbey church, witnesses to gifts and countergifts were invariably present. Except when an exchange was made on an important, well-attended feast day, when a gift of rights in a church was made before an entire parish, or when a large, crowded marketplace served as the forum for transactions of this kind,[136] the witnesses were surely known to at least some of the main actors. Indeed, some witnesses were relatives of the main participants.[137] The witnesses saw and heard what happened. Perhaps they also identified themselves formally by name or even conformed to the ritualized style of the occasion by arranging themselves in locations appropriate to their own social position. Sometimes, the division between witnesses and principals became blurred, when a lay witness spontaneously made a gift of his own in return for the usual countergifts.[138] At other times, the monks widened the scope of the ceremony by granting the privilege of confraternity to witnesses or consenting relatives, who then reciprocated by making their own gifts to a saint.[139] In any event, a witness could later swear an oath on a holy relic about what he had seen or even undergo a divinely sanctioned test of the truth of his testimony.[140]

Two things were essential to the future efficacy of these transactions. First, the transaction had to be properly performed, carefully remembered and scrupulously respected in ways that still allowed for subsequent modifications. In this period of significant social change in western France, it could not have been easy to balance the desire to maintain agreements strictly and the impulse to change them in response to the pressures of new needs. Second, a gift had to be periodically reenacted or reaffirmed.[141]

Several actions were taken to ensure that agreements would be observed in the future by people who, living in a society with relatively little formal government, had little reason to fear regularized secular sanctions against wrongdoing. Most importantly, terrible curses were invoked against those who might later dare to undermine the transaction. These people were also condemned in advance to pay unbelievably large, uncollectible, but still fearsome fines[142] or else to suffer the awful fate of proverbial sinners and troth-breakers such as Dathan and Abiron, Simon Magus, Julian the Apostate, and Judas the Traitor.[143] They could also be threatened with excommunication.[144] Then, instead of gaining the friendship of God, Christ, and the saints, they would incur the wrath and enmity of these supernatural beings, just as they would incur the anger and hostility of their own feudal lord if they broke faith with him.[145] Thus they would inherit eternal punishment, instead of a heavenly fief.[146] A gift could also be rendered more secure if the donor, his relatives, and, perhaps, his lord promised to defend it against challengers and to provide the monks with an equally valuable gift if they failed in their primary task of guaranteeing ("warranting") the monks' title to the original gift.[147] Sometimes, the task of warranting, acquitting, or defending the gift was assigned to small groups of people, whom the donor designated as pledges.[148] At the same time, measures were taken to ensure that monastic benefactors and those whom they designated would later receive the benefits due to them from the monks.[149]

To supplement and corroborate the memories of participants and witnesses, the knives, staffs, or other objects used in the ceremony were preserved by the monks as evidence or tokens of what had transpired. Occasionally, the donor's name was even scratched onto the knife or other object with which he had made his gift.[150] Monks also used another sort of object to perpetuate the memory of a gift: a piece of parchment on which the transaction was recorded by monastic scribes who wrote in Latin and often tried to use traditional or even antiquated formulae culled from older documents.[151] Although many such texts were drafted long after the rituals they recorded and thus served only an evidentiary function, others were produced quickly enough to be used in the exchange ceremony itself. When the gift was first made in the chapterhouse, the principal lay participants or their clerks made the sign of the Holy Cross next to the place where a scribe had written down their names.[152] Later, after the participants had passed from the chapterhouse to the church, the parchment could be placed on the altar instead of another object, so as to symbolize one side of the exchange between the lay people and the saint.[153] The charter was sometimes read aloud in its impressively incomprehensible Latin and was then explained in the vernacular to those present.[154] Finally, like the other objects used in these rituals, the parchment would be put away for safekeeping, only to be brought out for one of several different purposes: to have the names of additional *laudatores* inscribed on it; to be studied, sometimes along with related texts, by monks charged with overseeing the saint's estate and protecting it from attack or encroachment; to be produced as evidence at meetings convened to resolve a subsequent dispute about the gift;[155] or else to be copied into a cartulary or monastic history, where, in rare instances, it would be accompanied by a picture of the exchange ceremony the document recorded.[156]

Even in the absence of a charter, memory of a transaction, if not of its exact provisions, could be preserved by illiterate participants, witnesses, and neighbors and even by subsequent generations. For these people, symbolic actions and oral tradition were the primary means of maintaining continuity in culture and social structure. Rituals coinciding with deaths or other critical events in community life were especially likely to be remembered. Memory of a transaction was also reinforced by the continuing involvement of participants in the relationships that the exchange ceremony created, reaffirmed, or rearranged and by their participation in subsequent reenactments of the ceremony. On the one hand, the monks exploited their newly acquired possessions through public acts, such as the collection of tithes or rent, which were normally scheduled so as to coincide with major feast days. On the other hand, lay benefactors probably moved rapidly to enjoy the privileges that they had received from monks. Laymen who had been granted rights of hospitality at the abbey would appear there and feel wronged if they were turned away.[157] Lay recipients of burial rights must have either transported the corpses of their kin to the monastery for interment or called on the monks to do so. When a man who had been promised the right to die as a monk felt death approaching, he would ask for a monastic habit. Sooner or later, a benefactor whose son had been promised a place in the monastery would bring his child there to be admitted as a novice. Finally, some of the more durable countergifts that were made to monastic benefactors may have served as tokens that reminded their possessors of how, where, and why they had acquired these objects.

Efforts to stabilize gifts to saints and project their effects into the future, however, were often unsuccessful. Although lay and monastic participants generally did what they could to render gifts and countergifts immune from future disruptions, many gifts to saints became the subjects of prolonged and sometimes violent controversies, especially when a donor's relatives or lord challenged his gift.[158] As a result, ceremonies ostensibly designed carefully to create or reinforce solidarity and reciprocity among living and dead laymen, monks, and saints often became the cause or occasion of intense conflicts that disrupted the amicable relations that were supposed to exist among all the participants and their successors. Eventually, however, many disputes over gifts to saints were at least temporarily halted at ceremonies that closely resembled the ones at which gifts were initially exchanged. After brief or more prolonged discussion, the monastery's adversary often gave up his quarrel and made a concord with the monks, who, in return, usually accorded him benefits normally accorded to an abbey's more innocuous patrons.[159] His kin, moreover, would share in these benefits, when they joined in his "*guerpitio*," as these quitclaims were often called.[160] Agreements of this type were carried out slowly and ceremoniously and were recorded in charters that are sometimes hard to distinguish from records of new benefactions. Like the original transactions between lay people and monks, concords might either remain in force for generations or else become the subject of friction or open conflict.[161] Whereas some gifts to saints may ultimately have served to create or reinforce feelings of enduring solidarity between monks, their benefactors, and their benefactors' kin, others clearly generated or exacerbated social conflict.

This preliminary discussion of gifts to saints reveals that the *laudatio parentum* was associated with complex social transactions that served not only to transfer control of land and associated rights, but also to establish ongoing relationships between and among social groups. Subsequent chapters will consider the implications of this finding for efforts to determine whether the *laudatio parentum* was required by law, which relatives were expected to give it, why it was given at all, and what the history of this practice reveals about broader social developments in medieval France.

Chapter 3

Custom

STUDIES OF THE *laudatio parentum* can provide
general conclusions about eleventh- and twelfth-century land tenure, kinship, and social development only after historians have
established the legal or normative status of this practice. How the
laudatio is interpreted depends largely on whether the people who
secured it or gave it were following a legal rule, discharging a
religious duty, following custom, taking a practical precaution, or
simply behaving in a way that falls into a statistical pattern. Even
if we do not treat the *laudatio* as "the product of obedience" to any
kind of rule,[1] we need to know how medieval people viewed the
practice. It has proved difficult, however, to determine whether
the *laudatio* was essential to the legal validity of gifts to saints or to
identify the exact legal, moral, religious, or social consequences of
failures to make gifts in this way. These problems are hard to solve
not only because the available evidence is open to different interpretations, but also because the question of whether the *laudatio*
was a mere prudential practice or a legal institution—*"une prudence
habituelle"* or *"une obligation impérieuse"*[2]—is a useful one to ask
only if we make certain debatable assumptions about gifts to
saints and about earlier medieval law.

Moreover, even if a custom or legal rule required that some gifts
be made with the approval of certain relatives, its scope still has to
be delineated. Did it apply to all transfers of land? Or were there
circumstances in which individuals could make valid gifts without
the *laudatio*? Perhaps the rule applied only to inherited, as opposed to acquired, property, whereas gifts of property acquired
through a donor's wife, mother, or other female relative were subject to special restraints. But neither of these hypotheses has been
confirmed.[3] While an individual's power to alienate real property
may have depended on his own status, the status of his donee—
the recipient of the gift—or the nature and origin of the property
alienated, no one has demonstrated that the gifts of great nobles,

for example, were not governed by the same customs as the gifts of less powerful people.[4]

To answer these questions, we also need to gain an understanding of the normative context in which the *laudatio parentum* was practiced. If a rule or custom required that gifts to saints be made with the consent of relatives, did it form part of a system of real property law? Or did it instead regulate social exchanges in which the establishment or reaffirmation of social relationships was at least as important as the transfer of land? In other words, did the rule dictate how farmland, mills, vineyards, or other forms of landed property—along with power over serfs—were to be transferred from one person to another? Or did it regulate the actions of participants in more complex social transactions that entailed more than the transfer of land? Was the rule or custom primarily concerned with things or with people? Or is this distinction an unhelpful one to make for this period? At the same time, we must also determine whether the gifts that eleventh- and twelfth-century landholders so often made to monks and saints were ones that they were obliged to make and that their kin had a duty to support or whether the making and approving of such gifts were matters of purely personal choice or preference. Were a donor's relatives completely free to approve or not to approve his gift? Was their consent something that had to be extracted from them, because in giving it, they suffered a loss? Or did relatives have an active interest in approving gifts to saints? If gifts to saints were simply land transactions governed by a code of legal rules that were distinguished from mere customs or religious norms, then we should be able to determine whether a rule requiring the *laudatio* formed part of this code. If, however, we reject this way of looking at gifts to saints, then the normative status of the *laudatio* becomes more problematic and difficult to establish.

The more closely we examine the *laudatio parentum*, the more frequently and insistently the questions just posed present themselves. But several facts about the *laudatio* are well established, and the ones most central to this entire analysis can be conveniently reviewed here. To begin with, the great frequency with which the *laudatio* was given in many regions of France is not in doubt, provided that we make certain assumptions about scribal conventions and about the randomness with which monastic charters survive.[5] Although the *laudatio* was not as common a practice as some scholars have claimed,[6] studies of the Mâconnais, Picardy, and Poitou demonstrate that during the eleventh and twelfth centuries, many if not most gifts to saints were approved by relatives and that this practice only began to die out in the late twelfth or early thirteenth century.[7] Similar findings emerge from an analysis of gifts made to Marmoutier, La Trinité of Vendôme, Saint Aubin of Angers, Saint Vincent of Le Mans, and Saint Mary of Noyers.[8] In the seven quarter-century intervals between 1025 and 1199, the percentage of recorded gifts made to Marmoutier with the consent of at least one relative always falls within a range between 63 and 86 percent. At Saint Aubin between 1050 and 1199, 61 to 78 percent of all gifts were made with the *laudatio*, while at La Trinité, Saint Vincent, and Noyers, the figures are respectively 51 to 90 percent, 45 to 61 percent, and 64 to 90 percent.[9] Although it would be foolish to attach any importance to these specific figures, they certainly support the conventional view that the *laudatio* was a very common practice.

When considering how often the *laudatio parentum* was given, we should note that relatives were evidently more likely to approve new gifts to saints than they were to join in two other sorts of transactions between lay people and monks: quitclaims (or *guerpitiones*) that lay people made to abbeys at the conclusion of disputes,[10] and confirmations by lords of gifts that their tenants made to religious communities.[11] Nevertheless, transactions of these two kinds were still made with the *laudatio* fairly often. At Saint Aubin between 1050 and 1199, when two-thirds of all new gifts were made with the *laudatio*, more than half of all quitclaims were made in the same way, and more than one out of three confirmations were approved by at least one relative of the lord. Comparable figures for La Trinité, Saint Vincent, Noyers, and Marmoutier fall into more or less the same pattern. Quitclaims were rarely approved, as gifts were, more than 66 percent of the time, but the percentage of quitclaims made with the *laudatio* usually exceeded 50 percent.[12] Throughout our entire period at Saint Aubin, Marmoutier, Saint Vincent, and Noyers, familial approval of feudal confirmations is found in 36 to 47 percent of all recorded transactions, while at La Trinité, the figure is 60 percent.[13]

The fact that late eleventh- and early twelfth-century gifts to our five abbeys were often made with the *laudatio parentum* does not, of course, show that they were supposed to be made in this way. But other evidence suggests that considerable importance was attached to securing the consent of a monastic donor's kin. Besides showing that relatives frequently approved gifts to saints, charters also reveal how much trouble many monastic scribes took to record the participants in the *laudatio* precisely. While some documents refer only vaguely to the consent of a donor's relatives (*parentes*) or blood-relatives (*consanguinei*), for example, or to the approval of his family (*stirps, genus,* or *parentela*),[14] and while others simply name a few consenting relatives and then mention the approval of a donor's "friends by blood" (*amici*) or children,[15] charters usually list a donor's consenting relatives by name and indicate their relationship to him, either by using a single kinship term, such as *gener* (son-in-law), or else by tracing that relative's relationship to the donor and indicating, for example, that he was the husband of the donor's daughter.[16] Some of these lists are lengthy and complex. In recording a gift made to Noyers in c. 1130, by Johannes Alexandri and his sister Galiena, a scribe noted the consent of the following people identified only as relatives of these two siblings: Rabant and her brother Guillelmus; their mother, Guinosa; her husband, Josbertus; Johannes's wife, Petronilla; Petronilla's sister Amelina and her husband, Gano, and their son Bartholomeus; Galiena's sons Guillelmus and Matheus; her daughters Juliana, Maria, and Pelosa; and two men called Rainaldus Bigris and Fulcherius.[17]

Comparably complex consenting groups were described with precision by Marmoutier scribes, one of whom noted that a gift made in the late twelfth century by Ursio, the lord of Fréteval, was approved by his wife, Gricia; his firstborn son, Nivelo; his other sons, Fulcherius, Philippus, Matheus, and Bernardus; his four daughters, Isabel, Philippa, Persois, and Aalez; Aaliz, the wife of his firstborn son, Nivelo; and Ursiolus and Bernardus, the sons of Nivelo and Aaliz.[18] When recording a conveyance to Marmoutier in 1060–63 by Raherius, son of Guarinus and canon of Saint-Georges, another scribe carefully noted the approval of the following people: Raherius's sister Adeladis and her husband, Odo the Clerk; their sons Guarinus, Raherius, Simon, and Odo, who were the nephews (*nepotes*) of Raherius; Raherius's second sister, Hadvisa, the wife of Fulbertus Trusellus; her sons Petrus and Nihardus; and, finally, Raherius's third sister, Alsendis.[19]

When scribes provided what looks like incidental information about the donor's kin, their remarks sometimes imply that the *laudatio parentum* constituted an integral and significant part of the gift-giving ceremony. One Saint Aubin scribe, for example, probably had a good reason for inserting the following anecdote into a charter recording the gift that Philippus the knight made to the scribe's abbey. When Philippus made his gift at the castle of La Flèche, with the consent of his wife and his two younger sons, his two elder sons had left the castle to play—as boys, remarks the scribe, are wont to do. Later, however, the two errant youths returned to the castle and approved their father's gift. This story must have been meant to show that an initial flaw or anomaly in Philippus's gift had been speedily corrected.[20] Similarly, when a Saint Vincent scribe noted that a woman who had approved the gift of her father, Wido de Courtelard, had not yet been given to a husband, he was indirectly conveying a significant piece of information: at the time of the original gift, the main donor had had no daughter's husband or daughter's children whose consent could have been obtained.[21] A similar concern presumably lies behind the remark of a La Trinité scribe that at the time of Raoul de Beaugency's gift to that abbey, this knight had no heir born of his wife.[22]

Implicit in many remarks about the absence of relatives from a gift-giving ceremony is the assumption that gifts were normally approved—and, perhaps, were supposed to be approved—by such relatives. Why else would scribes have noted that the eldest son of Joscelinus Bodellus was absent when the latter first gave land to La Trinité,[23] that the son of Arnaldus Gruellus was so ill that his mother remained with him, while Arnaldus traveled to Saint Vincent to make a gift,[24] and that the husband of a benefactress of La Trinité had recently died?[25] The same assumption about the importance of securing the *laudatio* probably lies behind scribal notes that certain consenting relatives were infants. Although children too young to speak or understand what was happening could participate in a gift, the validity of their consent was always in doubt. Monks therefore thought it prudent both to note that a child had approved a gift as an infant and to secure his or her consent later on when the child was clearly old enough to understand, and to be obligated by, his or her own words and deeds.[26]

Many charters also mention measures taken to secure approval from kin who were either absent or reluctant to consent and from relatives who were born after a gift had been made. Some donors promised to carry out this task themselves;[27] others appointed pledges (*fidejussores* or *plegii*) to perform it and to indemnify the beneficiary if the gift in question became the subject of a costly challenge.[28] Sometimes, however, the monks themselves took the trouble to secure the approval of relatives and of others, usually feudal lords, whose approval was thought to be worth having.[29] This task was not always easy, as we can see from several stories indicating what it could entail. After Clarembaldus de Montfourmé had exchanged some property with Saint Vincent of Le Mans, he and the monk Bernardus agreed that on the eve of the feast of Saint John the Baptist, the exchange would be confirmed by Clarembaldus himself; his wife; his father, Vivianus; and Vivianus's wife. At the appointed time, Bernardus arrived at Vivianus's house in Laval, where Vivianus approved his son's transaction. But to find Clarembaldus, Bernardus had to travel to Château-Gontier. There, on the feast of Saint John, Bernardus caught up with Clarembaldus, who was feasting in the house of Fromundus de Chenevrolles. After finishing his meal, Clarembaldus came outside where Bernard awaited him and confirmed his earlier agreement with the monks of Saint Vincent. Clarembaldus then urged his brother Adelardus, who was eating inside, to come out to approve the transaction. Adelardus willingly gave his consent before a group of witnesses that probably included Fromundus's guests and household members. Later, Clarembaldus went to Bazougers to find his lord, Hamelinus de Bazougers. On the bridge of Bazougers, Hamelinus responded to Clarembaldus's entreaties by approving his tenant's exchange with Saint Vincent, as many witnesses watched. No record shows that Clarembaldus's wife or mother ever approved this agreement, as they were supposed to do. But perhaps the monk Bernardus made one or more unrecorded journeys to secure their consent.[30]

There was nothing extraordinary about Bernardus's efforts to ensure that a transaction benefiting his abbey was approved by people besides the main donor. Late in the eleventh century, other monks of Saint Vincent took similar pains to ensure that a gift made by Odo Donkey Neck was approved by his relatives and by others as well. In return for the right to die as a monk of Saint Vincent, Odo made his gift on the altar of Saint Vincent and Saint Lawrence at Le Mans in the presence of his son Vitalis, his *nepos* Robertus, his daughter Leta, and her husband, Guillelmus. After Odo was received as a monk, his gift was confirmed in at least five other ceremonies. First, because Odo held his property as a fief from Guillelmus de Braiteau, the latter, when he came to Le Mans, approved the gift by placing it on the high altar of the abbey church, in the presence of Odo Donkey Neck and many other monks of the abbey. Then, at Braiteau, Guillelmus's brothers Hugo and Gaufridus approved the transaction. At Le Mesnil, Odo's gift was approved by his brother's son Guillelmus Donkey Neck; by Guillelmus's three brothers Ernaldus, Hugo, and Albertus; and by their mother, Berta. Further approval of Odo's gift was given, first at Montigny, where another of Odo's *nepotes*, Haimericus Paganus, consented, and later at Luerzon, where Haimericus's brother Radulfus gave his approval. Each of these ceremonies was attended by at least one monk of Saint Vincent. Each was witnessed, remembered, and thought worthy of being recorded.[31]

Many monastic charters also suggest that the *laudatio* was itself a formal act more similar to giving than to witnessing. Although certain gifts were witnessed by the donor's relatives—whose kinship tie to him might be noted or ignored—we should not assume that every kinsman attending an exchange ceremony acted in the same capacity, for in any given ceremony, some relatives participated more actively than others did. Relatives approved conveyances orally and promised not to disturb them in the future.[32] Sometimes they even acted the part of donors, as they joined their kinsman in placing an object on the monks' altar. When Walicherius and his younger brother Johannis gave up a rent that the community at Saint Aubin owed them so that their father, whom the monks had just buried, would not seem to lie "in alms," the elder brother alone made the gift by placing a staff on the altar of a parish church pertaining to Saint Aubin.[33] In other instances, however, two or more relatives would act together in making a gift. This kind of joint investiture supposedly rendered gifts "firmer" than they would have been if only a single individual had made them.[34] When relatives made a cross on a charter at the appropriate place, they were again behaving more like benefactors than like witnesses.[35]

In fact, a significant number of gifts to each of our abbeys were made jointly by several relatives acting together, so that we cannot accurately represent them as donations made by a main donor, accompanied by one or more consenting relatives.[36] In other instances, gifts were made jointly by two or more kin and approved by one or more of their relatives.[37] Although it is unclear whether transactions of these two types differed significantly from each other or from gifts that individual donors made with the consent of their kin,[38] joint gifts—as they are called here—are worth noting because they show more clearly than other types of transactions do that a landholder's relatives sometimes played so central a role in alienating land that scribes obliterated the distinction between donor and *laudator*.[39]

In addition, the fact that many consenting relatives received countergifts from their kinsman's beneficiary suggests that they played an important and perhaps even indispensable role in exchange ceremonies. Like donors, they were sometimes accorded the society and benefit of the abbey in question[40] and the right to enter it later.[41] They, too, were given clothing, animals, or money.[42] Even if such countergifts—which were supposedly made out of charity[43]—did not balance a direct, material loss that the donor's relatives suffered by approving his gift,[44] countergifts to them formed part of an exchange between the saint and his people and the saint's benefactor and his people. Furthermore, even when consenting relatives received none of the material goods or spiritual privileges granted to the donor or his deceased relatives, they were really receiving a service from the monks. The monks helped them to discharge their obligation to procure prayers for relatives to whom they were indebted for their inherited property.[45]

In certain instances, the main donor himself either provided his kin with countergifts or else set aside money to be paid to any relative who later contested his gift.[46] Although the precise significance of countergifts to consenting kin is unclear, they supposedly rendered gifts to saints more stable. A Saint Aubin benefactor who gave money to his two consenting nephews did so, we are told, so that his gift would remain intact and inviolate.[47] When the wife of another Saint Aubin benefactor was given seven *solidi* for her consent, the scribe explained that this countergift was made so that her act would be "purer."[48] Other texts state that the bestowal of countergifts on a donor's consenting relatives made gifts firmer and ensured that these people would consent "more fully," "more willingly," or "more freely."[49]

The hypothesis that the *laudatio parentum* was much more than an empty convention or a prudent but inessential practice gains further support from the discovery that it was sometimes difficult to obtain. When Odierna, sister of the monk Petrus, wished to make a gift to Saint Vincent for the soul of her son Girardus, who had just been killed, her son Robertus de Montaigu opposed the gift and approved it only after the monk Gislibertus had pleaded with him to do so.[50] More than fifty years later, Simon de Beaugency encountered a similar obstacle to making a stable gift to the monks of La Trinité, who, in return, were to bury one of Simon's knights in their cloister. Initially, Simon's wife Adenordis refused to approve the transaction, which would have taken away part of her dower, and did so only when she became ill and felt close to death.[51]

Sometimes, recalcitrant relatives could profit by expressing disapproval of a kinsman's gift. In 1067, when Robertus the Burgundian's plan to give some property to Saint Vincent was blocked by his son Robertus Vestrul, who refused to approve it, the younger Robertus first demanded forty *solidi* for his approval. Later, responding to his father's plea, he approved the gift when the monks gave him twenty *solidi* and promised to bring him some wolf skins on Christmas Eve.[52] At a solemn ceremony at Saint Aubin, a woman who murmured disapprovingly about her brother's gift to the abbey was given ten *solidi* and then approved the gift "willingly."[53] From time to time, disapproval of a kinsman's gift was expressed more forcefully. When Raginaldus, son of Gedeo de Hischiriaco, asked his brother Paganus to approve his conveyance of a mill at Sermaise to Saint Aubin, Paganus did more than murmur and then get paid off. He rode to the mill, seized some money from the miller, and then tried to tear the mill down. Only after the bishop of Angers intervened did Paganus relent, confirm his brother's gift, and promise to defend the monks against future attacks of the sort that he himself had just made.[54]

When considered together, the frequency with which the consent of relatives was given, the care with which it was secured and recorded, the difficulties that were sometimes overcome in order to obtain it, and the benefits for which it was often exchanged all indicate that the *laudatio parentum* formed an integral part of gifts to saints. The same theory is also supported not only by charters stating that the *laudatio* could stabilize a gift, but also by much rarer passages indicating why this was so. One scribe stated directly that when a gift made to Marmoutier in 1194 was approved by the father, brothers, sisters, sons, and other *amici* and *proximi* (kin) of Guillelmus de Gémages, this approval was "necessary."[55] Another gift made to the same house more than a century earlier was allegedly approved by all those who were supposed to do so.[56]

Other texts hint at the significance of failures to secure the *laudatio parentum*. One Marmoutier scribe alleged that the wife and three sons of Giraldus Brunellus had approved his gift lest any dispute should later arise about it.[57] Another stated that a gift made by Raherius the canon was approved by all those who might later challenge it. This group, which has already been mentioned, included the canon's two sisters and their husbands, along with four sons of the first sister and two sons of the second.[58] After a man had given tithes to Noyers, he was asked by the abbot of that house whether he had any relatives who might later challenge his gift, and he responded that he had no kin at all.[59] In other cases, donors stipulated that they would indemnify their donees with money or property of equivalent value if their relatives failed to approve their gifts or caused trouble about them.[60]

Unusually vivid evidence indicating that a donor's relatives were likely to contest gifts that they had not approved comes from a charter recounting the background to a gift made to La Trinité in the early 1070s. In the *pagus* of Vendôme, we learn, a woman called Freducia held two estates that she had acquired from her progenitors by hereditary right, one in Listriacum and the other in the villa Sigonis. After her marriage to Guitaldus, she and her husband fell into poverty and decided that they would not be able to feed or clothe themselves without selling off Freducia's two

properties. But because Freducia did not wish to alienate her inheritance out of her own kin group, she first made a request of
Gervasius, son of Lancelinus, whose wife was Freducia's cousin
(*cognata*) and a daughter of Drogo, the brother of Matheus de
Montoire. In return for taking Freducia's two estates into their
own hands, Gervasius and his wife were asked to provide lifetime
support to Freducia and her husband, with the provision that after
Freducia and Guitaldus were dead, Gervasius, his wife, and their
offspring would possess the properties. Gervasius and his wife
refused this offer. Finding no close blood-relative of hers to aid
them, Freducia and her husband eventually decided to grant the
two estates to the monks of La Trinité on the terms previously
proposed to Gervasius and his wife. But Freducia, looking into the
future, said that she would never give a church any property that
her own kin could take away after her death. She therefore left the
estate in the villa Sigonis to the above-mentioned Drogo de Montoire, who was her blood-relative on her mother's side. The estate
at Listriacum, however, which she had received from her own
father and which, we are told, could not be rightfully challenged
by her cousins or by anyone else, she gave to La Trinité in
perpetuity.[61]

This story clearly shows that if Freducia and her husband had
given the estate at the Villa Sigonis to La Trinité, the gift could
have been challenged after her death by her matrilateral kin.
Along with charters expressing the fears of monastic benefactors
that their gifts would be challenged by their own kin, evidence of
conflicts between a donor's relatives and his monastic beneficiary
is very easy to find in eleventh- and twelfth-century monastic
charters. Many texts merely mention the anxieties of donors and
monks that the former's living or unborn relatives would disturb
gifts to saints and thereby jeopardize the benefits that donors and
donees hoped to secure by means of these transactions.[62] To allay
such fears, as we have seen, charters often invoked various sanctions on heirs, relatives, or other persons who disturbed gifts to
saints.[63] By themselves, provisions of this kind may show only
that a man's relatives were likely to challenge alienations that he
made without their consent and not that they were legally entitled
to do so.[64] But in fact, many such challenges (*calumniae*) were
made. Between about 1040 and 1100, Marmoutier was involved in

at least forty-six recorded disputes with people contesting their relatives' gifts to that abbey. During the same period, recorded familial challenges troubled La Trinité seventeen times, Saint Aubin twenty-eight times, Saint Vincent thirty-five times, and Noyers twenty-three times.[65]

In some of these cases, litigants challenged their kinsman's gifts on the grounds that they or their wives had not approved them.[66] In 1068, Hubertus, son of Robertus de Marrei, challenged the right of Marmoutier to land at Fontenailles which his father had conveyed to them, according to Hubertus, without his approval.[67] Four years earlier, when Drogo Cholet de Lavardin initiated a *calumnia* about other Marmoutier properties in the Vendômois, he contended that when his wife had approved her relatives' gift to the monks, she had been too young to give valid consent.[68] In the 1030s or early 1040s, Archembaldus challenged a gift to La Trinité that his elder brother Benedictus de Polinis had made with the approval of his cousin (*consobrinus*) Joscelinus and his lord, Hilgaldus, but that Archembaldus himself, being absent, had not approved.[69] A half century later, Bertrannus, the eldest son of Robertus de Montcontoire, seized property that his father had given to La Trinité in Bertannus's absence.[70] In 1064, Simon claimed a serf previously given by his brother to Marmoutier without Simon's consent.[71] A little later, after Agnes had given property to Marmoutier in return for money that her second husband used to help pay for a trip to Rome, her nephew, Jeremias de Turre, challenged his aunt's gift, claiming that he had never heard about it, much less approved it.[72] During the 1060s, Ebrardus, the viscount of Chartres, initiated a *calumnia* about properties that his brother and father had transferred to Marmoutier, allegedly without his authorization.[73]

When a knight or lord initiated a *calumnia* of this sort, he normally prosecuted it forcefully. Instead of visiting the abbey for a peaceful discussion or taking the monks to court, lay litigants often seized either the disputed property itself or other property held by their monastic adversary or else they used other forms of direct action.[74] One litigant tried to kill a man of Marmoutier with a spear.[75] To back up a claim that the dependents of Marmoutier did not have fishing rights in a stream running through a forest, another litigant, who had rights in that forest, destroyed the nets that the abbey's men were using there.[76] In a third case, when a lord claimed that the monks' serfs were obliged to go to his mill and not to the one recently built by the monks, he asserted this claim by having his men seize the goods of serfs going to the abbey's mill and by abusing them in other ways.[77]

Lay lords who claimed the right to impose various tallages, tolls, or other duties on dependents of our five monasteries simply had their *ministri* seize customs that the lords claimed but that monks regularly characterized as "evil customs."[78] In other instances, the monks' adversaries plundered the abbeys' lands and people. In these raiding expeditions, litigants took herds of cattle or pigs and burned crops and peasant dwelling places. Sometimes, they killed or wounded a monk or two, but their principal victims were almost certainly the monks' free or unfree dependents.[79] In carrying on disputes that monastic scribes sometimes characterized as *guerrae* and thereby likened to feuds between noble kin groups,[80] the monks' adversaries were engaging in an activity that was attacked by clerical leaders of "peace movements." The legitimacy of such disputes, however, went unquestioned by lords and knights, who regularly found reasons or pretexts for plundering the lands of their neighbors.[81]

Familial challenges provide corroboration for the conventional complaint made in the early twelfth century by the northern French monk Guibert of Nogent that "now, alas, those gifts which their parents . . . made to the holy places, the sons now withdraw entirely or continually demand payment for their renewal, having utterly degenerated from the good will of their sires."[82] To secure fifty quitclaims to properties in the Vendômois between 1050 and 1100, Marmoutier monks paid out almost 140 pounds of silver.[83] A payment of two or three pounds was common.[84] Payments of five, ten, or even fourteen pounds were not unknown.[85] Many quitclaims, as we have seen, were approved by the challengers' kin, in return for the same sorts of countergifts accorded to relatives who approved new gifts.[86]

Other evidence as well suggests that an individual landholder was not considered completely free to act alone in disposing of his land. Gifts to Marmoutier, Saint Vincent, Saint Aubin, Noyers, and La Trinité were sometimes approved not just by the donor's relatives, but also by his lord and overlord.[87] Although the *laudatio domini* or *dominorum*, as this practice can reasonably be called, was less prevalent in our region than was the *laudatio parentum*, it was common enough to merit attention. Between 15 and 25 percent of all recorded conveyances to these five abbeys were approved by the main donor's lord.[88] Like the *laudatio parentum*, the lord's consent could be costly to obtain,[89] and lords were almost as prone as relatives were both to challenge gifts that they had not previously approved and to discontinue their *calumniae* only when monks granted them valuable countergifts.[90] In the same sample, moreover, almost half the lords who approved their tenants' gifts were joined by their relatives.[91] These relatives sometimes challenged gifts made without their approval and only gave up their claims in return for the usual countergifts.[92] These forms of consent provide additional support for the general hypothesis that in this period, land was not always thought to be freely alienable by individuals.[93]

Similar attitudes toward the transfer of land may also be reflected in the methods used by monastic benefactors and monks to protect gifts against future challenges. In France during this period, neither donors nor their lords regularly promised that they and their heirs would perpetually warrant, acquit, or defend their gifts against future challenges. This practice, which became increasingly prevalent in England during the twelfth century,[94] did not develop as quickly in France. Even by 1200, the guarantees that French donors gave their donees were narrower in scope. A donor himself sometimes promised to warrant, defend, or acquit his gift,[95] while his consenting relatives and lord occasionally did likewise.[96] But before about 1250 a donor apparently lacked the power to impose this obligation on his unborn heirs or even on his own living kin, who might or might not assume it voluntarily.[97]

Lacking this power, a donor hoping to gain salvation for himself and his dead relatives by making a perpetual gift to a saint was in a precarious position. Although he and his monastic donees could try, as we have seen, to stabilize his gift by appointing *fidejussores* or threatening potential challengers with curses or excommunication,[98] these mechanisms were often ineffective, especially because such courts as there were at this time did not routinely uphold a dead man's gifts against the challenges of his kin.[99] As a result, a donor could only hope that after he died, his surviving kin and other friends would defend or at least respect the gift on which his own salvation and that of his deceased relatives were thought to depend.[100]

Although no charter from any of the five abbeys directly cites a specific legal rule that gifts to saints were to be made with the *laudatio*, a large body of charter evidence suggests not only that the *laudatio* was a statistically common feature of these transactions, but also that the people who gave it or secured it were conforming to a recognized norm. Even though the norm may not have been applicable to all land transfers and could assume different forms, depending on the nature or origin of the property being alienated,[101] the very fact that monastic scribes distinguished between different types of land with respect to their alienability may indicate that the *laudatio* was not an empty convention, but was instead a customary practice governed by norms that certain people could articulate fairly clearly.[102] When scribes distinguished inherited from acquired property and stated that gifts of the latter needed no kinsman's consent,[103] they were enunciating a principle that was not fully consistent with contemporary practice.[104] But in making the distinction, they demonstrated their awareness that certain norms were supposed to govern the alienation of land. Similar evidence can be found in scribal distinctions between other kinds of landed property. By noting that property conveyed to an abbey came from the dower, dowry, or inheritance of a donor's wife or mother, for example, they were presumably implying that gifts of these kinds of property were subject to special rules, which, moreover, were sometimes invoked, at least implicitly, by people who challenged the gifts of their kin to abbeys.[105] Unless these passages bear no relationship to actual practice, they indicate that certain norms governing land transfers were understood and sometimes articulated in this region by the mid-eleventh century.

Although the evidence just reviewed suggests that gifts to saints were supposed to be made with the consent of relatives, it does not prove conclusively that the *laudatio parentum* was essential to the legal validity of these transactions. It is possible that the *laudatio* was merely a precautionary practice and not a legally indispensable one. The existence of numerous charters that record gifts made by individuals acting alone raises doubts about the claim that a valid gift could only be made with the *laudatio*. Between 1050 and 1099, about half the recorded land transfers to La Trinité were apparently made without the *laudatio*, while solitary donors made several hundred gifts to Saint Vincent of Le Mans during the same period. Although gifts made without the *laudatio* were rarer at Saint Aubin, Noyers, and Marmoutier, these abbeys, too, received scores of gifts from single individuals.[106] Perhaps solitary donors had no living kin or had their gifts approved in unrecorded ceremonies. Or perhaps they were alienating acquired, rather than inherited, property, or properties so insignificant as to make familial consent unnecessary. While not totally implausible, these ways of explaining why many gifts were apparently made without the *laudatio* are unconvincing. To be sure, truly kinless people doubtless existed in the region, as they did in other parts of medieval Europe. But one wonders how numerous they could have been within the class of monastic benefactors, given the propensity of these people to recognize a wide range of kin and to keep close track of them.[107] To assume that all solitary donors were really kinless is also risky, because other evidence sometimes shows that they made their gifts while kinsmen of theirs were still alive.[108] To insist that donors acting without the *laudatio* must have been alienating acquired property is to resort to a circular argument.

Certain donors apparently acted inconsistently in securing the *laudatio*, making some gifts without it, others with the approval of certain relatives, and others still with the consent of a different kin group. Demonstrating conclusively that numerous donors with living kin made gifts without the *laudatio* would involve analyzing an unmanageable mass of genealogical minutiae. But this hypothesis is certainly consistent with some eleventh-century cases from the Vendômois, where several dozen people whose close kinship connections can be reconstructed gave, quitclaimed, or confirmed properties to Marmoutier and La Trinité. Of twenty-six gifts made to Marmoutier without the *laudatio parentum*, at least eleven were made by people who probably had at least one relative alive when the gift in question was made.[109] Of forty-eight

FIGURE 3-1: Salomon de Lavardin

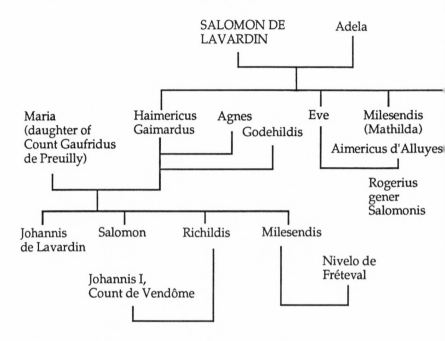

quitclaims or feudal confirmations made by solitary individuals, at least thirty-one were made by people with at least one or two living relatives.[110]

In the mid-eleventh century, Salomon de Lavardin was the principal figure in five transactions with Marmoutier and two involving La Trinité.[111] Twice, he acted with his wife and two daughters.[112] In a third instance, this kin group was augmented by one of his sons-in-law.[113] In making two other gifts to Marmoutier and one to La Trinité, Salomon acted alone.[114] None of these five transactions was approved either by Salomon's son Haimericus Gaimardus, who later succeeded his father as lord of Lavardin, or by Salomon's second son-in-law, Lancelinus.[115] (For Salomon of Lavardin's kin, see figure 3-1.)

Transactions involving Odo Rufus also seem to indicate that the *laudatio parentum* was not consistently secured from the donor's kin.[116] Odo made one gift to Marmoutier with his brother Rainaldus[117] and another on his own.[118] He made one gift to La Trinité

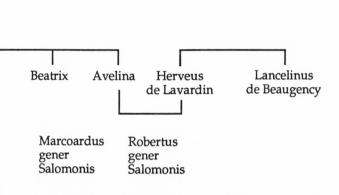

without the *laudatio*[119] and another with the approval of his wife, three sons, and an unspecified number of daughters.[120] When Odo approved gifts to Marmoutier or La Trinité by his feudal tenants, he acted alone.[121] (For Odo Rufus's kin see figure 3-2.) Transactions involving Archembaldus, the provost of the castle of Vendôme, tell the same story.[122] Archembaldus acted alone in making several gifts, confirmations, or quitclaims to Marmoutier and La Trinité,[123] but made one gift to the latter with his brother Hilgaldus.[124] Although Hilgaldus made a gift to La Trinité with his *consobrinus* Joscelinus,[125] the latter never approved any of Archembaldus's transactions, and Archembaldus failed to approve a gift by Joscelinus.[126] Neither Archembaldus's sister Adeleldis nor his brother Hugolinus figured in Archembaldus's gifts, nor did any descendants of his mother's sisters Helvisa and Christiana. (For Archembaldus's kin, see figure 3-3.)

A fourth set of examples from the same region makes the same point. During the mid-eleventh century, a knight of Montdou-

FIGURE 3-2: Odo Rufus

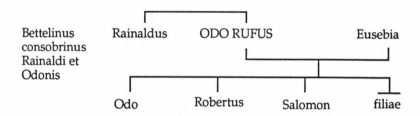

bleau called Tetbaldus, son of Leterius, repeatedly came into conflict with Marmoutier over rights in the church of Naveil, while
also acting as a benefactor of La Trinité.[127] His two transactions
with the latter abbey were not made with the *laudatio*.[128] But each
of his six different quitclaims to Marmoutier was approved by a
slightly different kin group. His wife, Helia, approved the first,
second, fourth, and fifth quitclaims. His son Arnulfus approved
all but the third, and his other son Tetbaldus joined in the last
two, as did his brothers Matheus and Robertus and his sister Agnes. Tetbaldus's son Burcardus approved the first, second, fourth,
and sixth transactions, while a daughter named Aremburgis approved the first, second, and fourth. Another daughter, Guitburgis, approved the second and the fourth, while the last daughter, Johanna, probably approved numbers one, five, and six.[129]
None of these transactions was approved by Tetbaldus's wife's
brothers, Arnulfus and Robertus. (For Tetbaldus de Vendôme's
kin, see figure 3-4.)

By examining transactions involving people whose kinship connections can be reconstructed even more fully, we can find further
reasons for questioning the unqualified contention that gifts to
saints were supposed to be made with the *laudatio parentum*. Because precise dates can rarely be assigned to these acts or to the
births and deaths of the relevant people, this analysis cannot yield
conclusive results. But it strongly suggests that a consenting
group did not always include all the people who could have been
considered the main donor's *parentes*. Included in figure 3-5 are
twenty people who were involved in at least one transaction with
Marmoutier or La Trinité.[130] By examining the kin groups that participated in these transactions, we can see that there was often a

large discrepancy between the kin group that gave the *laudatio* and the group of people who were probably considered the donor's kin, at least for certain purposes.

First, consider the gifts made to Marmoutier by Fulcherius Dives and his wife Hildeardis. Two of the former's gifts were approved by his wife and his sons Vulgrinus and Fulcherius II;[131] another was made without the *laudatio*.[132] Neither was approved by Fulcherius's other children.[133] Similarly, Hildeardis's gifts were approved by only a select group of her offspring. When she gave Marmoutier rights in a mill that she had bought from the husband of her daughter Adela I, her conveyance was approved only by her sons Fulcherius II and Vulgrinus and by Vulgrinus's son Arnulfus.[134] Another gift to the same abbey was approved by her son Fulcherius II, her daughter Agnes, and Agnes's son Hugo.[135] Hildeardis's deathbed gift to Marmoutier was approved by none of her children or other descendants.[136]

Early in the twelfth century, Fulcherius II made two gifts to Marmoutier, neither of which was approved by his children or by any other kin.[137] When his sister Adela I made a gift to the same abbey, it was probably approved by all her male and female children, including Odo Duplex, Hugo Duplex II, and Emelina.[138] The kin groups that approved two gifts to Marmoutier by Adela I's husband, Hugo Duplex I, took a different form. One consisted of Hugo's wife, Adela I, and his son Fulcherius II.[139] The other included five sons of Hugo's: the archdeacon Hugo, Odo, Herveus, Gaufridus, and Gislibertus.[140] Neither of these two gifts nor Adela I's gift was approved by Adela's and Hugo's daughter Emelina.

Similar inconsistencies are found in the composition of the kin groups that approved transactions involving members of the next generation of Fulcherius I's descendants. Odo Duplex and his brother Hugo Duplex II made one gift jointly to La Trinité.[141] But when Hugo the archdeacon twice confirmed gifts of his tenants to Marmoutier or La Trinité, he acted alone,[142] as did his brother Odo Duplex in making a quitclaim to La Trinité.[143] One gift and one quitclaim to Marmoutier by Guismandus I were both made without the *laudatio parentum*.[144] But when Guismandus sold to his wife's maternal grandmother, Hildeardis, some property that Hildeardis then conveyed to Marmoutier, the transaction was approved by his wife, Emelina, and her brother Gislibertus.[145] This

FIGURE 3-3: Archembaldus *prepositus*

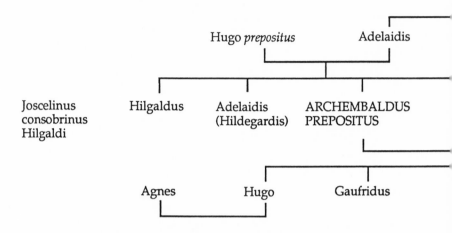

Gislibertus—who was the brother of Odo Duplex and the archdeacon Hugo Duplex II, the son of Adela I and Hugo Duplex I, and thus a grandson of Fulcherius Dives and Hildeardis—never approved any other recorded gift of his kin.[146]

Gifts by Vulgrinus, Fulcherius Dives II, Adela I, Odo Duplex, and Hugo Duplex I were all made without the approval of Adela II, Fulcherius de Turre, or other descendants of Fulcherius Dives I and Hildeardis. Moreover, gifts made by Fulcherius de Turre and his close kin were never approved by any of his matrilateral relatives, such as Fulcherius Dives II or Hugo Duplex II.[147] Of the two conveyances that Fulcherius de Turre made to La Trinité, one was approved only by his son Hieremias[148] and the other by his wife, Beatrix, his daughter Richildis, and his three sons, Herpinus, Hugo, and Hieremias.[149] Hieremias's gift to Marmoutier was approved by his sons Raginaudus and Fulcherius;[150] it did not receive the consent of his daughter Beatrix or of his sister Richildis, who had at least five children.[151] When Richildis's husband, Rotgerius, made a gift to Marmoutier, approval was obtained from Richildis and from four sons, Hugo, Rainaldus, Robertus, and Ivo.[152] But Richildis's deathbed gift to the same abbey was not approved by any of her kin.[153] Gifts of another man who married a female descendant of Fulcherius Dives I and Hildeardis were also approved only erratically by their relatives. Several convey-

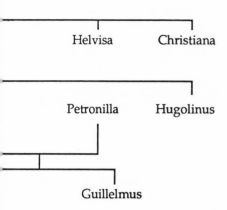

ances to Marmoutier and La Trinité by Ingebaldus Brito, who married a daughter of Fulcherius II, were approved by his wife and four sons;[154] others were made without the *laudatio*.[155]

Some of the apparent inconsistencies just noted can be explained away if we assume that the relatives whom we would have expected to approve particular gifts were dead when the gifts in question were made. But the more often this explanation has to be invoked, the less convincing it sounds. We should therefore ask whether the *laudatio parentum* was given with such regularity as to indicate that a legal rule required that it be secured. Other evidence raises the same question. The fact that the relatives of donors sometimes challenged gifts that they had not approved may suggest that gifts made without the *laudatio* were considered invalid or legally flawed; but on closer inspection, the significance of familial *calumniae* seems less clear-cut. Because a donor's kin, in recorded cases, almost never recovered property that he had allegedly alienated without their approval,[156] the legal significance of a failure to secure the *laudatio* remains unclear, unless we simply assume that monks routinely suppressed all records of fully successful familial challenges. Although the fact that familial claimants were usually given money or spiritual privileges for renouncing their claims may sometimes show that their challenges were not without merit,[157] some texts indicate that they were paid off

FIGURE 3-4: Tetbaldus de Vendôme

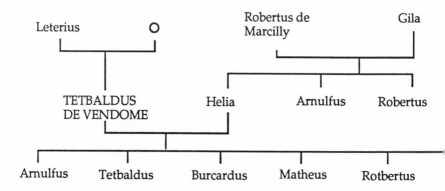

simply because they were causing trouble and not because their claims were considered well founded.[158] Familial challenges, moreover, were not always made on the grounds that the donor's kin had not approved his gift; they could be justified in other ways. Certain challengers asserted that their kinsman had given them the disputed property before conveying it to an abbey.[159] Others contended that because their kinsman had never even meant to transfer the disputed property to a monastery, it should have passed to them by gift or inheritance.[160]

If these claims are put aside, fewer cases remain in which relatives challenged gifts simply because they had not approved them.[161] These latter cases, while important, do not show that any relative of a donor could challenge a gift that he or she had not approved. Most disputes of this kind were initiated by sons, daughters, sons-in-law, or wives of monastic benefactors. Of the 150 eleventh-century familial challenges made against Marmoutier, Saint Aubin, La Trinité, Saint Vincent, and Noyers, almost one-third were made by sons of donors, while another quarter were made by daughters or sons-in-law. Challenges by wives and the second husbands of wives make up 6 percent of the sample, while the figures for claims by brothers and by sisters are, respectively, 12 and 2 percent. *Nepotes* initiated 12 percent of the familial claims in the sample and usually did so in cases where the donor had had no sons or brothers. Challenges by more distant kin or by ascendants were very rare.[162]

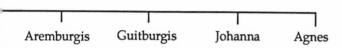

Aremburgis   Guitburgis   Johanna   Agnes

Because these findings raise doubts about the claim that the *laudatio parentum* was required by law, we should examine the hypothesis proposed by several scholars that practical considerations, rather than legal necessity, led most donors and donees to secure the *laudatio*.[163] Obtaining the consent of the donor's relatives made good sense, because they had a strong interest in challenging his gift and a good chance of successfully doing so. At least when viewed from a purely materialistic perspective, their interests directly conflicted with those of the donor's monastic beneficiary: they and the monks both hoped to control the same property. Relatives with blasted expectations may therefore have been eager to challenge gifts that directly or indirectly diminished their own resources. However unjust such challenges may have seemed to monks, they still threatened the stability of gifts to saints, because claimants could easily fabricate plausible, if inaccurate or mendacious, grounds for them.[164] Moreover, even if a donor's kin had no legal right either to invalidate his gift immediately or to challenge it later, they may have had a sort of moral claim to property that their kin had long possessed and were expected to pass on to subsequent generations. Finally, at a time when many disputes over property were carried on through raiding and plundering and led to compromises that were costly even to parties with strong claims, securing the *laudatio* may have been an effective way of preventing trouble from arising, both inside and outside kin groups. Once a donor's relatives had approved his gift

FIGURE 3-5: Fulcherius Dives

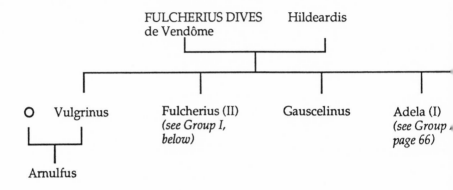

Fulcherius Dives, *Group I*

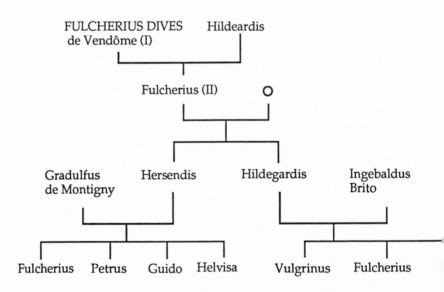

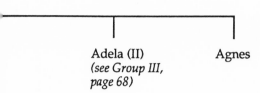

Adela (II)
(see Group III,
page 68)   Agnes

Gaufridus   Hugo
Paganellus

Fulcherius Dives, *Group II*

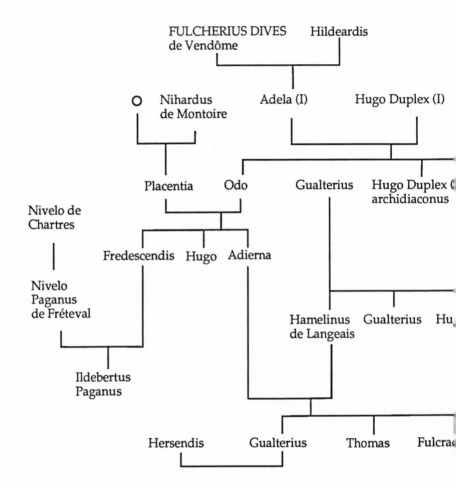

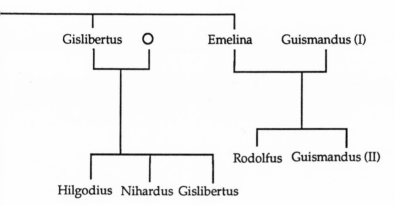

Fulcherius Dives, *Group III*

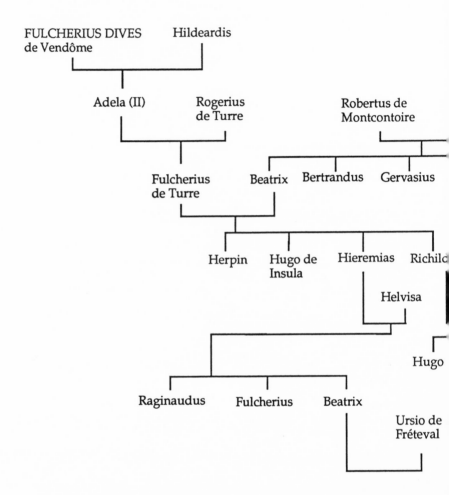

publicly and received countergifts, they probably had an incentive
and even a moral obligation to respect and defend it themselves.
The *laudatio parentum* can therefore be regarded as a precautionary
practice that flourished in a conflict-ridden society where knightly
strength often overcame monastic justice and where the moral or
customary rights of a donor's relatives sometimes overrode the
legal title of his monastic donee.

Haimericus

Rotgerius
de Turre

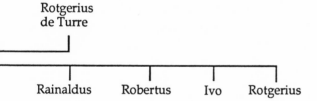

Rainaldus   Robertus   Ivo   Rotgerius

Because the available evidence provides only ambiguous answers to the question of whether the *laudatio parentum* was required by law or was instead procured simply out of prudence,
our initial inquiries into the normative status of the *laudatio* need
to be reformulated. In asking whether the *laudatio* was a legal institution or a mere prudential practice, historians are probably
making an unhelpful, anachronistic distinction. To show that a

legal rule required that gifts be made with the *laudatio*, we must do more than demonstrate that people generally made gifts in this way, that they were somehow obliged to do so, and that when they failed to observe this duty, there was trouble. We must also establish that their behavior was governed by a legal rule that was articulated clearly and distinguished from other rules having only moral, religious, or customary status, that the rule could be regularly and systematically applied to particular cases, and that failures to obey the rule regularly resulted in the invalidation of gifts to saints and in the imposition of effective sanctions. In other words, to establish conclusively that the *laudatio* was required by law, we must find in eleventh- and early twelfth-century France a particular type of legal order.[165] If this requirement cannot be met, we must abandon not only the claim that the *laudatio* was required by law, but also the contention that it was merely a precautionary practice that can be clearly distinguished from legal practices.

While French society in this period should not be characterized as totally lawless or anarchic, it lacked the sort of legal system that gradually took shape in later centuries. There was no strong governmental authority that could make law, punish transgressors against it, use it routinely to judge civil cases, and regularly afford redress to those whose rights under it had been violated.[166] No state monopolized the legitimate use of force. Nor was the law controlled by a group of trained professionals.[167] As a result, the criteria by which certain theorists identify legal rules and distinguish them from other sorts of norms cannot be found.[168] In addition, the legal *mentalités*, as well as legal institutions, of this period differed substantially from those of later periods. There is little evidence, for example, that legal rules were routinely and systematically differentiated from other sorts of norms or that people clearly distinguished between what would now be considered legal, moral, religious, or customary duties and rights. Social norms, moreover, were rarely articulated with sufficient clarity or regularity to be applied systematically to concrete cases; such rules as most people verbalized they knew in oral and not written form.[169] In this society, as in many of the ones studied by anthropologists, "the precepts of custom, very close in this respect to sayings and proverbs . . . have nothing in common with the transcendent rules of a juridical code: everyone is able, not so much to cite and recite them from memory, as to reproduce them (fairly accurately)."[170]

Finally, the process of establishing norms cannot be distinguished from the process of obeying them. In this type of society,

> the issue of what in fact happens can never be kept separate from the issue of what ought to be done. There is a point at which deviations from the rule remake the rule itself. Thus, every act leads a double life: it constitutes conformity or disobedience to custom at the same time that it becomes part of the social process by which custom is defined. Therefore, the distinction between the choice of rules and the making of decisions under the rules . . . remains ill defined.[171]

In hundreds of eleventh- and early twelfth-century disputes involving the abbeys of Marmoutier, La Trinité, Saint Aubin, Saint Vincent, and Noyers, it seems to have been very rare for litigants to refer explicitly to rules of any kind. In one case, a litigant claiming a serf from Marmoutier apparently cited a rule about seigneurial rights over children whose parents belonged to different lords. But disagreement immediately arose about what the rule actually was.[172] In another Marmoutier case, judges justified a ruling that a familial challenger's case was unjust by citing a rule that a man could alienate purchased property to whomsoever he wished.[173] But it is almost certain that this rule was not consistently observed in the period.[174] Normally, litigants invoked norms only implicitly, by reciting facts that would have been relevant to the dispute at hand only if participants in the case acknowledged the existence of an unstated norm and its relevance to that same dispute.[175] For example, a lay litigant who challenged Marmoutier's right to property that his father had given to the monks without his consent may have been implicitly invoking a norm that gifts should be made only with the consent of relatives.[176] A man who justified a *calumnia* against a kinsman's gift by alleging that he had approved it only as a boy was probably appealing to the norm that the consent of minors was not binding.[177]

Such norms, however, did not constitute part of an established legal code. They were only very general guides to action. Even in the few instances in which it is clear that litigants explicitly invoked specific norms, there is no reason to assume that they were appealing to legal rules that were distinguished from other sorts of norms and that would have pointed unequivocally towards a particular judgment, once certain factual issues had been settled.[178] Litigants who invoked a norm during the course of a dispute were not making legal arguments. Instead, like the disputants studied by certain anthropologists, they were employing more flexible methods of argumentation and legitimation. They were using fluid, variable "officializing strategies" in an effort "to transmute 'egoistic,' private, particular interests . . . into distinterested, collective, publicly avowable, legitimate interests."[179]

In responding to such arguments, moreover, and in making similar arguments of their own, judges, arbitrators, mediators, or other third parties were generally playing a role very different from the one attributed to judges by later medieval theorists. At least in disputes between upper-class people, even the most formal, ritualized methods of trial during this period did not proceed in such a way as to enable judges or litigants to distinguish clearly between law and fact. Unilateral and bilateral ordeals were supposed to establish whether a litigant's claim was just in the eyes of God; these procedures did not reveal whether his allegations were true or legally relevant or whether the rules he explicitly or implicitly invoked were accurately stated or had a direct bearing on the case at hand.[180]

Because trial by battle and trial by ordeal were used only rarely in disputes involving the five abbeys during the eleventh and twelfth centuries[181] and because the earlier stages of trials conducted under these procedures may have afforded opportunities for rules to be applied to the facts of a case,[182] the fact that neither trial by ordeal nor trial by battle themselves involved the application of rules to particular cases does not necessarily show that this method of settling disputes was unknown in this period. But the most prevalent methods of processing disputes did not involve the direct, systematic application of rules to facts so as lead to definitive rulings in favor of one party or the other. Most disputes between upper-class people ended in compromises that were designed to make peace.[183] In eleventh- and twelfth-century lawsuits, the people described in our texts as judges therefore performed a function very different from the one that Thomas Aquinas ascribed to judges two centuries later, when he wrote: "The person who delivers a judicial sentence interprets the wording of the law by applying this ruling to a particular case."[184] During the period when the *laudatio* flourished, people identified as judges did not proceed—and were not even expected to proceed—in accordance with the kind of "equity" that John of Salisbury would define in the 1150s as "a certain fitness of things which compares all things rationally and seeks to apply like rules of right and wrong to like cases, being impartially disposed toward all persons, and allotting to each that which belongs to him."[185] Before 1150, arbiters "did not normally decide on the basis of a set of impersonal rules rationally applied."[186]

The norms explicitly or implicitly invoked in our period therefore differed fundamentally from the laws and legal rules discussed by John and Saint Thomas. They were open to different interpretations, no one of which was distinctively privileged, and they served both as a way of organizing and constituting certain spheres of political experience and as a means of legitimating certain forms of political action. They were not conceived of as parts of an authoritative, rational system within which consistent interpretations of rules could be reached and the precedence of one rule over another could be established. Instead, these norms probably resembled the ones set forth in early medieval epic or didactic poetry.[187] Just as everyone knew, in some sense, that lords should reward their followers and act with counsel, they also knew that gifts to saints should be approved by relatives. But like the norms cited by poets, the rule or adage that gifts should be made with the *laudatio* articulated only a general standard of customary practice.

As we shall see more clearly in chapter 4, the rule did not indicate precisely which relatives should give the *laudatio*. It did not specify when, how, or why that standard should be followed. The fact that a donor's matrilateral kin or affines were most likely to participate actively in a gift when he was alienating property received, respectively, from his mother's or wife's kin group strongly suggests that the past history of the property being alienated was relevant to the question of how people would interpret or manipulate the general norm that gifts should be approved by kin. The same conclusion is consistent with the plausible hypothesis that gifts of acquisitions were less likely to be made with the *laudatio* than were gifts of inherited property. Instead of accounting for these findings by claiming that a clearly articulated legal rule requiring the *laudatio parentum* was qualified by special rules governing the alienation of land acquired in particular ways, it seems better to argue that the general rule itself was open to many divergent uses and interpretations, depending on various considerations that included the past history of the alienated property.

The rule, moreover, provided no guidance about what should be done when conformity to it would have necessarily entailed the violation of another norm or the flouting of another commonly observed practice. The question of how—or whether—such rules could be harmonized with one another and applied to concrete cases was not an object of systematic study; it was more likely to be a subject for poetry.[188] As a result, a man who made his gift with the *laudatio* could not be sure that it would be immune to later familial challenges, while a man who made a gift without the consent of his kin was not necessarily considered to be violating custom or acting improperly.

> Talk of rules, a euphemized form of legalism, is never more fallacious than when applied to the most homogeneous societies (or the least codified areas of differentiated societies) where most practices, including those seemingly most ritualized, can be abandoned to the orchestrated improvisation of common dispositions: the rule is never, in this case, more than a second-best intended to make good the occasional misfirings of the collective enterprise of inculcation tending to produce habitus that are capable of generating practices regulated without express regulation or any institutionalized call to order.[189]

To understand more fully the normative status of the *laudatio parentum*, we now need to look more closely at the purposes and functions of the transactions in which consenting relatives participated. As we saw in chapter 2, lay people who made gifts to saints were not simply alienating land. They were, among other things, discharging an obligation by conforming to an established religious norm that was apparently consistent with their own sense of familial duty. Whether they acted only for their own spiritual benefit or for that of their relatives and friends, they were thought to be obeying God's commands to give alms and to use their earthly wealth to make friends with God's saints.[190] To be sure, the people who heeded these commands were given hope of receiving something in return, both for themselves and for their kin and friends. But we should not treat biblical exhortations to give alms or to act charitably as completely unmediated directions about how to promote self-interest, rather than as injunctions to perform certain actions so as to avoid potentially dire consequences. Moreover, if the frequency with which gifts to saints were approved by relatives is treated as evidence that the *laudatio* was required by law (or custom), then the very fact that so many landholders made gifts to saints may show that people of their class were expected and even obliged to do so. Evidence previously presented about gifts made by people such as Fulcherius Dives I, Hildeardis, and their descendants suggests that in the eleventh-century Vendômois it was customary for wealthy landholders to make gifts to nearby abbeys such as Marmoutier or La Trinité. Other evidence demonstrates that among lords and knights various forms of generosity were considered obligatory and were not merely performed out of habit.[191]

If monastic benefactors were fulfilling an obligation and obeying a divine command when they made gifts to saints, we need to determine whether their kin could justifiably thwart their efforts to do so. Charter preambles sometimes answer this question in the negative, stating flatly that an individual seeking salvation has the right to give God and God's saints a part of his worldly wealth without necessarily securing the consent of anyone.[192] These statements might be dismissed as anachronistic survivals from antiquated legal sources. But given the number of gifts made to monasteries in this period, we should not ignore passages from charter preambles in which Christians are enjoined to give alms or to make gifts to saints so as to wipe out their sins and thus provide for a friendly reception in heaven.[193] Even if a landholder's obligation to heed these biblically based commands did not necessarily override whatever obligation he may have had not to alienate property without the *laudatio*, the first duty was not clearly limited or qualified by the second.

Even when a man had not approved his kinsman's gift to a saint, he was in a morally ambiguous position at best if he challenged it. Then, as many malediction clauses show, he ran the risk of being excommunicated and incurring the anger of the monks, their patron saint, and God.[194] In other words, his position vis-à-vis God, a saint, or a monastic community was identical with the one in which he would have found himself if he had harmed or otherwise betrayed a secular lord, such as the count of Anjou, and incurred that lord's anger.[195] He could also be charged with a serious offence against the relative whose gift he had challenged. According to one mid-twelfth-century English charter, a son who challenged his father's gift would break the bridge on which his progenitor could proceed to heaven and would thereby disinherit his father from the kingdom of heaven and kill him.[196] Benefactors of abbeys such as Saint Aubin or Marmoutier therefore had good reasons for threatening to curse any relatives who disturbed their gifts. A French text from an earlier period articulates the belief that people would first return from the dead when their own salvation had been jeopardized by attacks on the charitable acts that they had performed while alive and then would curse, threaten, and reprove the living people who were responsible for making them suffer. A man who had refused to confirm a gift that his mother had made before her death to the abbey of Saint Martin of Pontoise was supposedly admonished and threatened by his mother in a dream, whereupon he quickly confirmed her gift.[197]

At the same time, however, a man who gave away land without the *laudatio* could be charged with offending his kin, especially if his gift was so large that it effectively disinherited them. After a dying man had made a substantial gift to La Trinité of Vendôme, his wife and children induced the monks to return part of the gift on the grounds that it had disinherited them. Had this woman and her children acted properly or not? Several centuries later, jurists and judges had developed legal answers to this question. But during the period when the *laudatio* flourished, the question remained unresolved.[198]

Monastic sources, not surprisingly, do not fully or sympatheti-
cally represent the anxieties of lay people who feared that they
would be disinherited through the lavish gifts of their kin to abbeys. This concern, however, is clearly and forcefully represented
not only in later legal restrictions on deathbed gifts[199] but also in
the twelfth-century *chanson de geste Garin le Loherain*. There, at the
very outset of the poem, the inability of the Franks to offer effective resistance to Vandal invasions is explained partly by reference
to the propensity of dying nobles to impoverish their kin by making large deathbed gifts to monks:

> Ecoutez! écoutez! C'est une chanson de fortes races et de mer-
> veilleuse histoire. Elle remonte au temps où les Vandres
> vinrent dans notre pays et désolèrent la Chrétienté. Les Fran-
> çois ne pouvoient leur opposer de résistance; la longue guerre
> de Charles Martel contre Girart de Roussillon les avoient ré-
> duits à la plus grande foiblesse. Et puis alors, quand un
> prudhomme tomboit malade et se couchoit avec la pensée
> d'une mort prochaine, il ne regardoit ni à ses fils ni à ses
> neveux ou cousins germains: il fasoit venir les moines noirs
> de Saint-Benoît et leur donnoit tout ce qu'il possedoit en
> terre, en rentes, en fours et en moulins. Les gens du siècle en
> étoient appauvris et les clercs toujours plus riches; aussi les
> Gaules couroient-elles à leur perte, si le Seigneur-Dieu n'y eut
> pourvu.[200]

The morally ambiguous position of a son who challenged a gift
made without his approval by his father comes out clearly in the
record of a dispute between the monks of Saint Vincent and
Hugo, son of Burchardus de Sourches. When Burchardus was
gravely ill, he called the abbot of Saint Vincent to his bedside and
commended himself to the prayers of the abbot, to whom he then
confessed. Shortly after asking that some of his property be
granted in alms to Saint Vincent, Burchardus died. Later, the
transaction was actually carried out, perhaps by the knight's wife
Richildis, who had approved it in the presence of Hamelinus, her
younger son by Burchardus. The gift, however, was later challenged by Burchardus's eldest son, Hugo. The monks of Saint Vincent brought the matter before a group of people described as
"judges," whose decision in the case ran as follows. Hugo, they

thought, ought not to challenge or take away the alms of his father. But the monks, they thought, ought to give Hugo something
out of "charity." Accepting this decision, the prior and another
monk sought out Hugo in a nearby meadow and gave him ten
solidi, whereupon he formally approved his father's gift to Saint
Vincent by handing the prior a wooden fork that he was holding
at the time.[201]

What this and other less self-evidently ambiguous cases imply is
that there was no clear-cut way of resolving this very common sort
of dispute in favor of one party or the other. One could argue that
because Hugo got ten *solidi*, he had really won the case but had
bowed to political, moral, or religious pressures that were not legally sanctioned by agreeing to a compromise that would not leave
Saint Vincent and his monks empty-handed. Or one could contend that because Hugo's ten *solidi* had merely been given to him
out of "charity," it was really the monks who had won or should
have won the case and had then yielded to practical, rather than
legal, pressure and made a diplomatic concession to their benefactor's son.

However, because neither reading makes any more sense than
the other, and because both depend upon the invalid assumption
that legal obligations can be distinguished from other sorts of duties, it makes better sense to conclude that given accepted understandings of the situation in which Hugo, the monks, and Burchardus found themselves, neither side won the case or could
have won it. If neither party could have won, then it will be impossible—and not just difficult—to determine whether gifts to
saints were legally valid only if they were made with the *laudatio
parentum*. People were supposed to give alms. They were also
supposed to do so with the consent of kin. Ideally, these two
norms could both be observed. But a failure to observe the second
norm would not necessarily have invalidated an eleemosynary
gift. That gift, after all, had been given in accordance with a divine
command. There is no reason to assume that God's commands
were considered less imperative or binding than the commands of
custom, or, indeed, that the two sorts of injunction were clearly
distinguished from one another by contemporaries, who would
have unhesitatingly accorded some sort of legal primacy to customary, as opposed to religious, commands.

When assessing the status of norms governing gifts to saints, we should also bear in mind that a monastic benefactor normally procured spiritual benefits for his relatives as well as himself. Although in charter preambles a person's duty to help his kin attain salvation is not expressed as clearly as his duty to give alms, the first obligation is clearly articulated in texts such as Dhuoda's ninth-century *Manuel* for her son: "Pray for the kin of your father, who left him their property as a legitimate inheritance (*hereditas*). . . . To the extent of the goods that they left to him, pray for those who possessed these goods."[202] If landholders who regularly procured prayers for their relatives were fulfilling an obligation to those kin as well as to God and to God's saints, we should ask whether other kin could have rightfully frustrated this effort.

Could a knight's provision for his father's soul be justifiably undermined by the efforts of the knight's own son to prevent the former's land from being alienated in perpetuity? Did the knight's obligation to help his father attain salvation have to give way in the face of his obligation to make gifts only with his son's consent? To claim that the *laudatio parentum* was essential to the legal validity of all gifts implies that these questions should be answered affirmatively. On the other hand, the claim that the *laudatio* was simply a practical precautionary measure implies that neither the knight's son nor the knight's father had any real rights in this case, whose outcome would be determined solely by the knight's individual decision about how to dispose of property that he himself owned outright. Neither answer is satisfactory.

To pose the question in this way, moreover, is simplistic and misleading. If the knight in our hypothetical case had a duty to provide for his father's soul, his son would also have been obliged to do the same for the souls of his father and father's father and thus to aid his father, the knight, in procuring salvation for their common dead ancestor. In approving his father's gift to a saint for the benefit of his father's father, the son was doing more than agreeing to remove a legal impediment to a gift that his father wished to make. He was also fulfilling an obligation to his father's father and, perhaps, to God. In addition, the obligation of the knight and his son to provide for their common ancestor's soul takes on new meaning and new normative significance when we consider the means by which such obligations were discharged.

As Dhuoda's *Manuel* indicates, prayers for the soul of the knight's father could have been provided by means of a gift of property that the knight had gotten from his father by "hereditary right" and that the knight's son would otherwise have expected to receive in the same way from his father. The property was to be given to monks and their patron saint, through whose intercession the knight's father could gain from God an inheritance in the kingdom of heaven. In approving the knight's gift, the son would have been participating in an exchange not only with the monks but also with his own paternal grandfather. In effect, he would have been making a countergift to a dead ancestor who had already played a part in providing the knight and the knight's son with a gift in the form of an inheritance.[203]

To understand the context in which the *laudatio parentum* was given, we should also bear in mind that the son, in our hypothetical case, had expectations of receiving countergifts from his father's monastic donee and from his own heirs. Even if the monks, in return for the son's consent, gave him only a pair of shoes and no spiritual benefits, this countergift had more than material significance: it was a token of the son's social position and his relationship to the abbey. It may even have provided a tangible expression of the son's potential claim to establish at some future time a more substantial relationship with the monks, through which he himself could acquire in return for his own gift a heavenly inheritance comparable to the one that he was helping his father to acquire for their common ancestor. Furthermore, the son could assume or at least hope that his own descendants would discharge an obligation to him that was identical to the ones that he discharged to his ancestors when he approved his father's gift. For his descendants would have a duty to use some of the property that they received from him by hereditary right to procure prayers for him from a monastic community.

This analysis shows that people who gave the *laudatio* were doing more than approving a conveyance. They were participating in one phase of a long and complex process in which property and prayers were exchanged not just between their own kin group and an abbey, but also *within* that kin group. This conclusion does not imply that participants were ever oblivious to the proprietary or economic dimensions of gifts to saints; it does indicate, however, that analyses of the *laudatio* should consider more than the proprietary dimensions of these transactions. If a rule or custom provided that gifts to saints be made with the *laudatio*, it did more than regulate conveyances; it stipulated how certain religious and social obligations were to be discharged and how certain social and religious relationships should be created. When a donor's son refused to approve his father's gift to a saint, he was not simply deciding how property should be allocated; he was making a more complex choice about how to construe his own social obligations. Another implication of the argument presented thus far is that there was something fundamentally ambiguous about the norm that gifts should be made with the *laudatio parentum*. On the one hand, the norm could be taken to imply that a landholder should make only those gifts that his kin were willing to approve. On the other hand, the same norm could be taken as imposing an obligation on the landholder's kin to approve and support any reasonable gift that he made in return for spiritual benefits accruing to him and his kin.

In the conflicts that frequently arose between landholders and their kin over how inherited lands should be distributed, more than material wealth was at issue. Also at stake was the religious or "symbolic" capital that monastic benefactors hoped to acquire for themselves and their kin in return for their gifts of land to abbeys.[204] In principle, both forms of capital were valued. But in practice, the question of whether any particular exchange of landed wealth for symbolic capital was worthwhile could be answered in different ways by different kin, who inevitably viewed the same transaction from different perspectives but who could always invoke the same broad, ambiguous principle that gifts be made with the *laudatio parentum*. The practice that historians now reify by calling it an example of the *laudatio parentum* and by treating it as an act of obedience to an established custom was the social product of different actors with very different understandings of what the practice entailed. In most instances, decisions about the proper allocation of land involved more than the three people mentioned in our hypothetical case. Normally, a monastic benefactor had more than one dead relative for whom prayers

were needed and more than a single living relative with a claim on
the benefactor's property and consideration. In such circumstances, the problem of reconciling conflicting claims on limited
landed resources must have been far more complicated and troubling than any simple hypothetical case can show.

In the absence of any coherent system of real property law, it is
misleading for several reasons to say that property could be legally
or properly transferred in perpetuity only if the *laudatio* were secured. This claim seems unfounded if we consider both its logical
implications and some brute facts of eleventh- and early twelfth-
century life. First, the claim that the *laudatio* was required by law
or custom implies that a valid gift could be made, provided that it
was approved by the donor's relatives. But because absent, minor,
or even unborn relatives could challenge gifts that they had not
approved at all or had not approved as adults,[205] the group of
parentes whose consent was theoretically required was theoretically open-ended. As a result, no one could ever be absolutely
certain that the required consent had, in fact, been obtained and
that a gift had therefore been properly made. It was therefore vital for donors, donees, and even familial *laudatores* to supplement
the *laudatio* with other stabilizing mechanisms, such as curses,
threats, and promises to warrant and defend the gift. In this period, there was, in a sense, no totally secure or incontestably valid
way of making a gift in perpetuity, because there was no way of
conclusively barring later challenges to that gift by the donor's kin.
As a result, there was a potential conflict between the obligation to
make perpetual gifts to saints and the obligation not to disinherit
one's kin. A contradiction of this magnitude within a rational legal
system seems to be an anomaly, but within a customary legal order, contradictions of this kind can easily flourish.

Another reason for drawing back from the conclusion that the
laudatio was required by law or custom really amounts to a restate-
ment of the preceding argument. To say that a gift of land was
valid only if it was made with the *laudatio* implies that at any given
moment it could be authoritatively determined who had present
or future rights to any given piece of land. But the case of the
relative who challenged a gift that he had approved as a child or
that was made before he was born raises doubts about this hy-

pothesis. The same issue is raised by familial challenges justified by the assertion that at some time in the past, a kinsman of the challenger had held the disputed property.[206] Unless we contend that these claims were really valid and would have been successful had it not been for "religious" or other extralegal factors, or unless we argue that the challenges were really groundless and only met with some success because monks had extralegal reasons (such as fear) for granting money and spiritual privileges to these challengers, then we should acknowledge that property rights in eleventh- and twelfth-century western France were normally and continuously subject to adverse claims that could be enforced through various forms of self-help, including war. If this state of affairs seems incompatible with a system of real property law, then the claim that the *laudatio parentum* was essential to the legal validity of gifts to saints has to be abandoned.

It is important to remember, however, that the society in which the *laudatio parentum* developed was not static; that even before this practice died out a new legal order was slowly taking shape in much of France.[207] From about 1125 or 1150 onwards, more and more disputes involving Marmoutier, La Trinité, Saint Vincent, and Saint Aubin were being heard and decided both by episcopal courts, equipped with professional staffs and increasingly well-articulated procedures, and by legates and other papal representatives. By the reign of Henry II, some cases involving these abbeys were being argued out before royal seneschals acting under royal orders. Legal documents drafted at these different monasteries changed, as scribes adopted new phrases to describe disputes and the arguments made in what we can start to recognize as law courts. The rambling narratives characteristic of eleventh-century accounts of *calumniae* slowly disappeared, to be replaced by records that describe disputes through the use of concise formulae that conceal as much as or more than they reveal.[208] The last dozen years of the twelfth century saw the appearance of two legal custumals, one written in Angevin England and the other in Normandy,[209] and they were followed in the next several generations by further written works on the customs of various regions, including the ones in which the western French abbeys held property.[210] These thirteenth-century works, however, do not deal with the *laudatio parentum*, which had been gradually dying out while these fundamental changes in legal practice and legal thought had been taking place. By the time it starts to make sense to talk about the rules of medieval French property law, gifts of property were no longer governed by the general principle that a donor should act in concert with his relatives.[211]

While it appears, therefore, that the people who so frequently arranged for eleventh- and twelfth-century gifts to saints to be approved by the donor's relatives were conforming to a norm, this norm cannot reasonably be called a rule of law. Certain people could probably state it. But how it would be used or applied was a matter of doubt and uncertainty. Sometimes, people probably found ways of justifying actions that seemed to contravene it. Perhaps they sometimes argued that the requirement that gifts be made with consent should be set aside or ignored, when it conflicted with some other norm of equal status, such as one requiring landholders to give alms or help their ancestors to gain salvation. When this sort of conflict arose, there was no clear, uniform way of resolving it. In most cases, a compromise would have to be negotiated, or else a small local war might break out.[212]

By arguing that a rule probably called for gifts to be made with the *laudatio parentum* but that it existed within a distinctive sort of customary legal order and was implicitly qualified in ways that were too subtle and variable to be detected now, we can probably account for evidence that is otherwise puzzling or inexplicable. Moreover, by developing the implications of this view of eleventh- and earlier twelfth-century norms and principles, we can make a start at explaining the variations that are found in the composition of consenting familial groups. Like the general norm providing that rulers should act with counsel of barons or magnates, the norm that gifts should be made with the *laudatio parentum* designated only a general class of people whose approval might be called for; it left open the question of precisely which people should give their consent. But even if no definite rule specified precisely which kin were to approve every gift to a saint, studies of the groups of relatives who actually approved such gifts can illuminate the history of upper-class kinship in this period, provided that we find a satisfactory way of describing these groups and explaining how they were formed. This task is undertaken in chapter 4. Chapter 5 will then take up the implications of the view that those who gave or secured the *laudatio parentum* were doing something more than passively conforming to custom.

Chapter 4

Kinship

THERE ARE GOOD GROUNDS for thinking that during the eleventh and twelfth centuries, gifts to saints were normally supposed to be made with the *laudatio parentum*. In the absence of any developed system of real property law, no clearly articulated legal rule required that gifts be made in this way. But it was considered fitting, proper, and right for gift-giving to be carried out, not by solitary donors, but by people acting together with their kin. At the same time, gifts of this kind were ones that a landholder had a duty to make for his own soul and the souls of his kin and that his living and unborn relatives were obliged to support, provided that the gifts did not threaten the donor's kin with disinheritance.

If these hypotheses about the normative status of the *laudatio parentum* are correct, we must still consider four sets of important questions about the kin groups that participated in gifts to saints. First, what sorts of relatives belonged to these groups? Which kin appeared in them most frequently?[1] Second, what kinds of kin groups approved gifts to saints? Which ones did so most often?[2] Third, having established what kinds of relatives approved gifts to saints and how these relatives were grouped together on different occasions to form different consenting kin groups, we should try to discover whether any rule or principle specified which kin were supposed to give the *laudatio* or were at least eligible to do so. Did these groups normally include as many of the donor's kin as could be assembled?[3] Or were the members of a consenting kin group selected from a larger pool of potential *laudatores*? If recurrent patterns can be found in the composition of consenting groups, what do they reveal about medieval kinship and family life? If not, were consenting groups nothing more than randomly assembled collections of kin who were brought together haphazardly to approve gifts? Or can we account for irregularities in their composition in other ways? Fourth, what conclusions about kinship can we draw from the study of consenting groups? Does the study of the *lauda-tio*, as some scholars have suggested, provide direct evidence about the composition of medieval "families"?[4] If not, what does the study of this practice reveal about medieval French society? As these questions indicate, our problem is not merely to identify patterns in the composition of consenting groups, but also to find satisfactory explanations for the social practices of participants in gifts to saints.

A preliminary survey of thousands of kin groups that approved eleventh- and twelfth-century gifts to the five abbeys reveals some major obstacles to any effort to use statistical studies of the *laudatio parentum* as the basis for broad conclusions about medieval French kinship. To begin with, although the average size of these groups was less than three,[5] they included so many different kinds of kin as to suggest that there was something inconsistent or even arbitrary about the process of forming them. Between 1000 and 1199, gifts to Marmoutier, Saint Aubin, Saint Vincent, La Trinité, and Noyers were approved by more than sixty different kinds of kin, including, in no particular order, wives (W), sons (S) and daughters (D), brothers (B) and sisters (Z), fathers (F) and mothers (M), uncles (FB or MB) and aunts (FZ or MZ), nephews (BS or ZS) and nieces (BD or ZD), grandsons (SS or DS) and granddaughters (SD or DD), male first cousins (FBS, FZS, MBS or MZS) and female first cousins (FBD, FZD, MBD or MZD), fathers-in-law (WF) and mothers-in-law (WM), brothers-in-law (WB) and sisters-in-law (WZ), sons-in-law (DH) and daughters-in-law (SW), and stepsons (WS) and stepdaughters (WD).[6] If the selection of a few consenting relatives from this long list was an arbitrary process, then the kin groups that gave the *laudatio* need not have corresponded closely in composition to any kin group whose members acted collectively on other socially significant occasions.

The consenting kin groups in our sample, moreover, assumed a bewildering variety of forms. Although many of them, with the addition of the main donor, consisted of full or truncated conjugal families,[7] others, as we can see in figure 4-1, were different in structure. In this sample of the most unusual and complex groups mentioned in Saint Vincent charters, we find one consisting of the donor's sister, mother, and mother's brother's son. Another in-

FIGURE 4-1: Some Complex Consenting Kin Groups

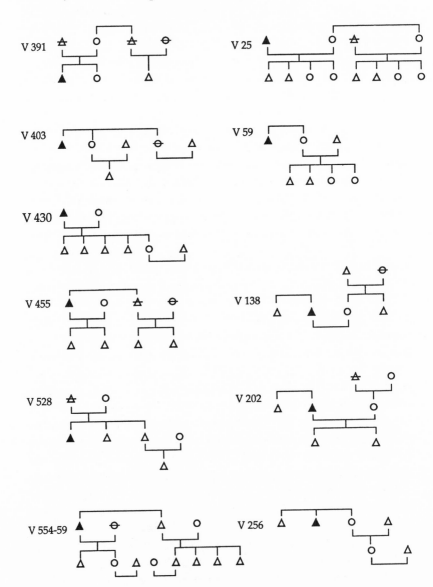

FIGURE 4-1 *continued*

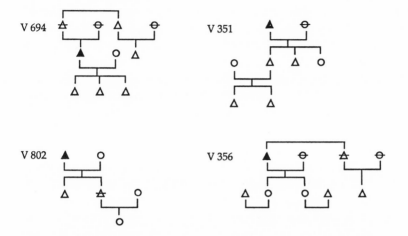

Key:

▲ Male main donor
△ Male member of consenting group
⚠ Deceased or nonparticipating male
○ Female member of consenting group
⊖ Deceased or nonparticipating female

cludes the donor's wife, two sons, and two sons of his brother. A third group is made up of the donor's wife, his two sons and two daughters, his wife's sister, and his wife's sister's two sons and two daughters.[8] Even though the members of these three groups were not necessarily selected at random from a larger set of kin, it is hard to believe that they were all recruited according to the same principle.

The hypothesis that the formation of consenting groups was a flexible or even arbitrary process receives further support from studies of different gifts made by donors whose kinship connections can be reconstructed in some detail. In Chapter 3, this type of analysis revealed that the *laudatio* was not consistently secured from the living kin of various donors to Marmoutier and La Trinité.[9] Here, a similar analysis of gifts to Noyers shows that the composition of consenting groups was not governed by a single, consistently applied rule of recruitment. For the purpose of locating within a single genealogical network a large number of donors to Noyers, figure 4-2 maps out kinship connections between benefactors who were linked by descent or marriage to one or more of the following people: Effredus de Mota and his wife, Agnes; Oggerius Modicus; Galterius, father of Adraldus; and three brothers called Bernardus Cauda Vaccae, Burchardus, and Acharias, lord of Marmande.[10] Although the people represented on this chart were surely not all considered to belong to the same kin group, many descendants of the people just mentioned were eventually linked together, after a fashion, by several marriages. Effredus de Mota's son Ansterius de Mota married Aldeburgis the Rich, daughter of Oggerius Modicus. After Bernardus Cauda Vaccae had first married Sophia and then predeceased her, leaving at least five sons and one daughter, the widow Sophia married Adraldus, son of Galterius, so that their three children became the half siblings of Sophia's six children by Bernardus. In the next generation, Simon de Nouâtre, son of Adraldus and Sophia, married a great-granddaughter (SDD) of Oggerius Modicus. We can now see which specific kin groups approved different gifts by any given donor, and by comparing each consenting kin group with the larger genealogical chart, we can see clearly how difficult it is to predict what form a consenting group would take.

The only recorded gift to Noyers by Effredus de Mota was made jointly with his wife, Agnes, without the consent of his son Ansterius or his two known daughters, Guitberga and Gelia.[11] When Ansterius later made a gift to the abbey, it was approved by seven of his children, three of whom were the offspring of Aldeburgis, while the others were probably born of another woman. Although the gift was also approved by Ansterius's niece (ZD) Milesendis, it was not approved by Aldeburgis or by his daughter Odila, his son Acfredus, his sister Guitberga, Guitberga's daughter Milesendis, Anterius's other sister, Gelia, or her daughter Milesendis.[12] When Ansterius's wife, Aldeburgis the Rich, confirmed a gift to Noyers by Gimo Carococta, she was joined only by her son Oggerius.[13] But her own gift to Noyers was approved by her other son, Herbertus, and her daughter Agnes, as well as by Oggerius.[14]

Other Noyers charters reveal that Ansterius and Aldeburgis had

various living kin who did not approve the transactions just mentioned. Around the time when Ansterius gave land to Noyers, his
niece Milesendis, daughter of Guitberga, gave the monks of Saint
Mary a gift that was approved by at least eight of her *parentes*,
some of whom were presumably considered to be relatives of Ansterius as well: Milesendis's mother, Guitberga; a certain Gelia,
who was either Milesendis's sister or her mother's sister; three
men whose relationship to Guitberga is unclear, and another Guitberga (probably Milesendis's sister), who consented along with all
her *infantes*.[15] No one who approved Milesendis's gift appears in
charters recording transactions involving the two sons of Ansterius de Mota. Acfredus made a gift to Noyers with the consent of
his mother, Aldeburgis; his wife, Agnes; his brother Ansterius,
the monk; and his other brothers; but neither his father's sisters,
nor their offspring, nor Acfredus's own sisters approved it.[16]
When Acfredus's brother Oggerius made a gift several decades
later, it was approved only by his sister's daughter's husband, Simon de Nouâtre.[17] Moreover, gifts of Oggerius's sister Odila and
those of her children were never approved by her siblings or her
siblings' descendants and did not invariably receive the consent of
all the children of these donors. One gift by Odila was approved
by her sons Aimericus, Girardus, and Thetbaldus and by her
daughters Lizina and Umberga.[18] Another one was made only
with the consent of Aimericus and Girardus.[19] Later, a gift by
Odila's son Aimericus was approved only by his brother Girardus,[20] while a quitclaim of his received only the consent of his
wife, Sizilla.[21]

Each gift to Noyers by Hubertus Petrosilus I, the husband of
Odila's sister Agnes, was approved by a different kin group; even
though his wife Agnes probably brought him a large dowry, neither her parents nor her siblings figured in Hubertus's gifts, confirmations, or quitclaims. An early gift of his was approved by
Agnes alone.[22] Another was made only with her consent and that
of their son Milo, who appears in no other Noyers charters.[23] A
third gift was approved simply by three of their children who had
not approved their father's previous gifts: Hubertus Petrosilus II;
Sarmannia, who is mentioned in no other Noyers charters; and
Aldeburgis Borilla, the wife of Simon de Nouâtre.[24]

Similar inconsistencies in the composition of consenting groups

FIGURE 4-2: Some Benefactors of Noyers and Their Kin

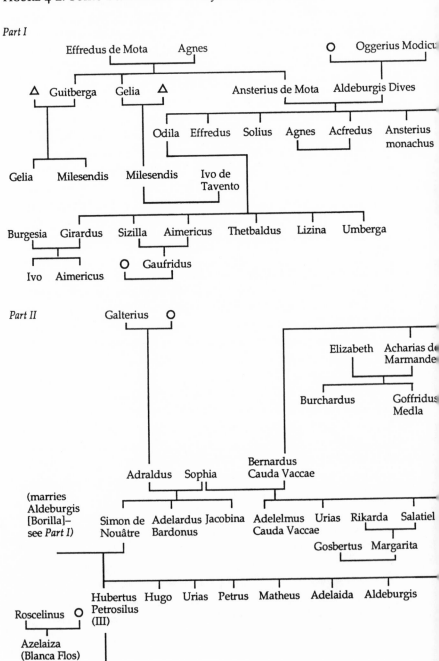

Part I

Part II

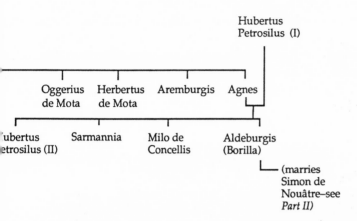

Hubertus
Petrosilus (I)

Oggerius   Herbertus   Aremburgis   Agnes
de Mota   de Mota

ubertus   Sarmannia   Milo de   Aldeburgis
etrosilus (II)   Concellis   (Borilla)

(marries
Simon de
Nouâtre–see
Part II)

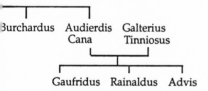

Burchardus   Audierdis   Galterius
                Cana   Tinniosus

Gaufridus   Rainaldus   Advis

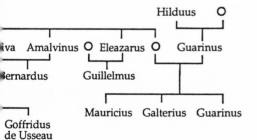

Hilduus   O

iva   Amalvinus O Eleazarus O Guarinus

Bernardus   Guillelmus

                    Mauricius   Galterius   Guarinus
Goffridus
de Usseau

are found in transactions involving several people linked to Simon de Nouâtre: his father, Adraldus; his mother, Sophia; several of Sophia's children by her first husband, Bernardus; Acharias de Marmande; and several others who were either married to or descended from people just mentioned. In the 1080s Adraldus made one gift jointly with Simon[25] and another without the *laudatio*.[26] Around the same time, a gift of Sophia's received the consent of Adraldus and six of her children by Adraldus or her previous spouse, but not the approval of three of her children by her first husband.[27] Transactions involving Sophia's sons were approved by many different combinations of her kin. A gift by Adelelmus Cauda Vaccae was approved only by Salatiel and Urias,[28] while a quitclaim by Salatiel and Eleazar was approved by none of their siblings.[29] One gift by Urias received the consent of Acharias de Marmande, Amalvinus, Eleazar, Salatiel, Adelelmus, and Simon.[30] Another was approved by Salatiel[31] and a third by Salatiel and Simon.[32] When Amalvinus Cauda Vaccae made a gift to Noyers after the monks there had buried his son Burcardus, it was approved only by his wife, Niva, and his daughters and not by any of his siblings.[33] Meanwhile, Guarinus, the brother-in-law (*sororius*) of Sophia's sons, made one gift without the *laudatio*[34] and another with the approval of his wife, her brothers Urias and Salatiel, and half brother Simon.[35] When Salatiel's daughter Margarita made a gift to Noyers, only her husband, Gosbertus, gave his consent.[36] Although Acharias de Marmande made a quitclaim that was witnessed by his two nephews Urias and Salatiel,[37] the latter did not approve a gift that Acharias made to Noyers,[38] or join him in confirming various gifts to the abbey by Acharias's tenants.[39] When Acharias made another gift to Noyers so that the monks would bury his wife, Helisabeth, only his son Burcardus approved it.[40] Around the same time, a gift that Acharias's brother Burchardus de Marmande made so that he could die in a monastic habit and be buried at Noyers was approved by Acharias, Burchardus's and Acharias's sister Audierdis Cana, Sophia, and four of Sophia's children, namely Adelelmus Cauda Vaccae, Urias, Salatiel, and Simon de Nouâtre.[41] This was done after Burchardus's death at the request of his brother, Acharias. Later, after Audierdis Cana and her husband, Galterius Tinniosus, had challenged the gift of Burchardus, they approved it along with their children Gaufridus, Rainaldus, and Advis, none of whom ever approved recorded gifts by their mother's kin.[42] Later still, when Acharias made a gift to Noyers for the soul of his brother Burchardus, it was approved first by Acharias's son Burchardus and later by Acharias's other son, Goffridus Medla.[43]

Finally, consider the numerous acts involving Simon de Nouâtre, who was linked by marriage or descent to the offspring of Hubertus Petrosilus I, the descendants of Oggerius Modicus and Effredus de Mota, and the descendants of his mother, Sophia. Simon—who participated in various transactions in which the principals were his mother, his father, or his half brothers[44]— made one gift jointly with his half brothers Urias and Salatiel.[45] Another gift was approved by his wife, Aldeburgis, and merely witnessed by Salatiel.[46] Two others also received only his wife's consent,[47] while a fifth gift was approved by his son Hubertus Petrosilus III, as well as by Aldeburgis.[48] Simon had at least six other children, none of whom approved any of these transactions.

These findings, which are completely consistent with evidence presented earlier,[49] merit attention because they suggest that consenting kin groups varied widely in composition and cannot be routinely equated with "families." This sort of evidence—which could be replicated many times over—indicates that when a gift to a saint was made, consenting relatives were recruited in what now appear to be unpredictable ways from a larger pool of potential *laudatores*.

Furthermore, what little we can learn from charters about the recruitment of consenting groups raises doubts about the hypothesis that this process was governed by any simple rule. Consenting kin groups were not formed under the direction of single individuals who alone decided who should or should not participate. Instead, the stories recounted in chapter 3 about the gifts of Clarembaldus and Odo Donkey Neck show that several people could play a role in determining who would approve a particular gift.[50] Some consenting kin were designated by donors. Others were sought out by the monks, while others still presented themselves. As a result, any patterns in the composition of consenting kin groups require a complex explanation.

In spite of the difficulties involved in analyzing the composition of consenting kin groups, we can still generalize about them in ways that allow us to formulate some hypotheses about medieval

French kinship. At the outset, we need to take a full inventory of all the relatives who ever gave the *laudatio*. The exact contents of different inventories are bound to vary somewhat, depending upon the region studied, the choice of charters to be analyzed, the meaning assigned to various vague or ambiguous kinship terms, and the solutions found for other technical problems of coding and counting consenting relatives.[51] Nevertheless, a list based on eleventh- and twelfth-century charters of the five abbeys does not appear to differ greatly from comparable lists that could be constructed from other documentary collections.[52]

The list in the appendix, table 4-1, and the kinship chart in figure 4-3 show clearly that membership in consenting groups was not limited to members of either the donor's conjugal family or patrilineal descent group. Gifts were approved by affines and matrilateral kin, as well as by patrilateral kin (such as sisters' sons) who were not patrilineal kin. Nevertheless, the group from which consenting relatives were usually drawn had relatively clear boundaries. Aside from affines,[53] virtually all relatives who consented to gifts rather than merely witnessing them[54] were descended from the donor's two sets of grandparents. No gifts were approved by people who can be conclusively identified as the donor's second or third cousins.[55] If affines are left aside, the composite group of consenting kin that can be formed by noting every type of relative who ever approved a gift or quitclaim to one of the five abbeys therefore resembles a cognatic kindred of first cousin range or a shallow cognatic descent group extending back only to the donor's patrilateral and matrilateral grandparents.[56] Within this group there is a clear masculine bias, as gifts were approved by more different types of male kin than female kin.[57]

Table 4-1 in the appendix also indicates which relatives usually approved gifts to the five abbeys. It suggests, for example, that gifts were approved frequently by spouses and by very close kin, such as children and siblings, and much more rarely by ascendants, collaterals, matrilateral kin, affines, and half-kin.[58] No matter which monastery we consider, this generalization holds. If we divide the number of relatives of a certain type who approved gifts to one of our abbeys by the total number of relatives who ever performed this act, the resulting figures vary little from monastery to monastery.[59] At Marmoutier, 36.5 percent of all consenting relatives were sons of the main donor, while at Saint Aubin, Noyers, La Trinité, and Saint Vincent these figures are, respectively, 33, 30.8, 36, and 35.9 percent. Similar calculations for consenting brothers at Saint Aubin, Marmoutier, Noyers, La Trinité, and Saint Vincent yield these figures: 16.8, 12.5, 14.5, 14.5, and 12.1 percent. Comparable figures for other close consenting kin are as follows:

Mothers: 3.7, 2.1, 2.7, 3, 3 percent
Sisters: 4.1, 3.1, 3.7, 2.5, 2.4 percent
Wives: 20, 18.2, 17.3, 18, 19 percent
Nepotes: 7.2, 2.4, 2.3, 3.3, 1.9 percent[60]

Similar patterns can also be found at all five abbeys with respect to the frequency with which other types of kin gave the *laudatio*. At Marmoutier, only 2 percent of all consenting kin were affines of the main donor, while at La Trinité, Saint Aubin, Saint Vincent, and Noyers, the figures are 2, 1, 1, and 1 percent. Matrilateral kin appear even less frequently.[61]

Figures in table 4-1 also confirm the hypothesis advanced above that consenting groups had a masculine bias.[62] Overall, eight males approved gifts for every five females; and if wives are placed in a special category and set aside, the ratio of males to females increases to almost three and one half to one. The large number of types of male relatives partly accounts for the predominance of males. In the total sample, at least twenty-nine kinds of male relatives are found, as against at least twenty-four kinds of female relatives.[63] The predominance of males, however, is primarily due to the fact that as between males and females related to the main donor in the same way, the former approved gifts more often than the latter did. For every seventeen consenting brothers in the total sample, there are, for example, only four sisters. The ratio of consenting sons to consenting daughters is only slightly lower, 4:1. Male children of the main donor's brothers or sisters outnumber the female children by ten to one. The masculine bias of consenting groups is also reflected in the fact that sisters' husbands appear far more often than brothers' wives. Because charters do not regularly distinguish between sisters' and brothers' offspring or between matrilateral and patrilateral uncles or cousins and because these sorts of kin did not, in any case, approve many

FIGURE 4-3: Factitious Consenting Kin Group

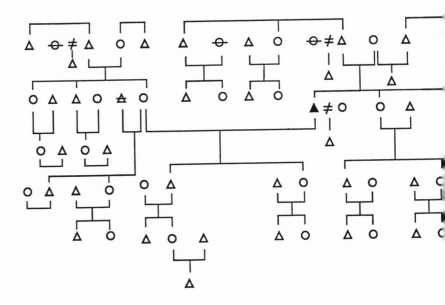

Key:

▲ Male main donor
△ Male member of consenting group
⚥ Deceased or nonparticipating male
○ Female member of consenting group
⊖ Deceased or nonparticipating female
≠ Illegitimate union

gifts, it is not certain that consenting groups were biased in favor of patrilateral or patrilineal kin. But because most consenting uncles were apparently fathers' brothers, it appears likely that patrilateral kin outnumbered matrilateral kin. This fact, along with the finding that brothers approved gifts more than four times as often as sisters did, may indicate that among patrilateral kin, patrilineal kin predominated.

Having analyzed rough, aggregate figures based on the study of hundreds of different consenting groups, we can now move on to form a clearer picture of who gave the *laudatio parentum* by exam-

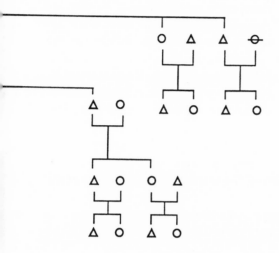

ining specific kin groups. Although their structure, as we have seen, could vary greatly from transaction to transaction, evidence already presented about specific gifts to Noyers, Marmoutier, and La Trinité[64] does not necessarily prove that relatives who gave the *laudatio* were selected at random or that donors and donees simply tried to secure the consent of as many kin as possible. If the process of recruiting consenting groups had taken one of these two forms, then certain statistical regularities in the composition of these groups would be very difficult, if not impossible, to explain.

In the Noyers charters discussed above, we find the same patterns discerned in our previous analysis of the total sample of relatives who approved gifts to the five abbeys between 1000 and 1199. In the small sample taken from the charters of Noyers, 83 percent of all gifts and 78 percent of all transactions were approved by at least one relative of the main donor. Consenting males outnumber consenting females by a ratio of 1.7:1 and, if wives are excluded, by 4.25:1. Mothers, although approving few gifts individually, appear more often than fathers, but brothers outnumber sisters, and sons are more common than daughters. Although brothers appear more often in the small sample than they do in the larger one and although sons consented in unusually small numbers (under 20 percent), these oddities are attributable to the fact that so many of these transactions involved Sophia's many sons, perhaps before any of them had grown children. This analysis therefore suggests that the recruitment of consenting groups was a complex and subtle process, rather than a random one.

Although consenting groups varied considerably in composition, certain statistical regularities in their structure can still be found. Of the hundreds of different kin groups that could, in theory, have been formed out of the types of relatives listed in table 4-1 and pictured in figure 4-3, relatively few approved gifts to the five monasteries. Even more significant is the fact that within this relatively small set of consenting groups, certain kinds of groups predominated. In particular, about half of the groups participating in gifts to Marmoutier, Saint Aubin, Saint Vincent, La Trinité, and Noyers consisted either of married couples or of full or truncated conjugal families.

In about half the gifts made to Saint Aubin between 1075 and 1099, for example, the *laudatio* was given by one of the following kin groups, which, for simplicity's sake, will be represented without regard to variations in the *number* of relatives of a given type (see figure 4-4, type 1): the donor's wife (12 percent),[65] the donor's wife, son and daughter (5 percent),[66] the donor's wife and son (18 percent),[67] the donor's wife and daughter (1 percent),[68] and the donor's son (11 percent).[69] In another eleven cases making up 15 percent of the sample, one of the groups included in type 1 also includes (see figure 4-4, type 2) a brother of the main donor (4 percent),[70] one or two of his affines (3 percent),[71] other unspeci-

FIGURE 4-4: Main Types of Consenting Kin Groups

Type 1

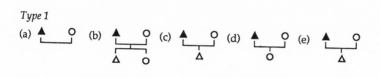

(a)   (b)   (c)   (d)   (e)

Type 2

(a)

(b)   (c)   and reliqua parentela
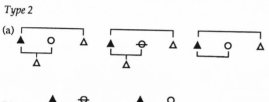

(d)
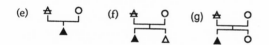

(e)   (f)   (g)

Type 3

(a)   (b)   (c)   and parens

Type 4

(a)   (b)   (c)   and cognatus
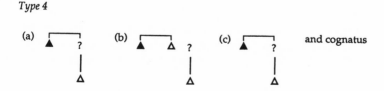

FIGURE 4-4 *continued*

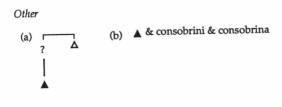

Key:

▲ Male main donor
△ Male member of consenting group
⊿ Deceased or nonparticipating male
○ Female member of consenting group
⊖ Deceased or nonparticipating female
? Relative of unknown sex

fied members of the donor's *parentela* (1 percent),[72] or a daughter's husband (3 percent).[73] Other consenting groups that can be conveniently classed together consist of a donor, one or more of his siblings, and sometimes an additional relative (see figure 4-4, type 3). In groups of this type, which make up 16 percent of the sample, we find a donor joined by a brother (11 percent),[74] a brother and sister (1 percent),[75] a brother, a sister, and an unspecified kinsman (1 percent),[76] a brother and a sister's husband (1 percent),[77] and a sister and mother (1 percent).[78] In cases of a fourth kind (see figure 4-4, type 4), the gift is approved by the donor's nephew (probably FBS, in most cases) (7 percent),[79] who is sometimes joined by the donor's brother (4 percent)[80] and once by the donor's brother's wife and the donor's *cognatus* (1 percent).[81] Groups of this kind make up 12 percent of the total. If these four types of groups are set aside, only 2 out of the 73 groups in our sample remain. One includes the donor and his uncle (*avunculus*),[82] while the other consists of the donor, two male cousins (*consobrini*), and a female cousin (*consobrina*).[83]

As the preceding analysis suggests, the vast majority of consenting groups in our total sample from all five abbeys can be fitted into one of the following categories:

1. Full or truncated conjugal families, including married couples
2. Conjugal families extended in one of several different ways so as to include affines, siblings, or one other type of relative
3. Groups made up of one or more siblings, sometimes accompanied by a spouse or the donor's mother
4. Groups in which the donor is joined by a sibling or a sibling's offspring

Of the forty-three groups involved in gifts to Saint Vincent between 1050 and 1075, forty-two fall into one of these five categories.[84] The only distinctive feature of the transactions in this sample, as compared with the Saint Aubin sample just considered, is that among the groups in type 3, the donor's mother appears with unusual frequency. Four gifts are approved only by the donor's mother,[85] while in two other cases (4.7 percent) the mother is joined either by the donor's sister or by the donor's sister and mother's *nepos* (see figure 4-4, type 3).[86] To demonstrate that neither the sample from Saint Aubin nor the one from Saint Vincent is unusual with respect to the types of kin who gave the *laudatio*, it should be noted that figures indicating the frequency with which different kinds of relatives approved gifts to Saint Aubin between 1075 and 1099 and to Saint Vincent between 1050 and 1074 (see appendix, table 4-1) are very similar to the ones based on an analysis of the total sample.[87]

Because charters never mention the precise ages of donors or consenting kin and rarely indicate their stage of life, and because they describe only brief moments in the lives of these people, we can hardly ever visualize consenting groups very clearly or trace their earlier or later history. When analyzing a gift approved by the donor's two brothers, should we imagine a trio of adult siblings who had lived together for years? Should we assume that their parents had recently died, leaving three young sons, at least one of whom would soon marry, while the other two would move away? Or should we speculatively construct other stories to make sense of the one recorded moment in the lives of monastic donors and their kin? The possibilities seem virtually endless. But if we assume that at least certain kin groups were more than temporary associations and developed in only a limited number of ways, we

FIGURE 4-5: Factitious Developmental Cycle of a
Consenting Kin Group

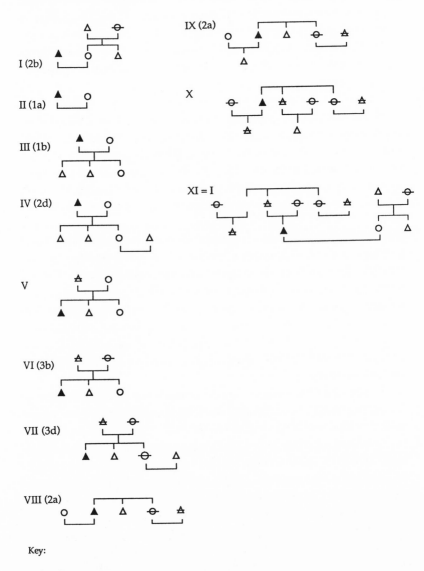

Key:

▲ Male main donor
△ Male member of consenting group
⚊△ Deceased or nonparticipating male
O Female member of consenting group
⊖ Deceased or nonparticipating female

can make what is admittedly a highly speculative effort to locate them at one of a limited number of stages in a few developmental cycles. These cycles will differ from one another in ways determined by a small group of variables: How many children of each sex are born to any given married couple? How many siblings and children marry? In what order do deaths, births, and marriages occur? At what point do certain group members either die or move away?

Although this conjectural method of classifying consenting kin groups, as we shall see, hardly explains all variations in the types of consenting kin groups, it can still help us to account for many of them. To illustrate this method, figure 4-5 pictures ten consenting groups that correspond exactly or very closely with groups pictured in figure 4-4 and that have been arranged so as to show how several different types of consenting groups could have developed into or out of each other. For simplicity's sake, figure 4-5 conflates into a single developmental cycle what could be best represented as several cycles. What follows is therefore a hypothetical but still potentially instructive account of how a single kin group could have evolved over many years through several different stages.

1. A man—referred to hereafter as the first donor—makes a gift with the consent of his wife, his wife's father, and his wife's brother.
2. After the deaths of his two affines, the first donor makes another gift, which is approved only by his wife.
3. After fathering three children, the first donor makes a third gift approved by his wife, his two sons, and his daughter.
4. After the daughter's marriage, the first donor's next gift is approved by his wife, his two sons, his daughter, and his daughter's husband.
5. After the first donor dies and is succeeded by his eldest son—who becomes the second donor—and after the death of the first donor's daughter's husband, the second donor makes a gift with the approval of his mother, his younger brother, and his sister.
6. Soon afterwards, when the first donor's wife has died, the second donor makes a gift with the *laudatio* of his brother and sister.

7. After the death of the second donor's sister, he makes a gift approved only by his brother.

8. After marrying, the second donor makes his next gift with the consent of his new wife and his brother.

9. Once the second donor has had a son, his next gift is approved by his wife, son, and brother.

10. As more time passes, the second donor's wife and son die, while his brother marries and fathers a son before he and his wife die. The second donor's next gift is therefore approved only by his nephew (BS).

11. Finally, after the death of the second donor and the marriage of his nephew to a woman whose father and brother are both living, the whole cycle can begin again.

With minor emendations, this hypothetical story could help to explain the composition of many consenting groups in our sample. Although this type of analysis has been most effectively used in discussions of coresidential kin groups with relatively clear boundaries,[88] it is not based on the assumption that all members of consenting groups necessarily resided together. Rather, it simply rests on the premise that *laudatores* were drawn from a bounded group of the donor's close kin and on the commonplace observation that as donors and their kin grew older, changes inevitably occurred in the composition of whatever kin groups they belonged to.

If we consider cases discussed earlier in this chapter and in chapter 3 in which different kin groups approved different gifts by the same donor, we can probably account for the varying composition of these consenting groups by postulating that the gifts in question were made at different stages in the developmental cycles of a donor's kin group. The gifts made by either the brother or the *consobrinus* of the provost Archembaldus may have been made without the latter's approval because Archembaldus had not yet assumed his father's position of provost, while those acts of Archembaldus himself that were not approved by any of his sons may have been made before the latter were born or were old enough to give valid consent.[89] A similar argument could explain why Odo Rufus made only one conveyance approved by his brother Rainaldus, several other conveyances without the *laudatio*, and others still with the approval of his three sons and all his daughters. Odo's brother Rainaldus may have died before Odo's children were born or had attained their majority, but between Rainaldus's death and the time when Odo's children approved Odo's gift, there was an interval when Odo had neither siblings nor offspring to approve his gifts.[90] Similarly, if we arrange the quitclaims of Tetbaldus, son of Leterius, in a certain chronological order and posit a particular birth order and death order for his children, certain variations in the kin groups that approved these transactions can also be explained.[91] Variations in the groups that approved transactions involving Salomon of Lavardin are explicable as well, if we assume that his son Haimericus Gaimardus was born well after Salomon's daughters Beatrix, Milesendis, and Avelina and that Salomon's daughter's husband, Rogerius, died an early death.[92]

Although these explanations for variations in the composition of consenting groups are admittedly speculative and could never be verified in most cases for lack of adequate data, there is some statistical evidence to support them. If we examine the frequency with which certain combinations of kin appear in consenting groups, several interesting statistical patterns emerge. First, it was rare for both sons and brothers to be included in the same consenting kin groups. Of 60 different groups in which brothers approved gifts to Saint Vincent between 1075 and 1099, only 8 (or 13 percent) included one or more sons, while only 8 (or 7 percent) of the 120 groups including at least one son also included at least one brother. At Noyers during the same period, only 6 (or 9 percent) of the consenting groups to which at least one brother belonged included one or more sons, while the percentage of groups including both sons and brothers was much lower. In addition, the fact that consenting groups only rarely included both wives and siblings of the main donor tends to confirm the hypothesis that once a landholder married and had children, it became much less likely that his siblings would approve his gifts.[93] It therefore seems reasonable to locate most consenting groups that included at least one brother at an earlier stage in a donor's life and to assign groups to which one or more sons belonged to a later stage.

Eventually, however, all of these exercises in speculative family history break down or lead to the formulation of circular arguments. When trying to explain anomalous findings about who gave the *laudatio parentum*, it is tempting, as we saw in chapter 3, to redate a charter, juggle with the birth order of children, postulate the existence of lost charters, invent unknown relatives, and send away a donor's kin either to an early death or else on a journey from which they can be recalled when needed.[94] In other words, to defend a hypothesis that supposedly explains certain findings about the *laudatio*, we must ignore, explain away, or transmogrify other evidence that fails to support it. When this procedure, which can legitimately be used from time to time, has to be carried out repeatedly, we should recast our hypothesis instead of the data.

In several instances, it is impossible to explain variations in the composition of consenting groups by locating different groups at different stages of a developmental cycle. This method cannot routinely explain why only certain gifts were approved by matrilateral kin, patrilateral collateral kin, or affines. Nor can it explain the structure of certain groups that participated in joint gifts. Finally, this method of explanation cannot adequately account for the consistent underrepresentation of females in consenting groups or the failure of a donor's living relatives to approve his gifts. These problematic cases have one thing in common: they all suggest that gifts to saints were supposed to be approved not by all the donor's *parentes*, but only by a select group of kin. In the case of gifts approved by affines or matrilateral kin, we can see more clearly than we can in other transactions that the participants must have been making choices about who should give the *laudatio*, rather than mechanically following a single, simple rule of recruitment.

This conclusion is consistent with what little we know about how consenting groups were formed and with more plentiful data about grants of spiritual benefits to donors and their kin. From stories related in chapter 3 about the efforts of monks to secure the *laudatio*, we know that the members of consenting groups did not necessarily approve gifts en masse. Sometimes, the *laudatio* was given piecemeal, as different relatives approved a donor's gift at different times in different localities and before different witnesses.[95] Even more significant is the fact that no single person or organized group necessarily decided who should or should not give the *laudatio*. Because the donor, some of his kin, and the monks all had a hand in determining who would do so, it seems unlikely that the composition of consenting groups was determined systematically.[96] Although evidence of a belief that gifts should normally be approved by certain kinds of kin can be found both in cases where relatives were pressed to give the *laudatio*[97] and in cases where they contested gifts made without their approval,[98] data of this kind also suggest that the question of which relatives should or should not consent to gifts was the focus of disagreement and even open conflict. This may imply, in turn, that the composition of consenting groups was not determined through the application of a rule whose meaning and scope were clearly defined. For these reasons, patterns in the composition of consenting groups could not have resulted from the blind obedience of participants to comprehensively applied rules. Instead, when such patterns can be found, they must have resulted from several different forces that frequently converged so as to produce similar results.

The hypothesis that the composition of consenting groups was not strictly regulated by binding customs is also indirectly supported by evidence about the groups of relatives who received spiritual benefits at exchange ceremonies, where choices had to be made about which dead or living relatives would receive prayers or other benefits in return for a donor's gift. Even when charters state only that a gift was made for the souls of the donor's *parentes*[99] or that "the society and benefit" of the monastery in question was extended to all his kin,[100] choices were probably made about who, precisely, the donor's kin were, so that the monks could pray for them by name.[101] The results of this selection process are described in charters providing lists of the kin who received prayers or other privileges. Just as genealogies of twelfth-century nobles included certain select kin considered worthy of remembrance while excluding others,[102] so these lists include only some of the donor's relatives and not others. At Saint Vincent between 1075 and 1099, for example, the privilege of "society and benefit" was accorded to people related to the main donor in different ways and grouped together to form different types of kin groups. The usual recipients were the main donor's wife, son, daughter, father, mother, brother, and sister.[103] But some grants were also made to a daughter's husband, a wife's father, a wife's first husband, a brother's wife, a *consobrinus*, and other types of kin.[104] Between 1050 and 1074, grants of privileges for the souls of benefactors and their kin took a similar form at Saint Aubin, where the main donor's spouse, father, mother, and sons were the usual recipients,[105] but where the privilege was also accorded to an *avunculus*, a *nepos*, and a sister's husband.[106]

The fact that spiritual privileges were granted only to a select group of the donor's kin and not to every conceivable relative becomes evident when we examine the gifts of men whose genealogies can be reconstructed from several charters. When Archembaldus the provost made one gift to Marmoutier for his own soul and the souls of his mother and wife, no provision was made for the souls of his two brothers.[107] Later, when his wife confirmed several gifts of his for which he alone had received confraternity from the monks of Saint Martin, the same privilege was granted only to her and their two small sons.[108] Later still, when a son of Archembaldus made a gift to Marmoutier with his wife's approval, he provided only for his father's soul, while his mother and brother went unmentioned.[109]

Although a gift by Adela I to Marmoutier was approved by several sons and daughters, it was made only for her own soul and not for the souls of her living or dead kin, such as her father, Fulcherius Dives, her mother, Hildeardis, or her husband, Hugo Duplex I.[110] An earlier gift by Hugo Duplex I was made for the souls of his father, mother, sons, and daughters, as well as his own, but his wife, Adela I, and his brothers went unmentioned.[111] Years later, a deathbed gift to Marmoutier by Richildis, a great-granddaughter of Fulcherius Dives I and Hildeardis (DSD), was made only for her own soul and the souls of her husband and five sons. No mention was made of Richildis's siblings, Herpin, Hugo de Insula, and Hieremias de Turre.[112] A gift made to Marmoutier during the 1060s by Hersendis, a granddaughter (SD) of Fulcherius Dives I and Hildeardis, and by her husband, Gradulfus de Châteaudun, was approved by the couple's three sons and their daughter but not by their other kin and was made only for the souls of this couple.[113] Gifts to Marmoutier by Salomon de Lavardin and his son Haimericus Gaimardus tell the same story.[114]

In certain respects, the kin groups that received the privilege of *societas* resembled consenting groups. Although the former were generally a little smaller than the latter,[115] they, too, could assume different forms. At Saint Vincent of Le Mans, grants of confraternity were made to different combinations of the following: the main donor, his wife, his father, his mother, his children, his brothers and sisters.[116] Some groups, however, included a brother's wife and children, a sister's husband, a *consobrina*, or an aunt (*matertera*).[117] Because grants of this kind could be made to both dead and living relatives,[118] whereas the *laudatio* could be given only by living kin, we cannot argue, as we can when analyzing consenting groups, that a known relative of the donor was left out simply because he or she was dead. It is therefore easier to show that group members were deliberately selected out of a larger pool of recognized or potentially recognizable *parentes*. Like grants of burial rights[119] or places in an abbey,[120] grants of "society and benefit" were made only to those kinsmen and kinswomen who were considered to have some sort of claim to them.

Because the practice of granting spiritual countergifts to only a select group of the donor's *parentes* had the effect of ranking certain kin ahead of others, it seems perfectly congruent with the widespread practice of making material countergifts of different kinds and values to different relatives who all approved the same gift.[121] The ranking system expressed in material countergifts, however, was sometimes more clearly articulated and more finely graded than the one implicit in the granting or withholding of spiritual benefits. Whereas a donor's relatives were either prayed for or ignored, different consenting kin who all received material countergifts were not necessarily remunerated with gifts of identical value or significance.

When Hamelinus de Montoire quitclaimed property to Marmoutier in return for ten pounds, his three sons received different amounts of money in return for their consent. Philippus got four pounds, while Petrus and Odo each received twenty *solidi*.[122] For their approval of a gift that Hugo, son of Gausbertus de Axia, made to Marmoutier in return for ten pounds, Hugo's brother Gislibertus received twenty *solidi*, while two other brothers got five *solidi*. Hugo's *avunculus* Widdio was given only six *denarii*.[123] A gift to Marmoutier by Ascelinus Jotardus was also approved by kin who received countergifts of significantly different values. The donor's wife got twenty *solidi*. His brother was given ten *solidi*. His daughter received twelve *denarii*. And only six *denarii* were accorded to Hugo's *nepos*. In return for confirming this gift, moreover, Hugo's lord, Ingebaldus Brito, and Ingebaldus's kin received payments of different amounts. The lord's wife received forty *solidi*, while two of their sons were given ten *solidi*. A third son was granted only a measure of oats, and the lord's *nepos* received but a single denarius.[124] A similar ranking system is expressed in the token countergifts made to the consenting kin of Tetbaldus, son of Leterius, when, in return for fifty *solidi*, Tetbaldus made one of his many quitclaims to Marmoutier. His wife got three *solidi*. One of his sons (who was probably the eldest) got six *denarii*. Three other sons were each given three *denarii*, while Tetbaldus's two daughters each got four *denarii*.[125]

The complexity of this kind of ranking system is best illustrated by a gift that Ervisus Chabruns made to Noyers with the approval of sixteen people who received countergifts ranging in value from six *denarii* to more than four pounds. The largest countergift went to Ervisus's *nepos* Hugo Rufus, who received four pounds and five *solidi*. Next, Hugo's two brothers Rogerius and Herveus each got fifty *solidi*, while Ascelinus, whose connection with Ervisus is not specified, was given forty *solidi*. The wife of Rogerius got twelve *solidi*, while Herveus's spouse got only three *solidi*. Both the son and the daughter of Ascelinus got five *solidi*, and Herveus's two daughters each got two *solidi*. Whereas Guiternus—whose connection with Ervisus is not explained—got only six *denarii*, his wife got twelve *denarii*, as did both her son and her daughter by Guiternus. Finally, a daughter of Guiternus's wife by a second marriage was given a pair of shoes.[126]

The practice of making payments of different sizes to different consenting kin indicates clearly that a consenting group was not treated as an undifferentiated mass of relatives. As the recipient of a payment that exceeded, equalled, or fell short of the ones made to other group members, each relative was openly ranked above, on a par with, or below his or her associates. When a countergift took the form of clothing, an animal, jewelry, food, wine, or some other kind of movable property, one of its functions, at least on certain occasions, was to symbolize the status of its recipient in a kin group. Shoes and other items of clothing were ordinarily given to children, while adult females were customarily granted hens or sows.[127]

In two instances, the use of countergifts as signs of status seems particularly clear. During the 1060s, a gift to Marmoutier by Robertus, the son-in-law of Guinemarus de Monte Hidulfi, was approved not only by his wife and her two sisters, but also by Robertus's lord, Ascelinus, Ascelinus's young sons Guillelmus and Guicherius, and Ascelinus's wife's younger sister Ermengardis, who was then very young and under Ascelinus's guardianship. While Guillelmus and Guicherius were each given a male piglet in return for their approval, Ermengardis received a female piglet, and when she approved the same gift many years later, the monk who had previously given her this gift gave her not only four *solidi*, but also a full-grown sow.[128] The social symbolism of countergifts was just as clear when a man called Gaufridus, upon succeeding to his father's fief, approved the latter's earlier gift to Saint Vincent of Le Mans. Of the three *nummi* handed to Gaufridus in the monks' chapterhouse, each was given for a particular purpose—one to buy a knife, the second to buy a sheath for the knife, and the third to buy nuts. Some would say that by making these gifts, the monks acknowledged that Gaufridus had truly come of age.[129]

One further fact about material countergifts supports the view that customs about giving the *laudatio* were flexible and variable. The same sorts of kin were ranked differently in different transactions. Although the donor's *major filius* was often distinguished from other consenting kin by the high value or special prestige of the countergifts made to him,[130] he sometimes received no more for the *laudatio* than did a younger son;[131] occasionally, he received even less than one of his sisters.[132] Similarly, while the donor's eldest brother, in the absence of sons, sometimes received more for his consent than did other relatives,[133] he was not always accorded this special status. In one Marmoutier charter, a brother was ranked above his siblings not because of his kinship position, but because he had helped the monks arrange the exchange with his brother, the main donor.[134] In another case, a donor's daughter received less money than the same man's nephew,[135] but in a different case involving different people, this ranking was reversed.[136] Sometimes, a donor's wife received a more valuable countergift than other consenting kin,[137] but at other times, she received less than the donor's eldest son.[138] These variations show that customs governing countergifts—and, by implication, the *lau-*

datio parentum generally—were more subtle and intricate than previous studies have indicated. For this reason, the question of which kin were expected to approve gifts to saints, like the question of whether the *laudatio* was required by custom, admits of no simple answer.

To address this question we should first reconsider the hypothetical kin group pictured in figure 4-3. This group includes all relatives who ever approved a gift to one of the five abbeys in this study. As we have seen, the relatives who might conceivably have been expected to approve a donation were the descendants of the donor's patrilateral and matrilateral grandparents and the close kin of his wife, including descendants of hers by previous marriages. Although this finding certainly does not imply that descendants of the donor's more distant ancestors were never counted among his kin, it indicates that consenting kin groups were almost certainly never larger than cognatic kindreds of first-cousin range. For various reasons, however, no group nearly as large or complex as this one ever approved a gift in our sample. In fact, of the more than sixty different kinds of kin pictured in figure 4-3, no more than ten ever approved any individual gift,[139] and in most groups, the number of different kinds of consenting kin was much lower, standing at three or less in most cases.[140] As a result, although consenting groups should not be automatically equated with either conjugal or coresidential families, they often resembled these sorts of kin groups very closely. At Noyers, most groups including three or fewer kinds of kin were made up of various combinations of the following relatives: wives, children, brothers and sisters, fathers and mothers.[141]

To see why only small subsets of the group pictured in figure 4-3 ever gave the *laudatio* in particular cases, we need to consider several different factors that resulted in donors having many fewer living relatives than the ones pictured in this chart. We can then consider the factors that resulted in only some of these living kin giving the *laudatio*. These two inquiries cannot be neatly separated, however, because the selection of consenting kin may have proceeded in different ways, depending on which kin were available. The most important factors relating to the first were, first, the donor's age and position in his own life cycle, and second, the demographic characteristics determining how many kin and what sorts of kin within the range of first cousins the donor had when he made his gift, and what sorts of living affines he had at this time. In a period of low life expectancy, kin groups including three generations must have been relatively uncommon, especially if we consider only those groups in which at least one member of the youngest generation was old enough to give valid consent.[142] It is not surprising, therefore, that grandchildren rarely gave the *laudatio* and that only two great-grandchildren are found among several thousand consenting kin in the total sample.[143]

In addition, by considering established customs governing the distribution of authority within kin groups, we can also see why mothers approved gifts more often than fathers did[144] and why gifts seem never to have been approved by both the donor's father and mother.[145] Because male landholders normally retained control over property until they died or became monks, they appear in charters only rarely as consenting fathers and never as consenting grandfathers.[146] Similar customs may also account for the fact that mothers approved gifts much more often than fathers did. When men died, their sons rather than their wives usually assumed their positions of familial authority, provided that the former were of full age. When women died, however, no such change in the distribution of familial authority occurred.

Although it is relatively easy to specify certain factors that determined what kinds of relatives were potentially available to approve a donor's gift, it is very hard to predict which members of this pool of potential *laudatores* would actually give the *laudatio* in particular instances. Still, rough correlations can sometimes be established between the composition of a consenting group and certain features of a gift, such as the origin of the alienated property.[147] Although, as we have seen, affines did not frequently give the *laudatio*, they were likely to do so, it seems, when the donor was alienating his wife's inheritance, dowry, or marriage portion.[148] When Hugo de Lupi Saltu gave Saint Vincent rights in a church forming part of his wife Maria's inheritance, both Maria and her mother gave their consent.[149] In a different kind of case in which Durandus gave Saint Vincent, inter alia, some properties that he had received as a dowry ("*in maritagio*") from Ansegisus Bletellus, the latter, as well as Durandus's three sons, approved the transaction.[150] Several Saint Aubin charters point to the same conclusion about the consent of affines. When Hubertus gave Saint Aubin some property that his father-in-law Gaufridus had given him "*in maritagio*," the gift was approved by Gaufridus and his son, as well as by Hubertus's wife.[151] A larger group of affines approved a gift that Robertus, son of Morehenc, made of property from his wife's *maritagium*. The group included not only Robertus's wife, Pagana, but also her brother Martinus, her two sisters, and her *avunculus*, along with five others who may also have been Robertus's affines. In making this gift on the altar of Saint Aubin, Robertus was joined by Pagana and by Martinus, who received a countergift, as did the two consenting sisters of Robertus's wife.[152]

In another kind of case, we can also see that the composition of consenting groups was sometimes influenced by the origin of the property being alienated. As table 4-1 in the appendix indicates, matrilateral kin rarely gave the *laudatio*. When they did so, it was often because the gift consisted of property in which the donor's mother possessed or had once possessed a particular interest. When Hugo gave Saint Vincent some land from the patrimony of his mother Beatrix, his gift was approved not only by his elder brother, Olivarus, but also by Beatrix herself and her own brother Fulcoius, both of whom received countergifts from the monks.[153] Although the failure of monastic scribes to record routinely the origins of all gifts to their abbeys prevents us from proving that mothers and matrilateral kin were expected to give the *laudatio* only in cases of this kind, this hypothesis is consistent with evidence found in several documents. After noting that Frotmundus had held by hereditary right some property that he gave to La Trinité with the approval of two brothers, a scribe went on to mention that the gift was also approved by Frotmundus's mother, even though it was not for her to approve it.[154] The passage probably implies that certain conventions governed the choice of *laudatores* and that it would have been appropriate for mothers such as Beatrix to approve other sorts of gifts.

A similar custom was cited obliquely in an eleventh-century dispute between Marmoutier and Nihardus, whose father, Gislibertus I, was a son of Hugo Duplex I and Adela and who was thus descended through his mother from Fulcherius Dives I.[155] Nihardus challenged a gift made to Saint Martin by his father's sister's son Guismandus II, on the grounds that the alienated property was part of the *maritagium* of Guismandus II's own mother, Emelina, who was Nihardus's father's sister (*matertera*). In one of the few recorded instances from this period in which a judicial decision is said to have been based on a clearly articulated custom, Nihardus's claim was judged unjust, because the disputed property was Guismandus II's acquisition (*emptio*), which he could rightfully give to whomsoever he wished. Although Nihardus lost his case, the decision may imply that he would have won if his allegations about Guismandus II's gift had been true.[156] This implies, in turn, that a married woman's natal kin group sometimes had a claim on her property. If so, we can now understand more clearly why, in a charter previously discussed in chapter 3, Freducia gave a matrilateral kinsman the estate that she had gotten from her mother and had wanted to give to La Trinité. Because her alleged reason for doing so was that her matrilateral kin could have challenged a gift of this property to an abbey, our hypothesis about the circumstances in which matrilateral kin were most likely to give the *laudatio* receives additional support.[157]

In a third kind of case, the past history and present status of property given to an abbey might have influenced or determined the composition of the kin group that participated in an exchange ceremony and even the way in which the transaction was carried out. As we have already seen, a donor's ascendants, siblings, and collateral kin were quite unlikely to be called on to approve gifts that he made after he had married and produced children, by which time he might have established an independent household.[158] This generalization does not apply, however, to cases in which men who had married and produced children continued, after their parents had died, to live with their siblings, among others, in groups sometimes called "fraternities" or "*frèrèches*."[159] In these instances, it appears that a decision not to divide a man's estate among his various children resulted in some gifts being made jointly by the latter, who were sometimes joined in these transactions by their wives and children.[160]

Nevertheless, the fact that joint gifts were almost never made by groups of first cousins and that gifts by individuals were only rarely approved by first cousins[161] suggests that in western France, at least, fraternities soon lost their corporate identity. After the siblings constituting the fraternity died, their estate was probably divided in such a way as to leave the children of any one of these siblings free to alienate land without the consent of children of the other siblings. In transactions carried out by fraternities, we occasionally encounter some of the largest and most structurally complex of the kin groups that ever participated in gifts to any of these five abbeys. At their largest and most complex, these groups resemble "joint families." They are worth examining, because they provide support for our finding that the largest group that could have been expected to give the *laudatio* consisted of a cognatic kindred of first-cousin range.[162] At their largest, these kin groups included a set of married siblings, together with their spouses and children. Because they did not later develop, it seems, into groups of cousins, accompanied by their spouses and children, we can probably assume that the group split up, and the land was divided. Family fission occurred at the precise moment that we could have predicted from an analysis of which relatives ever gave the *laudatio parentum*.

Neither this argument nor the finding that consenting kin groups often consisted only of full or truncated nuclear kin groups necessarily implies, however, that in most instances, the *laudatio parentum* was supposed to be given by the donor's coresidential family. Certain consenting groups clearly included kin who did not regularly reside with the main donor, as we can see from stories about monks who had to travel to secure the *laudatio*[163] and from the story of Freducia, who feared that kin who clearly did not reside with her would challenge her gift.[164] Kin from outside the donor's coresidential kin group were sometimes selected, or selected themselves, to give the *laudatio*, perhaps because they had a particular interest in the alienated property or a special reason for participating in an exchange between some of their kin and a monastic community.

Whereas consenting groups, as we have just seen, were likely to include additional relatives, such as affines, when certain kinds of property were being alienated, there were other circumstances in which these groups were smaller than we might have expected. Although a man who made a quitclaim or confirmed the gift of his feudal tenant sometimes did so in the company of relatives, he was more likely than donors were to act alone.[165] When his confirmation was made with the *laudatio*, the consenting group was usu-

ally smaller than the ones that approved gifts.[166] In addition, although gifts of acquired, as opposed to inherited, property were
sometimes made with the *laudatio parentum*,[167] the need to make
them with the consent of kin may have seemed less compelling
than it did when inherited property was being transferred. As a
result, gifts of acquisitions may have been made with the *laudatio*
less frequently than other kinds of gifts were, and the groups that
approved them may have been smaller than the ones that approved other kinds of gifts.[168]

In some cases, there may also have been a disposition to exclude
relatives who did not reside with the donor from participation in
his gift. Even though consenting groups should not be automatically equated with coresidential families, the overwhelming pre-
ponderance of conjugal pairs and full or truncated conjugal kin
groups in the total sample[169] suggests that, in many instances, no
one bothered to secure the *laudatio* from relatives who did not
reside with the main donor. The same conclusion is supported by
cases cited above in which gifts by donors with children were not
aproved by their living siblings, nephews, nieces, or cousins.[170]
Once a man had married, established a household, and produced
children (not necessarily in that order), he may often have acquired some measure of independence from his collateral kin, at
least for the purpose of making gifts to abbeys.

Many consenting groups, however, did not necessarily include
all members of the donor's coresidential kin group. Statistics in the
appendix table 4-2 show that daughters gave the *laudatio* far less
often than sons did. This discrepancy is so extreme that we should
probably not try to explain it simply by postulating that daughters
were more likely than sons were to leave their parents' household
and that they generally left at an earlier age. Daughters did not
give the *laudatio* only in cases where there were no sons to do
so,[171] but their underrepresentation in consenting groups is so
extreme as to suggest that there was no strong expectation that
they would approve their father's gifts. In addition, because the
consent of the donor's younger sons was clearly considered less
important to secure than that of his *major filius*, particularly in the
late twelfth century,[172] and because numerous gifts were approved by only a single son, it seems likely that younger sons
were left out of many consenting kin groups.[173]

It is also tempting to posit a causal connection between the timing of gifts to saints and the composition of the kin groups that approved them. As we saw in our earlier analyses of gifts to Noyers, Marmoutier, and La Trinité by specific donors, there were instances in which even a donor's living children or siblings evidently failed to approve gifts, with the result that these transactions were approved either by very few kin or no kin at all.[174] One way of accounting for these cases is to argue that a limited power of alienation was accorded to a donor when his gift was so small as to cause no threat of disinheritance to his kin or when he made his gift under circumstances preventing him from securing the *laudatio*.[175] An additional way of accounting for these failures to give the *laudatio* is to postulate that the gifts in question were made after the closer relatives who did not approve them had received from the donor as much land as they could ever expect from him. Under this hypothesis, a daughter who had been given with a dowry to a husband was even more likely to be excluded from a consenting group than a daughter who had yet to be so endowed. Similarly, the likelihood that a son would approve his father's gift was influenced by whether or not he had been provided with land to support him.

Neither in these cases nor in others, however, should we assume that the exclusion of potential *laudatores* from consenting groups was sanctioned by a binding legal rule or custom or that it was meekly accepted by the excluded kin. The fact that so many gifts to these abbeys were challenged by relatives who had not approved them suggests that the question of which relatives should participate in a gift was a source of controversy. Along with passages indicating that certain kin gave the *laudatio* only with great reluctance,[176] evidence of familial *calumniae* points clearly to the conclusion that the composition of many consenting groups may have been determined at least in part by intrafamilial struggles of which only faint traces can be found in monastic sources.[177]

Thus far, the composition of consenting groups has been explained primarily by reference to demographic factors and factors relating to the interests that different kinds of kin may have had in the property a donor gave to a monastic community. But because gifts to saints had religious and social dimensions, other factors may have also played a role in determining why certain kin and not others participated in these transactions. Having already shown that there was sometimes a correlation between the composition of a consenting group and the familial origin of the property given to an abbey, we now need to consider the possibility that these two variables were correlated, in turn, with the identity of the person for whose spiritual benefit the gift in question was made. If these three variables were, in fact, interrelated in certain cases, then the hypothesis that relatives were particularly likely to approve gifts of property in which they had a proprietary interest should be supplemented by the hypothesis that relatives were especially likely to give the *laudatio* in cases where they were linked by a significant tie of kinship to at least one of the people for whose spiritual benefit a gift to an abbey was made.

Sometimes, we can discern a close connection between the origin of the property given to an abbey and the identity of the relatives who received benefits from monks in return for the gift. In these cases, gifts were made in such a way as to provide spiritual benefits for people with special interests in the property exchanged for those benefits. This, in fact, may have been the norm. As we saw in chapter 3, Dhuoda's instructions to her son clearly indicated that the ancestors for whom her son was to pray or procure prayers were the people from whom he received the wherewithal to endow such prayers.[178]

When Rainardus made a gift to Marmoutier for the souls of his father, Odo de Daumeré, and his mother, Ermengardis, the alienated property came from Ermengardis's dower—the property that Odo had assigned to her when they were married.[179] A gift to Marmoutier by Helias, count of Maine, for the soul of his deceased wife Matilda and the souls of *her* ancestors consisted entirely of property from Matilda's inheritance, which she had presumably received from these same ancestors.[180] When Hugo the *vicarius* gave Saint Vincent some property from his wife's dower, he did not do so simply for his own soul; in return for Hugo's gift, his wife Hadvisa received the privilege of confraternity.[181] An even clearer connection between the origin of the property alienated and the recipients of privileges exchanged for it can be seen in a gift to Saint Vincent by Willelmus de Doucelles. In return for property from the dowry of his recently deceased wife, the monks agreed to sing a thousand masses for her within forty days of her death.[182] When the wife of Gausbertus de Joiaco died, her husband, acting for the sake of her soul, gave Saint Vincent some property that his wife's father, Warinus the provost, had given to him when he had married the provost's daughter.[183]

A story from a charter of Noyers makes the same point. After the death of Ganilo, who, like his mother, had both made a gift to Noyers and been buried there, the *honor* he had held with his brother Cleopa passed to Ervisus Cabruns, who had married their *neptis* Agatha. When Agatha and her husband had held the *honor* scarcely twelve years, she became mortally ill and approved what her *parentes* had given to Noyers and especially the gifts of her uncle (*patruus*) Ganilo. These things were also approved by Agatha's husband Ervisus and her sons Rainaldus, Gosbertus, and Poslardus. Ganilo's *nepos* Adraldus and Adraldus's son Simon also approved. Moreover, Ervisus, the husband of Agatha, knowing that it was through Agatha that he himself held the *honor* of Ganilo, gave for *her* soul to Noyers a certain serf.[184]

The belief that property pertaining to a landholder's wife should be given away to benefit her soul was slightly extended in a case where Hamelinus de Langeais made a gift to Saint Vincent for his own soul and for the souls of his wife Helviza, her ancestors as well as his, and Helviza's brother, Hugo Duplex II, who already lay buried in the monks' cloister. The alienated property almost certainly came from the inheritance or dowry of Helviza, whose natal kin group of Montdoubleau were influential in this region.[185] A similar method of allocating property for religious purposes is illustrated by a gift that Guicherius Tallahardus and his three brothers made to Marmoutier's priory at Lancé, when these four men brought the body of their father, Ivo, there for burial. In recording this transaction, a scribe went out of his way to note that the property alienated had been previously held by Ivo.[186]

Whereas the cases just cited show that some people who benefited from gifts to saints had had special interests in the property given, a transaction involving the abbey of La Trinité suggests that a connection can sometimes be found between the composition of a consenting group and the identity of the person or persons for whose spiritual benefit the gift in question was made. When Robertus de Insula made a gift to La Trinité for the soul of Bartholomeus, who was the brother of Robertus's father, Rainaldus, and whom the monks of La Trinité buried, the gift was approved by Robertus's brother Rainaldus; their mother, Berta; and their two uncles (*patrui*) Hugo and Hamelinus, who were presumably the brothers of Bartholomeus.[187] Because it was so rare for the *laudatio* to be given by uncles, it may not be farfetched to argue that Hugo and Hamelinus approved Robertus's gift at least partly because they wished to associate themselves with an act by which prayers would be procured for their brother.

In addition, a transaction between Saint Vincent and Robertus, son of Witnernus de Juillé, reveals clear links between the origin of the property given, the recipients of spiritual benefits, and the composition of the kin group participating in the exchange ceremony. At the time of the transaction, Robertus was closely associated with the abbey of Saint Vincent, where his father, Witernus, was a brother and where his brother Hubertus had previously died as a monk. On the advice of his father and mother, Robertus gave land to Saint Vincent for the souls of the following people: his maternal grandfather, Wauterius Bornus; his maternal grandmother, Lisoia; Gervasius Bornus, the son of Wauterius and Lisoia; Robertus's dead brother, Hubertus; and Robertus's deceased wife, Vigolent. In return for these benefits, Robertus gave Saint Vincent some property that he held by hereditary right from the patrimony of his maternal grandfather, Wauterius Bornus. The signatories to this act included not only Robertus, his present wife, Adeliz, and his children Willelmus and Hugo, but also a Wauterius Bornus, who was clearly a descendant of the elder Wauterius. The younger Wauterius, moreover, was the only signatory other than Willelmus and Hugo to be given a material countergift.[188]

Similar gift-giving practices are illustrated in a remarkable account of a gift that the youthful Willelmus, son of Hugo lord of Sainte-Maure, made to the monks of Noyers as he lay dying in Gascony, where he was serving the duke of Aquitaine. Hoping, according to the Noyers scribe, to be buried at Noyers next to his mother and to receive God's mercy through the prayers of the Virgin Mary, Willelmus told two of his companions that he would give the church of Noyers various properties, including one that had been given to his father, Hugo, by Johannes de Chinon, when the latter had given the former his daughter, Willelmus's mother, in marriage. This gift, moreover, was to be made not only for his own soul, but also for that of his mother. Later, after Willelmus's body and word of his gift had both been brought all the way back to the church of Noyers by the youth's two companions, Willelmus's father, Hugo, came to the abbey church of Noyers, where he made or confirmed the gift for the sake of Willelmus's soul, before Willelmus was buried. Present at this ceremony, at which a burial and a gift for the soul of the deceased were inextricably linked, was Aimericus Paganus, son of Johannes de Chinon. At Hugo's request, Johannes confirmed the gift and stated that he was doing so for the soul of his sister, as well as for the soul of his sister's son. After Willelmus's burial, moreover, Hugo made further gifts to Noyers and gave himself, as it were, to this abbey, stating that if he later became a monk, he would be a brother of Noyers and that if he were to die as a layman, he wished to be buried next to his son at Noyers. Finally, Hugo's present wife, Adenordis, promised that if she did not become a nun, she, too, would be buried at Noyers. In this way, the familial, the proprietary, and the spiritual interests of several monastic benefactors became neatly fused.[189]

In the unusually detailed documents just analyzed, we can see people acting in accordance with a broad principle very similar to the one articulated by Dhuoda. In one form or another, this principle probably lies behind many other, less well recorded transactions: Property should be used to benefit the souls of the people from whom it had been acquired. If Robertus, son of Witernus, had made a gift for the soul of his patrilateral kin, he would presumably have given property that he had received from his father, Witernus, and he might well have acted without the consent of his matrilateral kinsman Wauterius Bornus but with the approval of other kin. Here, as in other cases, there is no point in asking whether the reasons why particular relatives participated in a gift were juridical, religious, or social. We can only say that the gift had been made in a way that was considered fitting and proper.

Because the *laudatio parentum* was not routinely given by a kin group whose size and structure were determined by the application of a simple rule and can therefore be specified precisely, the study of this practice can provide no clear, unambiguous answers to the broad questions about medieval French kinship and family life that scholars such as Marc Bloch have repeatedly posed. Even though most consenting kin groups were small and included only the donor's spouse and children, the fact that certain gifts were approved by larger kin groups including more distant relatives makes it difficult to use studies of the *laudatio* to answer Bloch's question about whether the French "family" in our period bore a closer resemblance to the "vast clans" that supposedly existed in the early medieval period than it did to the small "conjugal" units of more recent times.[190] Moreover, because consenting groups sometimes excluded the donor's close female kin, while also including people who did not necessarily reside with him regularly, we cannot confidently employ evidence about the *laudatio* to determine the normal size and structure of eleventh- or twelfth-century households.[191] Furthermore, although consenting groups in our region rarely included matrilateral kin and probably did not contain many people linked to the donor through his female relatives, the prominent role assumed by matrilateral kin in certain transactions makes it difficult to give a definitive answer to the recurrent queries of medievalists about whether "the family" at this time was cognatic (i.e. bilateral) or agnatic (i.e. patrilineal).[192] Finally, because consenting kin groups occasionally included first cousins or even more distant kin whose precise relationship to the donor is not clearly specified in our sources, analyses of these groups cannot help us to determine precisely "how far along the lines of descent," as Bloch put it, "the obligations towards 'friends by blood' extended."[193]

These conclusions, however, will seem disappointing only if we conceive of the medieval "family" and medieval kinship generally in ways that create certain rigid and highly problematic expectations about how investigations of medieval kinship groups should proceed and what conclusions they should reach. From scattered passages in which monastic scribes at the five abbeys and elsewhere indicate that certain gifts to saints were approved by the donor's family (*parentela* or *genus*),[194] we are likely to conclude that the relatives who gave the *laudatio parentum* sometimes constituted—and were supposed to constitute—a clearly delimited, enduring social group whose composition was regulated and determined by a set of clearly formulated rules that were, in these cases at least, being strictly observed. This way of looking at medieval "families" seems to be justified, moreover, by other medieval sources, such as legal documents specifying the rights and duties of a person's kin,[195] canon law doctrines defining the kin group within which marriages were forbidden,[196] poems in which noble *lignages* are apparently represented as coherent and enduring social groups, chronicles and charters describing feuds involving opposing *parentelae*,[197] and genealogical writings designed to glorify a particular *lignage*.[198] The same approach is also consistent with "the structural-functional view of society as a system of *enduring groups* composed of statuses and roles supported by a set of values and related sanctions which maintain the system in equilibrium,"[199] with the view that "kinship" is a "mechanism in terms of which . . . the rights and duties of *specifically denominated actors* are defined and enforced,"[200] and with the view that regularities in social practice can be explained as the product of obedience to rules.[201] If we therefore conclude that our primary objective in studies of the *laudatio* should be to identify the rules governing the composition and structure of the "family" viewed as a basic, if elusive, unit of eleventh- and twelfth-century society, we will find, for reasons already given above, that many, if not most, gifts were approved only by fragments—or mutated forms—of true *parentelae* and therefore provide only fatally flawed evidence about the medieval "family."

This conclusion, however, is not the only one that can be drawn from the study of the consenting kin groups in our sample. If we regard the *parentela* or *lignage*, not as a real social group, but as a cultural category that medieval people could use in different ways in different contexts,[202] if we reject the claim that medieval people in our period had a "kinship system" of "moral and jural norms" that they applied more or less comprehensively,[203] and if we treat any rules of kinship that may have existed in our period primarily as idioms in which particular people could make claims to various forms of "capital,"[204] then evidence about the kin groups that gave the *laudatio parentum* will appear in a new light and can then be used as the basis for some useful generalizations about medieval kin groups. Moreover, if we keep these same ideas in mind when reviewing the other kinds of texts mentioned above, we will see that the evidence they contain about kin groups can be interpreted in the same way as evidence contained in charters about what kinds of kin groups gave the *laudatio*.

If we treat the *parentela* as a fluid cultural category or ideological construct and distinguish it radically from the many different "practical kin groups"[205] that actually engaged for longer or shorter periods in such activities as making a gift to an abbey, participating in a burial ceremony, or prosecuting a feud, we can see from our study of consenting groups how large a discrepancy there often was between kinship ideology and actual practice. We can also see that even imaginary representations of kin groups could assume different forms. French nobles of this period may have wished to imagine themselves or others as being surrounded, especially at moments of crisis, by large groups of kin, who were sharply distinguished from non-kin and were supposedly bound together by powerful sentiments of solidarity and reciprocity. The kin group of a nobleman could be imaginatively represented in several different ways. Sometimes, it assumed the form of something resembling a patrilineal descent group, whose members were usually, if not invariably, linked to the nobleman through males.[206] At other times, it could include many relatives linked to him through his mother or other females and might therefore resemble a cognatic kindred.[207] When a lay nobleman, moreover, imaginatively represented his own family for the purpose of assessing the propriety of a proposed marriage, he did not necessarily define his own family in the same way as clerics did, when they were called upon to pronounce on the legitimacy of such a marriage.[208]

When we shift our attention from "the family," conceived of as a cultural or legal category, to the "practical" kin groups that actually engaged in particular social activities, we find not only that the latter differed in composition from the former, but also that they could assume different forms, depending upon the nature of the activity in which they were engaged. For example, when a nobleman's kin assembled to avenge his death or to support him in a major political struggle, this group probably included a substantial number of people related to him in various ways, including, perhaps, the bonds of spiritual kinship.[209] In practice, however, a man's kin group could take a very different form: when he was making a gift to an abbey, the kin group with which he acted might include only a handful of very close relatives who came together or were brought together for a certain limited purpose and then dispersed.

If, moreover, we consider the composition of the kin groups that actually assembled to give the *laudatio*, we can see that their structure and their size could vary considerably. Whereas many consenting groups were so small and included such a narrow range of kin that evidence about them seems to show that "the small family" was the characteristic kinship unit of this period, others were so large and complex in structure as to suggest that large kin groups continued to play important social roles in the eleventh and twelfth centuries. In certain situations, a man might be associated with some of his wife's kin or mother's kin. But at other times, neither his affines nor his matrilateral kin were relevant to his purposes and did not associate themselves with him. Sometimes, a monastic benefactor acted together with all his children. At other times, it was only his sons or merely his eldest son who acted with him. Women were not routinely excluded from a man's kin group, and wives, in particular, frequently played a central role in it. But there was a strong and consistent bias against including many females in consenting groups.

Some of these variations, as we have seen, can be correlated with the stage in life at which the donor made his gift, with the demographic characteristics of the people descended from his grandparents, or with the origin of the property that he alienated. In other words, the composition of the donor's kin group could assume different forms in different situations and at different stages in his life cycle. As donors grew older and fathered children, their ascendants and collateral kin were less and less likely to participate in their gifts to abbeys, while donors who had no children were far more likely than donors with offspring were to associate themselves with their siblings and siblings' children. Although consenting kin groups did not routinely include the donor's matrilateral kin or affines, people related to the donor through his wife or mother were expected to join with the donor when he was acting in a way that touched the lives of these women. The organization of any particular kin group was significantly determined by the nature of the action in which the group was engaged.

Although there were evidently certain loose conventions about the kind of kin group that should participate in a gift to an abbey, both donors and their kin had a certain amount of freedom to constitute consenting groups in accordance with their own interests and desires and, more particularly, with their views about whether participation in a particular transaction was a privilege or a burden. In exercising that freedom, a donor was constrained both by a need to secure the *laudatio* from kin who did not necessarily wish to associate themselves with his gift and by a fear lest someone excluded from the consenting group would resent his or her exclusion and cause trouble on account of it. At the same time, however, neither the donor nor his monastic donee were necessarily inclined to extend the privilege of participating in an exchange ceremony to anyone who could conceivably claim kinship with the donor. Meanwhile, those who were considered the donor's kin had to decide whether, in a particular case, the act of giving the *laudatio parentum* was a privilege or a burden. To understand more fully why certain kin and not others were likely to be included in a consenting group and why excluding them could be dangerous, we must directly confront the question of why so many gifts to saints were made with the *laudatio parentum* and not by solitary individuals.

Chapter 5

Earthly and
Heavenly Inheritances

INTIMATELY RELATED TO questions about the
normative status of the *laudatio parentum* and the composition of
the kin groups that gave it is the question of why this practice
should have been observed, in particular instances or in general.
This problem is even more difficult than the ones considered in
chapters 3 and 4, partly because the available sources are so frus-
tratingly uninformative and partly because it is hard to decide
what constitutes a truly satisfactory explanation for a practice as
complex as the *laudatio*. If charters are reticent about whether gifts
to saints were supposed to be approved by a donor's relatives and
if so, by which ones, they are almost completely mute about why
this practice was followed. What little evidence they contain on
this point, moreover, is the product of an official monastic perspective on transactions that may have looked very different to
different lay people and even to different monks. In any event,
most charters indicate only that the *laudatio* supposedly made gifts
to abbeys "firmer," without clearly revealing why this was so.[1]
Historians are therefore left free to explain the *laudatio* in ways
that are generally constrained less by empirical evidence than by
their own assumptions about how land was held in earlier European societies and about how medieval customs can best be explained. As a result, these assumptions, along with the available
evidence, need to be examined critically.

Although previous scholars have proposed different ways of explaining the prevalence of the *laudatio parentum* during the eleventh and twelfth centuries, they have been virtually unanimous in
assuming that because transactions made with the approval of
relatives served primarily to transfer interests in landed property,
explanations of the *laudatio* should focus on the question of why
land at this time was supposedly not legally alienable by indi-

vidual landholders. Proceeding on this assumption, they have tried to explain this practice by associating it with a particular system of land tenure. Because explanations of this type do not indicate why people should have established, followed, and maintained a rule requiring that conveyances be made with the *laudatio*, legal explanations have often been supplemented by arguments designed to show that this alleged rule served important economic and social functions and that it both reflected and reinforced pervasive feelings of "family solidarity" within the landholding classes of this period.

As we shall soon see, none of the competing legal explanations for the *laudatio* accounts satisfactorily for all the available evidence. In addition, they all rest on assumptions about medieval law and gifts to saints that have been called into question in previous chapters. Furthermore, both legal and functional explanations of the *laudatio* proceed from the debatable premise that the practices of particular people can be explained as the outcome of consistent efforts to obey rules or to meet certain general social needs. As a result, although explanations of both types help to identify some of the ideological and practical pressures that made it likely that a donor's kin would participate in gifts to saints, they need to be substantially reformulated; they should also be supplemented by other arguments that take account of distinctive features of gifts to saints and earlier medieval legal culture and that do not purport to explain social behavior simply by reference to rules or general social needs.

In their purest and simplest form, legal explanations for the prevalence of the *laudatio* are implicitly grounded on several preliminary assumptions. Such explanations, summarized in chapter 3, supposedly show that because a custom or legal rule required that valid alienations in perpetuity and perhaps even for shorter terms be made with the approval of the alienor's kin, landholders who wished to prevent their alienations from being invalidated had good legal grounds for closely following this rule by seeing to it that their conveyances were made with the *laudatio parentum*. At the same time, monastic beneficiaries and other alienees either aided alienors in procuring the *laudatio* or acted independently to achieve this objective because they had a strong interest in ensuring that alienations were properly made and would not later be undermined by familial challenges.

It was not, therefore, on their own initiative but in response to pressure from alienors or alienees that relatives gave the *laudatio*, according to the legal explanations. Although some alienations, as various documents show, were evidently made without the consent of the alienor's kin[2] and although others were probably aborted when it became clear to the prospective parties that the *laudatio* would not be given,[3] there were thousands of cases in which alienors and alienees succeeded, by one means or another, in securing the *laudatio* from the kin of the former, so that most alienations conformed to the rule that land be alienated only with the *laudatio parentum*.[4] The prevalence of this practice, the argument runs, can therefore be attributed mainly to the relatively successful efforts of alienors and alienees to promote their own interests by following an established rule governing alienations of land.

Because legal historians suggest that they can best explain the *laudatio* by positing the existence of a rule enjoining this practice, their main objective has been to show how this rule fitted logically into a system of real property law. Although legal explanations of the *laudatio* can take different forms and be developed with greater or lesser rigor, they all start from the premise that the reason why a landholder could not legally alienate land without the consent of his relatives was that his legal rights in the land he held were somehow limited. In most cases, this premise is supplemented by the further assumption that a donor's relatives were supposed to approve his alienations, especially those made in perpetuity, because they themselves had rights of one kind or another in the property being alienated. The task of providing a legal explanation for the *laudatio parentum* has therefore entailed efforts to reconstruct speculatively from fragmentary evidence about medieval practice the postulates of a system of land tenure that is consistent with the first premise and, in most cases, with the second one as well. As a result, the main question considered in this kind of analysis is: What sorts of rights could a donor and his relatives conceivably have had in land that he could alienate only with their approval?

This question can be answered in more than one way, not only because the available evidence is scanty, hard to interpret, and often ambiguous, but also because some of it points clearly in different directions. As legal historians have acknowledged, this finding suggests that by itself, legal analysis can adequately account for only a fraction of the social practices recorded in charters.[5] Evidence about the *laudatio* can be used *either* to show that individual proprietorship was the norm in eleventh- and twelfth-century France *or* to demonstrate that a communitarian landholding system prevailed there. In addition, the problem of determining what rights a donor and his kin could have had in property alienated with the *laudatio* is complicated by the fact that in regions such as western France, where feudal property was prevalent and allodial property (property owned absolutely, rather than being held from a lord) rare, substantial numbers of gifts to saints, as we have seen, were approved by the donor's lord or lords and by their relatives, as well as by the donor's own kin.[6] Although previous studies have not fully treated these additional forms of consent, explanations of the former need to be compatible with explanations of the latter. This issue, moreover, is closely related to another one that has arisen in legal analyses of the *laudatio*. During the period when this practice was prevalent, was feudal property heritable? To resolve this question, legal historians must consider the property interests that may have been held in fiefs by the donor, his heir and other kin, his lord, and perhaps even his lord's kin. In doing so, they must solve the problem of heritability in a way that is compatible with their theories about the *laudatio*. Because there are good grounds for thinking that conventions governing the transmission or "devolution" of property from generation to generation did not remain unchanged during the long period of two or more centuries when the *laudatio* was commonly practiced, different legal explanations for the *laudatio* may have to be constructed for different periods.[7]

Any global explanation for the prevalence of the *laudatio parentum* must also solve three additional problems. First, the explanation must be compatible with evidence already presented about the composition of consenting groups, because certain methods of allocating rights in land among kin are easily workable only when certain kinds of kin groups are present.[8] Second, the problem of identifying the rights of most monastic benefactors and their consenting relatives is all the more difficult because it concerns the landholding practices of a class of people who had land, but who did not themselves use land for productive purposes and whose property rights cannot, therefore, be illuminated by evidence about their access to land, their use of it, or their direct control over its immediate products. In other words, in trying to analyze real property rights of lords and knights and their kin, legal historians are faced with a more intractable problem than the one encountered by scholars concerned with land tenure in more egalitarian societies, because any rights in land that noble donors and their kin may have had were more abstract and less continuously exercised than ordinary use rights.[9] Third, there are grounds for thinking that the property interests of a donor's kin varied, depending on whether the property in question was acquired through his father, mother, or wife.

In spite of these difficulties, if cases involving property associated with a donor's wife or mother are temporarily set aside for separate treatment, and if questions about why lords and their kin sometimes approved gifts are deferred for the time being as well, it is possible to outline a set of alternative hypotheses about the property rights of landholders and consenting kin. While these explanations are, in most cases, based on arguments proposed or considered by previous historians, they have been freely adapted in such a way as to illustrate the main legal theories that can be used to account for the *laudatio parentum*. These hypotheses can be conveniently represented as lying on a continuum running from the individualist theory that land was held by individual donors to the communitarian theory that land was held by family corporations. Whereas the individualist theories rest on the premise that those who gave the *laudatio* either had no rights at all in the alienated property or merely consented in their capacity as prospective heirs with possible future claims to that property, the communitarian theories generally treat at least some consenting relatives as having present interests of some sort in this land. What follows, then, is a highly schematic summary of possible legal explanations of the *laudatio parentum*.

According to theory 1, a hypothesis located at the individualist end of the spectrum, the alienor's relatives had no present or even future interests in the land he held.[10] However, as members of a society in which land was the main source of wealth and social position and in which family solidarity was highly prized, a landholder's kin had a strong practical, as opposed to legal, interest in the disposition of their kinsman's land. Prevailing custom recognized this interest and protected it by barring landholders from alienating land without the consent of their kin. A landholder's right of alienation was thereby restricted, not because his relatives themselves had any legally enforceable rights in land, in which the landholder may have had only a life estate, but only because land was not treated as a commodity over which landholders were legally empowered to exercise full rights of alienation.[11]

Under a variant of theory 1, theory 1a, only the interest of the alienor's heir in the alienor's land was recognized by established custom. The alienor was therefore barred from conveying real property without his heir's consent.[12] Other relatives approved alienations only because the alienor or alienee thought it prudent to guard either against unlawful but still potentially vexatious *calumniae* by kin other than the heir or against the possibility that the alienor's prospective heir would predecease the alienor, leaving someone else who had never approved the alienation to inherit the alienor's property. Even the presumptive heir, however, had no present or future rights in the alienated property. He simply benefited from a custom in which a strong social bias—as opposed to a legal rule—against disinheritance was articulated.[13]

Theory 2 postulates that although none of the alienor's consenting relatives, under existing custom, had any present interest in the alienated property or even any clearly recognized right to get it after the donor's death, each of them had a sort of contingent reversionary interest in the land that might supersede any right that the alienor could create by himself for his alienee. Here, it is assumed that throughout the period when the *laudatio* was prevalent, landholders had heritable interests in their land. As a result, if the land was alienated without the *laudatio* of any relative whose consent was required, that relative might have a better claim to it, at least after the donor's death, than the alienee and could therefore challenge the alienee's right to the land as soon as the donor died, if not earlier.[14]

According to a variant of theory 2, theory 2a, only the alienor's heir had the reversionary interest just described, and only he had the right to challenge alienations made without his approval. Other kin approved alienations only for the reasons postulated in theory 1.[15]

The argument advanced in theory 3 is that, at least in cases where gifts were made jointly by two or more relatives acting as equals, relatives held land as joint tenants. Because they all had present interests in the land, they all had to join in conveying it to third parties. They may also have lived together, although retaining the option of dividing their joint holding and becoming individual proprietors whose powers of alienation would then be restricted in the ways explained by theories 1, 1a, 2, or 2a.[16]

According to theory 4, a theory differing substantially from the ones already considered, rights in the alienated property were vested, not in the individual donor or in a set of potentially independent joint tenants, but in an ongoing family community including not only the principal alienor (if there was one) or the coalienors, but also the consenting relatives of the principal alienor or the coalienors, whether or not they all lived together. The land could therefore be legally alienated only if the alienation was approved by every one of these people, each of whom could claim property alienated without his or her approval even before the donor's death.[17]

According to a variant of theory 4, theory 4a, it was only the donor's coresidential kin who formed, along with the donor, a family community with collective rights in the alienated property.[18]

Under theory 5, which resembles the preceding one, rights in the alienated property were held not only by the alienor and his consenting kin but also by past, present, and future members of a corporate kin group that had previously been represented by the donor's ancestors and was now temporarily represented by the donor and that would, after the donor's death, be represented by his heir, his heir's heir, and so on. As the current representative of his corporate kin group, the donor had some power over the land. But he could not legally make an alienation that would last beyond his own death, at which time his heir would replace him as the head of the *lignage*. If the alienation was to be a perpetual one, the heir's consent was vital, because he would acquire rights in the alienated property the moment his father or other ancestor died.

The heir could therefore challenge an alienation in perpetuity that had been made without his approval.[19]

Because the five theories just outlined do not cover cases involving property in which the alienor's wife or mother possessed or had possessed special interests, they need to be supplemented with an explanation of the legal or proprietary basis of the *laudatio parentum* in these instances.[20] In cases involving property that came from the dowry or inheritance of the alienor's wife or mother, we can explain the consent of the alienor's affines or matrilateral kin by postulating that members of these groups had retained reversionary interests in this property when it had passed to the alienor, so that they could claim it if it ceased to be used for the support of their kinswoman or their kinswoman's children. How long these reversionary interests lasted and whether they could ever be extinguished is unclear.[21]

In addition, because the legal theories just presented do not account for the fact that substantial numbers of gifts, as we have seen, were approved by the donor's lord or lords and even by relatives of his lord or lords, they need to be extended to cover these findings.[22] To explain why a donor's lord or lords sometimes approved his alienations, any one of the theories outlined above could simply be supplemented by the postulate that because a donor's gift or other alienation could conceivably have abridged the fief that he held directly from his lord and indirectly from one or more overlords, interests of lords and overlords were protected by a custom requiring all of a tenant's alienations to be approved by his lord and even by his overlord.[23]

This supplementary postulate, however, does not explain why relatives of the donor's lord or overlord sometimes joined their kinsman in approving a tenant's alienations.[24] This objective can be attained by combining theory 2a or theory 5 with an existing explanation that accounts for the approval given by both Anglo-Norman lords and their heirs to gifts by their feudal tenants.[25] Fundamental to this modified theory is the postulate that when a lord followed the conventional practice of granting a fief to a new tenant *and to that tenant's heirs*,[26] he was not alienating a fully heritable estate that the new tenant would own and could therefore freely alienate in perpetuity. Instead, the lord was giving the tenant only a life-estate in property that would pass, on the tenant's death, to his heir, who would also hold a life-estate in it. In effect, the lord was creating a potentially endless series of life-estates that were to be held in succession from the lord and his heirs by the tenant, the tenant's heir, the heir's heir and so on. As a result, when the tenant died, his fief would eventually pass to his heir. But the heir would not, strictly speaking, "inherit" it from his ancestor; instead, he would succeed to it by virtue of a "hereditary right" created by the original grant to his ancestor by his ancestor's lord.[27] On the death of the ancestor, the fief he had been granted reverted to his lord, who was then obliged to regrant it to the ancestor's heir.[28]

The property to which the heir had right did not consist of whatever part of the fief the original tenant was holding at his death; instead, the heir was entitled to the entire estate that the lord had originally granted to the tenant. Lacking the power, by himself, to alienate his fief in perpetuity or, indeed, for any term longer than his own life, the most the tenant could do was to create a short-term interest for his alienee. Even to accomplish this limited objective, he had to secure his lord's consent, because any alienation that he made would diminish (or "abridge") the fief that his lord had granted him. In addition, if the tenant wished to make an alienation that would endure beyond the time of his own death, as he would have to do in order to make a perpetual gift to a monastic community, he or his donee would have to secure the consent of his own prospective heir and hope that all subsequent heirs to his fief would later approve his gift as well.

The donor's lord, too, had been in the same position when he had given a fief to the tenant and the tenant's heirs.[29] He, too, had only a life-estate in the fief that he had received from his own lord. As a result, if the lord wished to give part of his estate to a tenant and the tenant's heirs and thereby create a tenancy that would endure after the lord's own death, the lord would have to secure the consent of his heir and then hope that his subsequent heirs would confirm the alienation and respect it. Because a perpetual alienation by the tenant would therefore threaten the interests of the tenant's lord's heirs, as well as the tenant's heirs and the tenant's lord, it finally becomes clear why gifts were sometimes approved by relatives of the donor's lord or lords.

As just presented, this theory closely resembles theory 2a. But it could be modified to fit with the communitarian postulates of theories 4 and 5. This modification could be effected if, instead of seeking the key to the *laudatio parentum* and to the consent of the lord and lord's relatives in a gift that the lord had made to the tenant and the tenant's heirs, we regard this conveyance as part of a more complex and encompassing transaction through which an enduring relationship was established between the lord and his kin on the one hand and the tenant and his kin on the other. We could further maintain that medieval kinship ties had just as much potential as lordship ties to serve as the basis of rights and duties that would inhibit both tenants and their lords from acting alone, without the consent of their kin. As Maitland suggested, we could argue that in a legal order recognizing the birthrights to land, "a child acquires rights in the ancestral lands, at birth or, it may be, at adolescence; at any rate he acquires rights in the ancestral land, and *this is not by gift, bequest, inheritance or any title known to our modern law.*"[30] In this way, we could show that at least some of the donor's kin and lord's kin had a direct interest in transactions that, under individualist theories, involved only the lord and the lord's heir and the tenant and the tenant's heir.

When viewed in their own terms as efforts to provide legal explanations for the *laudatio parentum*, each of the theories just outlined has strengths and weaknesses that can only be briefly outlined here. If we modify theory 1 by allowing for the possibility that familial restraints on a landholder's power of alienation were not universally operative, so that without the *laudatio* he could alienate acquisitions, for example, or make small, reasonable gifts of inherited land that would not disinherit his heirs, this theory could account for cases in which donors with living kin apparently made gifts without the *laudatio*.[31] This same modification might also help us to understand why some consenting relatives received only token countergifts[32] and why certain familial challenges were sometimes judged unjust and never resulted, in recorded cases, in the familial challenger's recovering all the property alienated without his approval.[33] Nevertheless, the theory that kin had no rights whatever in property alienated with their consent is hard to reconcile with other evidence already cited in chapters 2 and 3, notably the valuable countergifts sometimes made to consenting kin,[34] the prominent roles of certain relatives in many exchange ceremonies, the gifts made jointly by several kin acting as equals, the familial challenges to gifts allegedly made without the *laudatio*, and the substantial payments and privileges accorded to litigants and their kin when the former, with the latter's approval, quitclaimed rights in lands allegedly alienated without their approval. Unless we argue that all these practices were observed out of practical prudence, rather than out of a desire to conform to custom, we must consider the possibility that consenting kin had veritable rights in the alienated property. But what kinds of rights?

Theory 2—which holds that consenting relatives had contingent reversionary interests that would only support valid claims to the property under certain conditions—is useful in explaining the role that affines and matrilateral kin occasionally played in gifts made to abbeys. The theory is also consistent with the finding that the countergifts made to many consenting relatives were so small that they resembled tokens more than payments for veritable legal interests. Moreover, the fact that certain familial challenges to alienations were made only after the donor's death[35] suggests that before he died, consenting relatives had only contingent rights in the property that they later claimed. However, because the relative who was most likely to initiate this kind of dispute was the main donor's heir,[36] it is worth considering the merits of theory 2a, which holds that only he—and not other consenting kin—had this kind of reversionary interest.

In spite of their virtues, theory 2 and its variant, theory 2a, are both hard to reconcile with the fact that consenting relatives other than the heir sometimes received more valuable countergifts for his approval than other consenting relatives did.[37] Moreover, the fact that certain familial *calumniae* antedated the main donor's death[38] and were made by relatives other than his heir[39] suggests that certain consenting relatives did not acquire whatever rights they allegedly had in the alienated property by inheritance from the main donor.[40] Instead, they may have gotten them by being born into a property-holding corporate kin group. Furthermore, these two theories are inconsistent with evidence indicating that in certain instances, gifts were made jointly by several kinsmen acting as equals.

Whereas theory 3 can be supported by evidence about joint gifts, it does not satisfactorily account for most of the data just cited in support of the first two theories and their variants and seems particularly difficult to reconcile with evidence concerning transactions in which the position of most consenting kin, especially as indicated by the countergifts they received, was subordinate to that of the main donor and, in some cases, the main donor's heir.[41] Finally, without reconstructing long, detailed histories of properties held by codonors, the contention that these people retained the option of dividing their joint holdings is no more plausible than the claim that as members of a family community, they were not free to divide their lands.

Although theories 4 and 4a—along with theories 3 and 5—are open to various objections grounded on evidence already cited in support of such "individualist" theories as 1 and 2, they are particularly vulnerable to the criticism that they give insufficient attention to the structure of numerous consenting kin groups. If property alienated with the *laudatio* had previously been held by a family community, rather than by an individual, it should be possible to show that that community was defined with some precision and was structured so as to allow it to endure over several generations. Even though certain anthropologists maintain that unilineal descent groups are not the only kin groups that can ever function as property-holding corporations,[42] it is hard to see how some of the consenting groups discussed in chapter 4 could, given their structure, have maintained their corporate identity over time, instead of breaking up, at the very latest, upon the death of the main donor, around whom they seem often to have been organized.[43] Finally, while theory 4a helps to explain why many consenting groups consisted of small conjugal units, it does not account for the fact that many kin did not approve gifts at the same time or place as the donor and that substantial countergifts were made to people who did not necessarily reside with the main donor.[44] Although theory 5 is well-suited to explain evidence indicating that the main donor and his prospective heir were the central figures in gifts to saints, it can serve as a comprehensive legal explanation for the *laudatio* only if we find ways of dismissing evidence indicating that relatives other than the heir sometimes played important parts not only in exchange ceremonies but also in familial challenges.

Each of the theories just outlined explains some of the available evidence about the *laudatio parentum*, but even when modified in the ways just outlined, none of them satisfactorily accounts for all of it. Moreover, they are all open to a series of objections, each more serious than the preceding one. For one thing, the previous discussion has already shown that each theory is too rigid to allow for changes that evidently occurred in the form of the *laudatio* between c. 1000 and c. 1200[45] or for variations with respect to how gifts, *calumniae*, and quitclaims were made within a single segment of this two-century period. If the consent of the donor's son and heir gained increasing prominence in this period,[46] then theories giving special weight to this particular practice may be better suited to explain late twelfth-century evidence,[47] while alternative theories work better for the eleventh century.[48] Moreover, evidence presented in earlier chapters suggests that even within a relatively short period running from, say, 1075 to 1099, the *laudatio* assumed different forms, each of which calls for a different explanation. In cases where no main donor can easily be distinguished from his consenting kin, theories 3, 4, and 4a may have special explanatory power, whereas theories 1a, 2a, or 5 can better account for transactions in which only the donor's eldest son joined his father in making a livery of seisin and received a substantial countergift. For these reasons, a comprehensive legal interpretation of the *laudatio parentum* during virtually any segment of the entire period running from 1000 to 1200 should combine elements from two or more of the theories outlined above.

Further modifications in legal explanations of the *laudatio parentum* would not serve, however, to validate the general assumptions on which arguments of this type depend. First, the validity of these explanatory theories depends on the assumption that land transfers in the period were regulated by rules that constituted a system of land tenure and that differed in content but not in nature from rules found in later periods of French history. Regularities in the practice of making gifts to saints are seen as reflections of rules of real property law, rather than as elements in a distinctive legal culture in which there was no systematic way, even in theory, of reconciling certain kinds of conflicting claims to land. As a result, the solution to the problem of why the *laudatio* was so prevalent in this period is sought through efforts to reconstruct a single system of land tenure, and practices inconsistent with that system are ignored or explained away.

Second, legal explanations for the prevalence of the *laudatio* merely tell us how an alleged rule requiring the *laudatio* may have fitted into a particular system of land tenure; unlike the functional explanations that will be considered shortly, they do not clearly indicate why this rule or practice first came into being or why it was later maintained and reproduced for several centuries. Third, legal explanations take no account of the fact that at least in recorded cases, the *laudatio* was associated with transactions involving far more than the transfer of land. The motives of participants in gifts to saints are ignored, as are the religious meanings that at least some contemporaries attached to these transactions. Finally, explanations of this type give no consideration to the timing of gifts to saints or quitclaims or to the extraeconomic significance of land and land transactions in earlier medieval societies.

To meet the first of the objections just outlined, legal explanations of the *laudatio parentum* need to be significantly modified and supplemented so as to take account of the fact that in the societies in which this practice first developed, no system of real property law existed. Second, to determine how the practice of making gifts with the *laudatio* was maintained, we should first analyze and criticize functional explanations of this practice and then reformulate them in the light of this critique. Third, having considered both legal and functional explanations for the *laudatio*, we should then consider explanations for this practice that acknowledge the religious dimensions of gifts made with the *laudatio*. We must also examine the timing of gifts and of challenges to them as well as the social or extraeconomic significance of land and gifts of land in this period. Finally, we should consider the pressures that may have led so many people to participate in the practice of making gifts to saints with the *laudatio parentum*.

Although legal explanations of the *laudatio* involve the formulation of theories of land tenure that are probably foreign to elev-

enth- and early twelfth-century ways of thinking and talking
about rules, rights, and duties, they can still provide insights into
the various competing methods by means of which claims to land,
as well as to spiritual benefits and social status, were made by
participants in both gifts to saints and familial challenges. Individualist theories suggest that in certain instances individual rights of
donors or heirs were asserted and maintained, while other theories show that at other times the claims of groups were stronger. If
we think of exchange ceremonies and disputes over gifts to abbeys
as being, among other things, processes through which certain
people tried to assert their own rights to participate in exchange
ceremonies, although at times acknowledging the rights of others
willingly or grudgingly, and if we allow for the probability that
exchange ceremonies were always open to differing interpretations, both at the time and after the fact, we can find useful ways
of establishing the different and sometimes mutually inconsistent
normative bases of the *laudatio parentum*. Because of the multi-
dimensional character of gifts to saints, the possible implications
of asserting a right of participation in these ceremonies cannot be
specified precisely and may not always have been clear to the participants themselves. But according to the theory advanced here,
assertions of a right to participate implied, at least in certain instances, that the person making them had at least a potential
claim to the property being alienated.

In this kind of analysis, the discovery that no single theory or
set of theories can account for more than a fraction of the practices
recorded in charters is not a drawback—as it normally is in legal
explanations for the *laudatio*—but a virtue, because evidence of
disputes over the granting or withholding of the *laudatio* and evidence of both familial and feudal challenges to gifts to saints provide good grounds for thinking that in this period, there were
several different and sometimes competing ways of thinking
about rights in land, no one of which held uncontested primacy.
When viewed in this way, the *laudatio parentum* and associated
practices can be seen as being as much the product of social conflict as they were of social consensus. Finally, because our immediate concern is with the proprietary dimension of transactions carried out with the *laudatio*, the following discussion will be focused
primarily on the issue of right in, or claims to, land. But as we

shall soon see, the religious and social dimensions of the *laudatio* should ultimately be considered in any comprehensive effort to explain its prevalence.

Instead of further revising the legal explanations just outlined, simply by trying (and failing) to determine what sorts of present or future legal interests a donor and other participants in his gift must have had in the alienated property, we should attempt to reconstruct part of the normative basis of the *laudatio* in a different way by identifying those normative principles pertaining to land-holding that could have been explicitly or implicitly invoked, before or after the fact, to justify practices that legal theories supposedly explain by positing the existence of certain systems of land tenure. In doing so, we should try, not to reconstruct a consistent system of real property law, but to find or reconstruct several different and potentially conflicting norms or adages about land-holding. This method, while speculative, is no more so than the one commonly adopted by legal historians, who have found little evidence indicating that eleventh- or twelfth-century participants in gifts to saints all entertained a single theory about the ownership of land.

The approach proposed here should at least lead to conclusions more in keeping with the legal culture in which the *laudatio* was actually practiced. To demonstrate the general plausibility of this approach, we can cite not only the arguments proposed in chapter 3, but also the famous letter of 1020 in which Fulbert of Chartres responded to a request from the Duke of Aquitaine "to write something about the character of fealty." Here, a leading scholar and jurist chose to explain the mutual obligations of lords and vassals, not by constructing a coherent theory of lordship and vassalage or propounding legal rules, but instead by setting forth a set of general norms. In explaining the duties of vassals to their lords, Fulbert wrote:

> He who swears fidelity to his lord should always keep these six terms in mind: safe and sound, secure, honest, useful, easy, possible. Safe and sound, that is, not to cause his lord any harm as to his body. Secure, that is, not to endanger him by betraying his secrets or the fortresses which make it possible for him to be secure. Honest, that is, not to do anything

that would detract from his lord's rights of justice or the other prerogatives which have to do with his honour. Useful, not to cause him any loss with regard to his possessions. Easy and possible, not to make it difficult for his lord to do something that would be of value to him and that he could otherwise do with ease, or to render it impossible for him to do what was otherwise possible.

Fulbert then went on to assert that a vassal was obliged to do good, with respect to his lord, as well as to abstain from evil, and that "the lord, in turn, should be faithful to his vassal in all these [six] matters."[49] What this passage presents is not anything approaching a legal theory of vassalage, lordship, and the fief, but a set of proverbs conveniently grouped into two triads. Although Fulbert's remarks may well have been based on "the authority of books" ("*ex librorum auctoritate*"), they are perfectly in keeping with the methods of speaking and remembering in an oral culture.[50]

They are also consistent with the style of argumentation sometimes found in *chansons de geste* and also documented, from time to time, in charters describing the challenges that a man's relatives, his lord, or his lord's kin made to gifts that he had made without their approval. In a chapter recording a familial challenge dated c. 1090, a scribe of Saint Aubin noted down several simple but significant statements about the transmission of landed property and perhaps even about rights in land. When some vineyards quitclaimed to the abbey by a man called Vivianus Dives in return for twelve pounds were challenged on several different grounds by Vivianus's wife Aremburgis, his son Rigaldus, and his daughter's husband Sevinus, the case was argued out by these four people in the presence of two important lords. Of the arguments made on this occasion, two are relevant to the present discussion. First, Aremburgis said that she claimed the vineyards because her husband had given them to her as a marriage portion. Next, Rigaldus challenged his father's quitclaim on the grounds that, as he put it in a revealing statement, his father's property ought to be his after his father's death. Although it is not clear that either Aremburgis or Rigaldus was really contending that she or he was entitled to hold the disputed vineyards, and although both challenges were ultimately rejected by the two lords judging the case on the grounds that Vivianus, through whom both claimed, had never had any right to the vineyards, these two simple arguments provide interesting evidence about how people in this period asserted their rights.[51] The norm or adage underlying Aremburgis's claim was simply this: A woman was entitled to a marriage portion and should not be deprived of it. The adage more directly invoked by Rigaldus was virtually identical with the one invoked in *Raoul de Cambrai* by Raoul the younger after asking his lord, King Louis, to give him a pledge that "I may hold my own land as my valiant father held it before me."[52] Addressing the king, Raoul declared: "Everyone knows that the land of the father ought by right to pass to the child."[53] In making such claims, Aremburgis and Rigaldus, as well as Raoul, were neither citing legal rules nor merely expressing their own personal values. They were explicitly or implicitly invoking certain norms whose force is often reflected in the practices of donors, their consenting kin, and those who initiated familial challenges.

Even if everyone knew, however, that the land of the father should pass to the son and that a woman should not be deprived of her marriage portion (or her heritage, for that matter), these general adages were not necessarily in perfect accord, in all cases, with others that were probably current in our period. Nor did the general validity of the norms just cited necessarily ensure that anyone who invoked one or the other of them would have his or her way in a dispute or exchange ceremony. For one thing, such norms, like the ones discussed above in chapter 3, were lacking in specificity on important issues. Moreover, in opposition to them, there were other norms that could be cited as well. Although the first or the second of these two adages could be used, as they were in the case of Vivien the Rich, to justify a challenge to a donor's alienation by an heir or wife who had not approved it, a donor and his monastic donee could have defended a gift or quitclaim made without the *laudatio* by citing the former's obligation to give alms, and could, in some instances, have cited as well the duty, mentioned by Dhuoda, to procure prayers for one's ancestors.[54] A donor, moreover, could have argued, as Guismandus II did in a case cited above, that a man had a right to give to whomever he wished any land he had purchased with his own money.[55] Furthermore, he may also have been able to justify a gift made without the consent of his kin by claiming, much as the author of the Anglo-French treatise *Glanvill* did in the late twelfth century, that "any person may freely give in his lifetime a reasonable part of his land to whomsoever he pleases."[56] If the latter norm were cited, then argument could continue on the question of whether the gift had been a reasonable one. An heir such as Rigaldus could have argued that the gift was unreasonable because it disinherited him. But because disinheritance was a relative matter, there must have been considerable room for argument about whether an heir had been disinherited by a particular gift. Such arguments could well have proceeded in different ways and led to different outcomes.

Just as the norm cited by Rigaldus and Raoul was unclear about how much of a father's land should pass to his son, so, too, it was vague on the question of whether anyone other than the father's firstborn son had any claims on the father's land. In cases where a donor's gift was approved only by his eldest son or where a consenting son and heir was accorded special primacy, a principle of primogeniture was probably being asserted. The same is true of cases in which a donor's gift was challenged only by his heir. The participation of a donor's other kin, however, could have been justified by a norm specifying that a landholder should not disinherit his children or his kin generally. This norm merely implied, in turn, that a man's children and other kin were entitled to some kind of support from him. More specifically, the rights of daughters may have been asserted in norms that either took the more extreme form of stipulating that a woman's husband was entitled to a dowry from her father or other kinsman or the weaker one of holding that a man and his wife should not be deprived of the dowry promised them.[57] In addition, all the donor's relatives, including his heir and wife, could have contested a gift made without the *laudatio* by citing the general adage that a man should act with the counsel of his kin. Furthermore, to support a challenge to a gift made from property pertaining to a close kinswoman of the challenger, a general adage, such as *"materna maternis"* could have been cited as well.[58]

Finally, in asserting a right to challenge a gift that the donor had made without anyone's consent, the donor's lord could have relied on one of the general adages or norms articulated by Fulbert of Chartres in the passage cited above: "He who swears fidelity to

his lord" should not "cause him any loss as regards his possessions."[59] After citing this general principle, the donor's lord or
overlord could then have asserted that because the donor's gift
effectively abridged the lord's fief, it injured him in his property.
In justifying a challenge to the gift of the lord's tenant, moreover,
the lord's brother, for example, could have first invoked the same
principle cited by his brother in the preceding case in order to
demonstrate that his brother had an interest in the brother's tenant's fief. Then, to show that he himself had an interest in the
same property, the lord's brother could have invoked the adage
used in several earlier cases to show that a man's kin had an interest in his property. In considering these justifications of feudal or
feudal-familial challenges, we should remember that there was
nothing conclusive about them. In response, a donor could always
invoke his duties to give alms and to procure prayers for his kin.
Moreover, because there was presumably no more consensus
about what constituted abridgment of a fief than there was about
what disinheritance was, the donor, with support from his monastic donee, could have argued that his gift was sufficiently small as
to cause no harm to his lord or his lord's kin. As in the cases
already discussed, there would have been no systematic, legal
way of determining which of these conflicting norms should take
precedence. For this reason, as well as others, the dispute was
likely to end in a compromise.

Even though the preceding argument helps to clarify the normative bases of the *laudatio parentum*, it does not indicate why or
how the practice of making gifts with the *laudatio* was established
or why it was followed with any regularity. In the absence of a
legislature to establish the rule, courts to apply it systematically to
particular cases, or officials to enforce court decisions made in accordance with it, these questions are even more difficult to answer
than they are in discussions of legal rules found in modern legal
systems. For this reason, legal explanations can be supplemented
with functional ones designed to show, first, that the *laudatio parentum* was an integral part of a particular social order and, second, that it served to maintain this order by preventing the fragmentation of upper-class estates, and thereby protected the position of upper-class kin groups.[60]

The rule supposedly requiring that gifts be made with the consent of relatives has therefore been interpreted by proponents of theories 4, 4a, or 5 both as the expression of so-called "family solidarity" and as a means of repressing threats to that solidarity by the individual members of kin groups. According to this functionalist interpretation of the *laudatio*, an intensification of long-standing sentiments of family solidarity among upper-class people constituted an effective adaptive response to the new political conditions of the post-Carolingian era, when a breakdown in the ability of state institutions to maintain social order made it necessary for many people to band together with their own kin even more tightly than before in order to protect themselves. Changes associated with this response to shifting political conditions were manifested in many spheres of life, including individual and group psychology, kinship organization, social ideology, and land law.

As a result, medieval people supposedly became strongly predisposed to act collectively with their kin and to repress the individual initiatives of particular group members. They also came to believe that group interests in property overrode individual interests, to the extent that the latter were recognized at all. When an individual family member contemplated making a conveyance of land, it was therefore considered fitting, proper, and right that he carry out his wish only if his conveyance were acceptable to his entire kin group and could therefore be considered a collective, as opposed to an individual, act. In cases where a particular landholder was rash or thoughtless enough to proceed with an alienation before securing the *laudatio* or after failing to secure it, his kin were entitled to contest and invalidate his gift.

According to this theory, the main effect or function of the *laudatio* was therefore to restrain alienations of landed property by lay members of kin groups and to protect a kin group's lands from being depleted by the alienations of individual group members, whose feelings of generosity and piety might otherwise have overridden established sentiments of family solidarity and led them to act against the interests of their own kin. What was, perhaps, the most serious threat to a family's landed wealth arose when the head of the family was approaching death and could be persuaded by monks to provide for his soul by giving an abbey some lands that would otherwise have been transmitted to his heir or to his other kin. The anxieties of lay landholders about the possibility of losing land to monks are expressed in later legal rules restricting a landholder's power to make deathbed gifts,[61] in Carolingian legislation,[62] and in the passage from *Garin le Loherain* already quoted above.[63]

Like legal explanations for the *laudatio parentum*, the functionalist theory that a rule requiring the *laudatio* met certain social *needs* has only limited value. For one thing, this theory takes no account of the religious or social dimensions of gifts to saints and must therefore be supplemented in the ways discussed below. Moreover, even after showing that the *laudatio* truly performed certain socially valuable functions, we still face the problem of determining how the alleged need to have these functions performed was mediated in practice. This is a difficult task, particularly when monastic charters show that hundreds of donors and consenting relatives repeatedly disregarded the alleged need to conserve family property.

In addition, functional explanations of the *laudatio* are vulnerable to more specific criticisms. If the rule requiring the *laudatio* was supposed to prevent a kin group's landed wealth from being substantially diminished by the piety and generosity of individual group members, then it does not seem to have effectively performed its supposed function. During the eleventh and early twelfth centuries, the rule did not prevent substantial transfers of wealth from upper-class landholders to French abbeys such as Marmoutier, Noyers, or La Trinité. At most, it retarded this process. Moreover, it is not clear, as we have already seen, whether the norm requiring the *laudatio* was designed to prevent landholders from making gifts that their kin opposed or to ensure that a donor's kin would approve gifts that he wished to make. In either case, the norm would have promoted a certain sort of "family solidarity." But if family solidarity could take such different forms and was so malleable a principle that it could legitimate efforts to give land to abbeys as well as efforts to block these gifts, then its value as an explanatory principle becomes questionable.

A third, related set of objections to the functionalist approach to the *laudatio* is more complex. Because gifts to saints made with the *laudatio* not only depleted a kin group's landed resources but also provided certain living or dead group members with material, political, or spiritual benefits, transactions of this kind did not precipitate clear-cut conflicts between individualism—as represented by individual landholders—and family solidarity—as represented by these landholders' kin. Sometimes, a donor's gift provided monks with wealth to support the donor's kinsman when the latter became a monk. In ways that were sometimes less direct but were no less significant, gifts to saints also served to enhance a kin group's local power and prestige by associating its members with an abbey that possessed political, as well as spiritual, power. Furthermore, because valuable and prestigious material countergifts were sometimes made to a donor's consenting relatives, gifts to saints did not necessarily entail even a material loss for the donor's kin. In fact, certain consenting relatives may have felt that they had made a good bargain with their kinsman's donee. Finally, in those instances where relatives giving the *laudatio* were the recipients of spiritual privileges such as confraternity, their position in the transaction they approved did not differ appreciably from that of the main donor. They, too, were participants in an exchange of land for prayers—an exchange of material for spiritual capital.

It is therefore mistaken to assume that gifts to saints *necessarily* damaged the interests of a donor's kin, especially if we accept the premise that in the society where this practice flourished, the acquisition of spiritual capital rivaled in importance the acquisition of material capital and that what nobles strived for was not to maximize their wealth but to maximize prestige by controlling the circulation of wealth. For this reason, gifts did not necessarily entail a clear-cut conflict between group (or so-called "family") interests and individual interests. Conflicts generated by such gifts, moreover, were not always clashes between a solitary donor on the one hand and his kin group (or "family") on the other. Conflicts of the latter kind arose only when a donor wished to make a gift in return for which *he alone* would receive countergifts from a monastic community.[64] A different and more common sort of conflict arose when a transaction involved, for example, the bestowal of countergifts on some of a donor's dead relatives, but not on his consenting kin.[65] Here, the dispute could be represented as taking place between living and dead members of a single kin group. In cases where countergifts were accorded only to certain living relatives, but not to others, gifts may have threatened to spark a conflict between two subgroups of living relatives.[66]

To argue that gifts to saints automatically posed a threat to "familial" interests is also misleading, not only because two or more relatives often benefited from these transactions, but also because, as we have already seen, many consenting kin groups were unstable, ad hoc assemblages of the donor's relatives, rather than cohesive, enduring corporate groups. As a result, even in cases where some of a donor's kin blocked his alienation, it is hard to say in whose interests they were acting. Any claims they may have made to be defending the interests of their family or *lignage* should be seen as ideological justifications for the interests of particular people. For who was to say who constituted the donor's *lignage* or what its interests were, when there were different and competing ways of representing a kin group and defining its interests? As a result, the claim of a donor's expectant heir to preeminent status among his kin could be countered by arguments based on a different model of kinship, such as one that acknowledged the place of younger sons, daughters, affines, matrilateral kin and, finally, the dead. For these reasons, we should treat many disputes precipitated by gifts to saints as reflections of competing views about how kin groups should be defined, not as conflicts between "the family" and "the individual." For all the reasons just presented, we should abandon the unqualified contention that the main social function of the *laudatio* was to defend families against the actions of individuals.

Whereas the legal and functionalist theories just considered emphasize the proprietary dimensions of the *laudatio parentum*, we can also provide a partial, complementary explanation of this practice by considering the religious significance of the transactions with which it was associated. Even though there was probably no consensus in this period about the nature and purpose of gifts to saints, a relatively consistent picture of them emerges from monastic sources—one that differs dramatically from the one implicit in legal and functionalist explanations. By piecing together passages from many different charters, we can construct a composite picture of gifts to saints, as monks evidently wished to represent them.[67] We can then see that a gift of landed property to an abbey was part of a complex exchange process whose official rationale lay in certain Christian teachings about sin, death, divine punishment of sinners, and the attainment of posthumous salvation. In this process, a donor's relatives had a significant role to play, not only because they could help the donor and other designated beneficiaries gain certain benefits from monks, but also because their participation was appropriate in transactions in which kinship was a crucially important concept.

According to the monastic ideology articulated by the scribes of the five abbeys,[68] both donors and the relatives and other friends for whose benefit donors often acted were living in a state of sin and were therefore liable, after they died, to become the objects of God's anger and enmity. Instead of attaining salvation, they would be punished.[69] Their mortality and sinfulness constituted an inheritance from their forefather Adam,[70] who, for his sin against God, had been condemned with all his posterity to live and die in a state of sinfulness.[71] Adam and his descendants thereby lost the paternal inheritance of eternal life in heaven that God the Father had originally granted to Adam, and instead, they received from God only a transitory inheritance on earth.[72]

Through God's grace, however, and, in particular, through the incarnation, humans could still attain salvation if they followed certain scriptural precepts[73] that scribes quoted or paraphrased in charter preambles and in formulaic passages describing the motives of monastic benefactors. The most significant of these scriptural passages for our purposes are these:[74]

"Give alms; and behold, all things are clean unto you."[75]
"Water quencheth a flaming fire, and alms resisteth sin."[76]
"Shut up alms in the heart of the poor, and it shall obtain help for you."[77]
"Redeem thou thy sins with alms."[78]
"Alms deliver from all sin and from death."[79]
"The ransom of a man's life are his riches."[80]
"Give and it shall be given to you."[81]
"There is no good for him that is always occupied in evil and does not give alms."[82]

"Give alms and they will pray for you."[83]
"Honor the Lord with your substance."[84]

The most revealing of these passages for our purposes is:

"Make unto you friends of the mammon of iniquity, that
when you shall fail, they may receive you into everlasting
dwellings."[85]

By following these precepts and, in particular, by giving alms,
men could supposedly attain salvation after their deaths. Almsgiving entailed an exchange process in which humans gave away
the transitory earthly wealth they had initially received from God,
in return for an eternal inheritance in God's kingdom.[86] In making
this exchange, human beings were not to deal directly with God
the Father; instead, they had to act through several intermediaries. First, there was Christ (or God the Son), who, as both God
and man, was the mediator between God and humankind.[87] Next,
between Christ and humans there stood the saints, who were
God's *amici* and the appointed mediators between Christ and human sinners.[88] Finally, between the saints on the one hand and
sinners on the other were monks belonging to religious communities dedicated to particular saints. Because these mediators, as
well as God himself, were directly or indirectly involved in the
process of almsgiving, a scribe could properly represent a gift to
his abbey as being made to God, to the abbey's patron saint or
saints, or to the abbot and monks of the monastery.[89] As people
who were poor by choice rather than by necessity, monks were, in
the opinion of the monks themselves, the most appropriate beneficiaries of almsgiving.[90] In return for the alms from sinners that
monks used to support themselves and distributed to those who
were poor involuntarily,[91] monks, as we have seen, would pray to
their patron saint on behalf of their benefactors or those whom
their benefactors designated. Monks could also provide these people with ancillary religious services in ways that usually entailed
enduring, regularized relationships between monastic communities and lay people.[92]

Although gifts of alms to saints, according to monks, were the
best form of alms and the main means by which a man or woman

could obtain salvation, prestations of this kind were not guaran-
teed to have their desired effect. The original monastic donees or
their successors might fail to intercede with prayers to a saint on
behalf of the intended beneficiaries. To guard against this eventu-
ality, records of a community's benefactors were to be carefully
kept in charters, martyrologies, and other documents.[93] Because
each succeeding generation was supposedly more evil and de-
praved than its predecessor, monks assumed that a man's gift
would be challenged by his sons or other relatives.[94] To guard
against this second threat, several measures could be taken. From
a spiritual perspective, the most significant of these devices were
the curses of donors and donees against the traitors who undermined particular gifts. When cursed, these false *calumniatores*
would incur the anger of God, Christ, and the saint whose property they had disturbed, and be condemned to eternal punishment.[95]

To appreciate the complex religious meanings ascribed to gifts to
saints, we need to consider the various ways in which the items
exchanged could be represented, the structure and interrelationships of the participating groups, and, finally, the temporal dimensions of the entire exchange process. The earthly wealth that
donors gave to monks could be represented in several ways, each
of which entailed a different way of viewing the total exchange.
The land given to an abbey could be seen as earthly wealth that
donors had received ultimately from God[96] and were thus return-
ing to him. It could also be viewed as an earthly and therefore
transitory inheritance from the donor's ancestors,[97] who had either died or become monks and to whom it was being returned
after being converted into prayers. To the extent that sinfulness
or sin itself was considered an item of exchange, it could be seen
both as an essential attribute of the lay participants[98] and as
something that participants inherited from Adam through their
ancestors.[99]

The items of exchange that donors received or hoped to receive
in return for gifts of earthly wealth could also be seen as taking
different forms, depending upon the perspective from which the
transaction was viewed. These items included the prayers and
other spiritual services that monks provided to both living and
dead donors, along with the nominees of the latter, as a means of

wiping away sin; the right of the donor or the person he designated to undergo a conversion in status that would make him a
brother and therefore a kinsman of the monks to whom the donor's gift was made; the privilege of being recognized as a friend
or kinsman (*amicus*) by the monks' patron saint; intercession with
God by God's *amicus*, the saint, on the donor's behalf; and, finally,
a heavenly inheritance of eternal life that was granted by God
himself. At the same time, the eternal punishment that a man
would posthumously suffer if he disturbed another's gift or failed
to make a gift of his own could also be represented as an infernal
inheritance that could be considered the birthright of postlap-
sarian man, standing in total opposition to the heavenly inheritance or birthright that other humans could acquire through God's
grace.[100]

Furthermore, the full meaning of gifts to saints was rendered
even more complex by the fact that the recipients of the earthly
wealth that a donor gave away could be represented in several
different ways, each of which was associated with a different representation of the entire exchange process. The recipients could be
identified as the present abbot and his monks; their successors in
later generations, who could be considered the heirs of the monks
to whom the gift had been directly given; the abbey's patron saint;
God; the living and dead relatives for whose benefit the donor
gave alms; unborn relatives who supported the donor's gift or
augmented it; and even the donor himself.[101]

When viewed from one perspective, most of the main parties to
the exchanges were not individuals but complex groups that
played several different roles simultaneously. In representing all
participating groups, moreover, the language of kinship was used,
sometimes in mysterious or at least paradoxical ways, to indicate,
explicitly or implicitly, the obligations and entitlements of various
participants. The immediate recipients of gifts to saints were
monks living together as brothers under the rule of their father
the abbot. In some cases, the community of brothers included
people who were also relatives of the lay donor,[102] although in
other instances, the donor himself was, or at least eventually became, a brother of the house and thereby became a recipient of his
own gift. As members of the present generation of monks died
off, they were supposed to be replaced by monks of a subsequent

generation, who became not only the successors or heirs of their predecessors, but also the prospective recipients of the donor's gift. In addition, because one important obligation of living monks was to pray for their monastic predecessors or ancestors,[103] the latter, too, could be considered part of the monastic kin group that received the donor's gift. Furthermore, all past and future monks, including the abbots, could be seen as members of the family of their abbey's patron saint.[104] That saint belonged, in turn, to a group of "the very special dead."[105] Moreover, because all saints could be considered to be God's friends and kin and because some of them, such as Saint Mary, were close relatives of Christ, the patron saint of the donor's monastic beneficiaries could be seen as a member of several overlapping kin groups of supernatural beings.[106]

For reasons already adumbrated, the temporal dimensions of the exchanges initiated by gifts to saints were complex. Although the exchange itself was initiated on earth at a particular moment, it took on its full meaning only when located temporally in relation to the Creation, the Fall, and the Last Judgment.[107] Moreover, as the mortal participants in the exchange passed through different stages of existence separated by the boundaries of birth and death, their own positions in the exchange process changed, as did the exchange itself. Although the donor and his monastic beneficiaries would eventually die and join their ancestors or predecessors among the dead, their heirs, descendants, or successors would be born and succeed to some of their ancestors' or predecessors' obligations. When the dead donor and dead monks were no longer able to pray or procure prayers for anyone, it was up to their successors to continue the transaction initiated by the original parties.

The preceding analysis of the religious significance of gifts to saints corroborates and supplements the previous claim that transactions carried out with the *laudatio parentum* differed fundamentally from the modern conveyances that have previously served implicitly as models for transactions carried out with the *laudatio*. Gifts to saints differ clearly from modern gifts simply because in the former, both the giver and the recipient took it for granted that the gift was made in return for specific services. The differences between gifts to saints and modern sales are more complex. In a sale, the buyer gets real property from a seller, who receives a price for his land. The two parties then part company with no enduring tie between them, except for the the seller's obligation to warrant the buyer's title. They may meet again in the land market or elsewhere, but there is no necessity that they do so.[108] Gifts to saints took a different form. Although they usually involved only two parties directly—a lay group and a religious one—each group, as we have seen, was complex in structure. Moreover, the exchange in which the two groups participated was not straightforwardly bilateral, because it was supposed to set in motion a series of further exchanges within, as well as between, each group and, if properly performed, to implicate God, who did not automatically become a party to the transaction. Unlike a modern sale, therefore, a gift to a saint could not be completed, even in theory, in an instant.[109] At the same time, gifts to saints employed media of exchange quite different from those used in land sales and operated within very distinct topographical and social spheres of exchange. Neither prayers nor property were fully alienable commodities.[110] Both, moreover, traversed the boundaries between the living and the dead, between the secular and the sacred, and between heaven and earth, while gifts, hospitality, prayers, visits, and burial ceremonies involved the crossing of the lines dividing the lay and monastic worlds. Even though no party to the transaction was expected to profit at the expense of the other, the exchanges were not straightforward examples of "balanced reciprocity" that provided for "returns of commensurate worth or utility within a finite or narrow period."[111] No gift of an earthly inheritance, supposedly, could ever truly balance God's gift of a spiritual inheritance. Nor could the ultimate value of prayers relative to property be definitively established. Nor would the transaction be completed within a finite period, because it was not clear when heavenly inheritances would vest.

Gifts to saints can therefore be treated as "total social movements." Like the exchanges studied by many anthropologists, "they are at the same time economic, juridical, moral, aesthetic, religious, mythological and socio-morphological phenomena. Their meaning can therefore only be grasped if they are viewed as a complex concrete reality, and if for convenience we make abstractions in studying some institution we must in the end replace what we have taken away if we are to understand it."[112]

If we simply restore to our picture of the *laudatio parentum* those aspects of gifts to saints that have sometimes been excised from previous studies and consider more than the economic and juridical elements of these transactions, we can see that in exchanges endowed with the religious meanings discussed above, the *laudatio parentum* was not out of place and played a significant role. The involvement of a donor's kin in gifts to saints served, in several ways, to endow these transactions with a certain balance or symmetry that rendered them more complete and comprehensible, as well as more practically viable. First, through the involvement of kin in gifts to saints, the notion that guilt, sin, and indebtedness to God constituted an inheritance that passed ineluctably from ancestor to heir was balanced by the notion that a person's kin could and should help him to discharge his debts. At the same time, the participation of a donor's kin in his gift increased the chances that his own death would not deprive the transaction of supporters, because relatives who participated in it renounced their right to challenge it later and might also defend and maintain it even though they were not automatically obliged to warrant any gift they had approved.[113] The role of consenting kin was therefore analogous to that of future monks, who, without having participated in the original transaction, would eventually assume a binding obligation to provide the original donor and his nominees with whatever prayers and other services had originally been stipulated. Furthermore, the material benefits that could be expected to pass from ancestor to heir in the form of landed property would be balanced by the spiritual benefits that heirs could procure for their ancestors by giving part of the land they had received from their ancestors to a monastic community. As a result, it was fitting that a donor be supported by any relatives who claimed the same descent as he did.

Whether the consenting relatives were actually conveying their own rights in the alienated property or merely supporting the donor's gift, their position in the exchange was closely analogous to that of the main donor, because both he and they were exchanging something earthly and transitory for the hope of an eternal, heavenly reward. Some consenting relatives, moreover, stood in the same relationship to the donor's ancestors as he did, for they were helping to provide the dead members of their kin group with valuable spiritual services. At the same time, they were supporting their kinsman, the donor, just as he was supporting his own ancestors. Furthermore, the donor's relationship to his consenting kin was parallel to that of living monks to their successors or heirs. Finally, by joining together in a group of kin to make an exchange with living monks, an undying monastic corporation, a saint, and God, a donor and his consenting relatives were behaving in a way that was perfectly consistent not only with the behavior of living monks, but also with the actions routinely attributed to supernatural beings.

When placed in an even broader social context, moreover, the beliefs associated with gifts to saints and therefore with the *laudatio* can be seen as a form of ideology—as a set of powerful and compelling ideas, authoritatively articulated by representatives of a privileged and restricted social group, about how the supernatural and human worlds were ordered, should be ordered, and had to be ordered. For one thing, gifts to saints provided both a model of and a justification for an established mode of medieval political action whereby a person who had incurred the anger of a superior or lord could recover his social standing by approaching or making friends with a friend of the lord or superior and then inducing his friend to intercede with the lord or superior on his behalf. This established method of seeking reconciliation with superiors through the mediation of third parties is clearly illustrated in a letter of Archbishop Lanfranc.

> Lanfranc, archbishop by divine favor and not his own merits, sends prayerful greetings to Abbot Baldwin.
>
> The man who brings this letter says that he has incurred your anger and so has left his home, where he was born and brought up, and his family and friends. Because he thought that for me you will do much, he begged me to write to you, father, on his behalf. May our intercession move you in your goodness to show him mercy, so that he may know that the man to whom he has turned to find pardon for his fault is indeed your friend.[114]

At the same time, both kinship and property rights in this period were accorded paramount importance in the supernatural world, as well as on earth. In religious discourse, momentous significance was therefore attached, in several important contexts, to the concept of "inheritance," which neatly combined and simultaneously represented ideas of kinship, property, entitlement to kinship, entitlement to property by virtue of kinship, and an obligation to assume an ancestor's duties and guilt. In addition, because exchanges between upper-class monks and the members of an emerging and increasingly well-defined class of nobles supposedly involved supernatural beings as well and because the earthly inheritances used in these transactions often consisted of legitimated power to take various forms of feudal rent from lower-class people and sometimes assumed the unmediated form of serfs and all their posterity,[115] the underlying economic and political logic of gifts to saints rendered them an effective means of legitimating and reproducing an entire social order. In these transactions, members of upper-class groups to which access was restricted by birth were supposedly able to conform to God's precepts only by transferring power over lower-class people and their offspring from one upper-class group to another.[116]

It would be simplistic and misleading to treat eleventh- and twelfth-century ideas about salvation as mere elements in a superstructure of religious ideology. The people of this period did not develop their ideas about the acquisition of both heavenly inheritances and influential friends in God's heavenly kingdom simply by projecting onto a fictive supernatural world several important features of their own society. Nor did they formulate and propagate these views simply for the purpose of legitimating the existing social order in France, where nobles were anxiously interested in forging and reforging close political alliances with influential friends and in gaining rich inheritances that they could then maintain or expand by asserting their power over peasants. It would be equally misleading, however, to insist on the total autonomy of medieval religious ideas about sin and salvation, to ignore the way in which these ideas endowed certain features of medieval life with an aura of legitimacy and inevitability that they did not inherently possess, or to forget the practical role of medieval rituals in reproducing medieval social structure.

On those occasions when gifts to saints were made with the *laudatio parentum*, we can sometimes see an integral connection between two sets of ideas: ideas about how men and women could gain salvation and thus enter God's kingdom as subjects rightfully possessing heavenly inheritances and ideas about the rights or claims of these same people to be included in particular social groups and to share in the continuing enjoyment of privileged social and political status. In a smaller but still significant number of cases, we can also see that both the continuing enjoyment of such status and an ability to enter into exchanges with the supernatural were facilitated by the dominance that lay lords maintained over a hereditary class of unfree people.

Although an understanding of the religious ideology of gifts to saints can help to explain why it was considered fitting, proper, and right that gifts to saints be made with the *laudatio parentum*, this type of explanation does not deal fully with the social significance of exchange ceremonies either for lay participants or for any of their kin who were somehow excluded from participation. It reveals little about the timing of gifts to saints or the secular significance of certain kinds of land transactions. For lay people, the import of gifts to saints and of the *laudatio parentum* was probably not unrelated to the times when gifts were made. As we saw in previous chapters, these times were not chosen haphazardly. They usually coincided closely with significant changes in the lives of individual donors and their kin. Because lay people were most likely to give gifts to saints when they or their close friends were about to die or enter a monastery and because they also occasionally made them before going on pilgrimages or crusades, it is clear that transactions of this kind were often closely associated with important status changes in the lives of individuals and kin groups. At these times, certain social roles, obligations, and rights had to be rearranged, while others were in need of reaffirmation. These occasions, however, need not all have been experienced by different parties to a gift in precisely the same ways. As a family elder lay dying, his kin, his close connections, and certain monks were likely to gather by his bedside on their own initiative or at the behest of the dying man himself.[117] But not every person, presumably, had come there simply out of obedience to the convention that people of a certain class were supposed to die in the presence of others. On the contrary, each person could simultaneously follow custom and yet experience the family gathering in ways shaped by his or her own particular perspective. The same could be said of attendance at other ceremonies when gifts to saints or quitclaims were made.

Of all the occasions with which gifts to saints were closely associated, by the far the most significant, both statistically and culturally, was death. Although monastic scribes did not always specify the circumstances under which gifts to their abbeys were made, it is clear that in the eleventh and early twelfth centuries, numerous monastic benefactors were sick or dying at the time of their gifts. When Mainardus Mala Barba made a gift to Saint Vincent for his own soul and the souls of his *parentes*, he was at Montfort, suffering from the illness that eventually killed him, and was surrounded by eight witnesses, including his sister's husband, Odo de Nouans, who had urged him to make the gift.[118] Gaufridus de Chouha, too, was dying when, with the approval of his son, he made the second of his two gifts to Saint Vincent, and received in return the right to be buried in one of the abbey's churches.[119] On his deathbed, Odo de Sceaux was visited by Peter the monk and then gave some property to Saint Vincent with the approval of his wife, his son, and his son's daughter.[120] When making his last confession, Hugo Duplex II confirmed in the presence of two priests and his own son and daughter-in-law a gift to Saint Vincent, in whose cloister he was later buried.[121] Although Normannus, a knight (*miles*) of Mosteriolum, was too ill to make a gift to Saint Vincent himself, he was able to send his son Robertus to the abbey of Saint Vincent to ask the monks to grant him the society and the benefit of the monastery. When they did so, Robertus made a gift to the community on his father's behalf.[122]

Even when a gift was not made just before or just after the death of a kin group member, lay participants in exchanges with saints had good reason to look back in time to earlier deaths of kinsmen and kinswomen and forward to the time of their own deaths and the deaths of people close to them. Intercession for the dead in the form of prayers was the main thing that lay people could directly procure from monks in return for gifts of land. Moreover, many gifts were made in return for burial rights that the donor or his kin could exercise immediately or later.[123] In what appears to be a somewhat smaller class of cases, landholders made or confirmed their gifts to abbeys when one of their close kin had recently died or was about to die. It was just after the funeral of his father, for example, that Orricus de la Barre confirmed gifts that the former had previously made to the monks of Saint Vincent, who then promised Orricus that they would bury his mother as well.[124] When the wife and small children of Rogerius the *miles* brought Rogerius's body for burial at Saint Vincent, they gave the monks a small parcel of land.[125] Upon the death of his sister, whom the same monks buried, Hubertus de Théligny gave Saint Vincent the third part of some tithes, the other two-thirds of which he had given them some years before,[126] while a similar transaction was carried out by Fulcoius de Calceia upon the death of his son.[127] Gaufridus the *miles* of Saint-Jean gave various lands to Saint Vincent for the benefit of his wife, who died soon afterwards and whose funeral the abbot of Saint Vincent celebrated in one of the monks' cemeteries.[128] Finally, other gifts to monasteries were timed so as to coincide with the entrance of the donor or his close relative into an abbey[129] or the benefactor's departure for Jerusalem.[130] Whether or not the exchange ceremonies themselves constituted real rites of passage, their close association with moments of significant social transition is clear.

Once we realize that gifts to saints were often associated temporally with rites of passage, notably death, burial, or entrance into an abbey, the problem of explaining why they were often made with the *laudatio* resolves itself into the more general problem of why relatives participated in burials or deathbed gatherings. Without exploring this issue in detail, it seems plausible that relatives attended on such occasions to mourn and provide for the soul of the deceased, to establish connections of their own with an abbey, and, above all, to establish their own social standing at a critical moment when both property and social roles were about to be redistributed.[131] Whatever their motives, the relatives who gave the *laudatio* on such occasions were most likely doing more than approving an alienation of land. If this is so, it is not fanciful to suggest that relatives consciously excluded from such ceremonies or inadvertently left out of them might harbor a sense of grievance, not only because land to which they might have a claim had been alienated without their approval, but also because the kinship status on which claims to property as well as other things of value was based had been denied them. Any relatives of a donor who had not approved his gift were in a position closely analogous to that of relatives in other medieval societies who were denied their shares in a wergeld payment. For excluded kin of these kinds, what was of primary importance was not simply property but a kind of status that might or might not serve as the basis for a proprietary claim but that was nonetheless important.[132]

To grasp the possible significance of gifts to saints for a donor's kin, whether or not they gave the *laudatio*, we should consider not only the official religious significance of gifts to abbeys and the times when such gifts were made, but also prevailing attitudes toward certain items exchanged in these transactions. Exchanges between lay kin groups and abbeys were constituted in such a way as to make them important occasions for a donor's kin, not only because of their religious meaning, but also because of the special symbolic significance that was apparently attributed, in the course of an exchange ceremony, to the items exchanged, including goods, money, and, above all, land. In previous discussions of material countergifts, we have seen that the goods and coins that were often given to consenting relatives had something more than use-value or exchange-value. Like the pledges employed in various archaic legal cultures, they acquired through their incorporation into exchange ceremonies "a personality." They were not "inert" but "live."[133] A countergift consisting of a sow or a war-horse, for example, did not serve only to recompense a consenting relative for a loss that he or she may have sustained through his or her kinsman's gift; it also symbolized and memorialized his or her social status and kinship position and his or her role as participant in an exchange ceremony. In many cases, the primary function of most goods given to consenting relatives was to serve as tokens of status and social relationships. Because the female kin who were given sows or chickens, for example, were neither swineherds nor chicken-keepers, but the wives or daughters of lords and *milites*, it is hard to see how the exchange of their consent for these goods can be intelligibly construed simply as a form of barter in which one right was exchanged for another of equivalent price or value. In these transactions, value and price were not the only things at issue. Even when more valuable countergifts, such as horses, were made to consenting kin, they had more than economic value. For present purposes, the fact that certain material countergifts could serve as tokens of status and of social relationships created through an exchange ceremony is important for the following reason. If receipt of such a countergift served to symbolize status and relationships, then deliberate or inadvertent exclusion from the ceremonies at which such countergifts were distributed may well have entailed a denial of status as well as a denial of the right to enjoy certain relationships.

Even when money was used as a countergift in these ceremonies, it did not serve merely as a medium of exchange or store of value; instead, like sows or chickens, it had a symbolic function as well. The hypothesis that coins of the same value were not considered interchangeable for all purposes is supported by the following episode from a Saint Vincent charter. When a castellan from Maine gave up his claim to impose a certain tallage on the dependents of the abbey, he made a point of making his quitclaim by placing what was supposedly the first *denarius* he had received from this disputed tax on the altar of the monastery's patron saint.[134] Coined money, moreover, lent itself to the expression of finely graded ranking systems that may have had much in common with the ones implicit in earlier medieval rules about what shares in a wergeld payment would go to different kin[135] or in customs about the distribution of bridewealth payments in certain tribal societies.[136] If this analogy holds, then we have a further reason for doubting that consenting kin were simply alienating some sort of proprietary interest in the land being donated.

Property rights, too, were apparently viewed in ways that distinguish them clearly from the estates conveyed in modern realty transactions. Whereas medieval European monastic communities could, in theory, have been supported with grants of produce by lay benefactors, land evidently had various characteristics that made it an appropriate medium of exchange in transactions between monks and lay people. The mere fact that monks and their dependents lived off the produce of the land given to them hardly proves that the land had only economic significance, because it is perfectly possible for the same thing to serve simultaneously both economic and symbolic functions, as certain countergifts to donors and their consenting kin clearly did.[137] As we have seen, biblical metaphors in which posthumous salvation was represented as a heavenly inheritance for which an earthly inheritance could be exchanged held great meaning for medieval Christians and may well have been construed as being more than metaphorical. Even though land acquired through purchase was generally considered to be more freely alienable than inherited land, several charter preambles indicate that it was the latter kind of property that landholders were supposed to give to abbeys.[138] This preference, while perhaps explicable in purely utilitarian terms, can be most plausibly attributed to the belief that there was a special kind of connection between inherited land and the person or persons who held it. This hypothesis receives additional support from our previous finding in chapter 4 that spiritual privileges for a particular person were sometimes acquired through gifts of property to which that person had a special relationship. Finally, the fact that monastic recipients of a perpetual gift of land were sometimes explicitly barred from selling, exchanging, or otherwise alienating it, on pain of losing it to the donor or his kin, suggests that the land in question was considered to have something more than mere economic significance.[139] Like the material and monetary countergifts discussed earlier, the land itself or lordship over it could serve as an enduring token of a relationship between donor and donee.

This hypothesis is supported by an early twelfth-century charter recording a dispute involving Saint Aubin. In around 1102 Waldinus, lord of Malicornant, wanted the monks of Saint Aubin to acknowledge formally that they held from him all their property in Arthezé, including the church there. Because the monks claimed that according to their ancient charters, their rights in this village came from Frankish kings, they refused Waldinus's request. After this lord had caused much damage to the abbey, various "judges," including the bishops of Le Mans and Angers, upheld the monks' position. Initially, Waldinus refused to abide by this judgment, but after being excommunicated, he repented and called the abbot of Saint Aubin to his castle, where he pledged to return what he had taken from the monks and, along with his wife and son, gave up his original claim.

According to the source, Waldinus and his wife and son were

willing to do this for the following reason. All three were eventually convinced by the monks or third parties that they would lose no favor with God if the alms that they thought were theirs or those of their kin (*parentes*) turned out to be the alms of others. This passage implies that initially, Waldinus, his wife, and his son all believed that their relationship with God had to be mediated not simply by the monks of Saint Aubin, but by a particular property right that they or their kin had previously granted to Saint Aubin and that served as a bridge—to use an image we have encountered before—between them and God. Waldinus, therefore, had not claimed lordship over the monks' rights in Arthezé simply for the sake of exercising political power over them and extracting certain profits from this position. Treating rights of lordship over the village as a kind of token, he claimed them so that he could claim a relationship with God on behalf of himself and his kin.[140]

In secular life as well, land was endowed with more than mere economic significance. It yielded more than rent and produce. According to one scholar, members of certain medieval European kin groups were thought to be tied in an almost physical way to land that they and their kin held,[141] and this attitude may have been shared by members of French kin groups in this period, particularly in cases where members of a noble kin group had become so closely tied with a particular house or heritage that they took their name from it.[142] When viewed from this perspective, the belief that acquired land was more freely alienable than inherited land can be attributed less to a practical concern to keep holdings compact—they were often widely dispersed already, in any case—than to a belief that members of a kin group had a special relationship to land that had been passed on to them by their ancestors.

Closely correlated with this attitude toward land and land-holding were particular attitudes about transfers of land. Because ceremonies of alienation took a form that seems not only highly ritualized, but also magical, symbolic liveries of seisin can be seen as efforts to control property rights and the social relationships bound up with property rights by manipulating certain objects symbolizing those rights and relationships.[143] Moreover, if rights in land served, inter alia, as tokens of social identity and social relationships, so that to possess or be associated with certain lands was to have a claim to a particular place in society, then the transfer of such rights may have constituted not just a conveyance, but a significant rearrangement of—and threat to—existing social relationships. Like our previous argument about the symbolic role of countergifts, the one advanced here suggests, first, that the involvement of relatives in exchange ceremonies may sometimes have had as much or more to do with claims to status than with claims to property, and, second, that exclusion from exchange ceremonies in which land was transferred could be interpreted as a denial of the excluded person's social identity.

By treating gifts to saints as "total" exchanges, rather than as conveyances of land, we can provide a better framework for analyzing the *laudatio parentum*. Starting from the initial premise that the donor's relatives were participating in a complex socioreligious transaction, it is possible to formulate more complex and satisfactory answers to the questions about whether the *laudatio* was necessary, who was expected to give it, and why it was considered proper for it to be given. Because the question of whether relatives were supposed to participate in these transactions is broader than the question of whether land could be legally alienated with the consent of kin, it requires a complex answer involving more than legal analysis. What is now at issue is not how a valid conveyance could be made, but how an intricate ritual was supposed to be carried out. Instead of simply following a rule about conveyancing, those who secured or gave the *laudatio* were reproducing, within the context of a particular kind of ritual, practices shaped, in part, by norms that cannot be easily disentangled from one another. In particular, the belief that relatives should give the *laudatio* because they had claims of one kind or another on the alienated property is hard to distinguish from the belief that relatives should approve gifts to saints because they were entitled or obligated to participate in and benefit from exchanges of this kind.

If consenting relatives were participating in total exchanges, then questions about which kin should give the *laudatio* also appear in a new light. It becomes easier to see why, within certain limits that are important to specify, consenting kin groups could vary considerably in composition. For the transactions in which a donor's relatives participated not only involved different sorts of property rights, in which different relatives might or might not have a claim; they also provided different kinds of spiritual benefits for different living and dead relatives of the main donor and were carried out at times that may have had different meanings for different relatives of the donor. In addition, at a time when the definition of medieval kin groups and the proper distribution of power and authority within them were both contested, it is not surprising that the general norm that gifts should be approved by kin was used in different ways. A more complex understanding of what a donor's relatives were doing when they approved gifts to saints also requires the formulation of several different strategies for explaining why such participation was called for and considered appropriate. Any such explanation must address several distinct questions: Why was it generally considered proper and right that gifts to saints be carried out by kin groups and not just by isolated individuals? What motives did benefactors or beneficiaries have for securing the participation of kin in these exchanges? What motives did relatives have for fulfilling the expectation that they would participate in their kinsman's gift? What were the effects on society as a whole of the recurrent practice of making gifts to saints with the *laudatio parentum*?

When approving a conveyance, a consenting relative was also entering into a special relationship with a monastic community and a saint as well as helping to provide for the spiritual welfare of some of his relatives. He was also participating, in many cases, in a funeral or in some other ceremony marking a major change in the life of his kin. Moreover, the conveyance he approved resulted in the exchange of property rights associated with his own kin for a contingent interest in a heavenly inheritance. In the rituals through which the exchange was carried out, the consenting relative also played a visible, openly recognized role at a time when it was especially important that his own kinship position be acknowledged.

At the same time, the main donor and the monks had reason to think it both right and advantageous that the donor's relatives be included as participants in exchange ceremonies. Monks had an interest in establishing amicable ties with the kin of their beneficiaries, not only because the latter would be thereby dissuaded from later initiating familial challenges, but also because it was often in the monks' interest to widen the network of the abbey's connections. In addition, monks may have encouraged the participation of kin in gifts to saints because, given the religious symbolism of these rituals, isolated individuals seemed out of place. Donors, too, should not be seen as encouraging the participation of their kin simply for instrumental purposes. For here, as in other spheres of medieval life, individual action for individual benefit was probably considered wrong or unfitting. In a period when dying alone, cut off from friends, was considered inappropriate, how proper would it have seemed for an isolated person to give alone and receive alone? Why should men who customarily made their gifts at least partly for the benefit of their dead kin wish to exclude their living relatives from an important occasion? It hardly ever happened, however, that gifts to saints were approved by as many kin as possible. While this finding is partially attributable to difficulties of travel and communication between relatives who resided far apart, it may also be partially explained by postulating that both monks and donors sometimes had reasons to restrict access to exchange ceremonies, just as relatives of a benefactor sometimes had grounds for abstaining from giving the *laudatio*.

Gifts to saints should not be viewed as untroubled, conflict-free feasts of familial and religious solidarity. While the giving of gifts in medieval societies was associated with the creation or recreation of social ties that were supposed to endure and to link givers and recipients together, these relationships could be established for different reasons, assume different forms, and undergo significant changes over time. Just as ties that nominally entailed reciprocity and mutuality could actually entail the subordination of one party to the other, so gifts to saints could be made for different reasons and produce different results. A vast number of medieval transactions were clothed in the forms of reciprocity. But these forms could be used by either party to attain different ends and could be undermined in different ways. As a result, there is really nothing paradoxical about the fact that all parties to these transactions expected trouble from each other and often got it.

Monks had reason to fear that the benefactor himself might go back on his word and take back what he had given. They had even more reason to fear that their benefactor's relatives—especially the absent, the unborn, and the infantile—would later undermine the gift. The benefactor's kin were worried lest he leave them disinherited or else exclude them from participation in what was potentially an advantageous and socially significant exchange. While fearing that his relatives might upset his gift, the benefactor also worried that his monastic beneficiaries would be too slothful or corrupt to carry out their appointed religious obligations. Even the dead and supernatural parties to the exchange were somewhat mistrusted. Dead relatives could return in dreams to curse or reprimand their living descendants for having denied them access to heavenly benefits. The saint or God could unleash wrath against the benefactor's relatives if they upset his gift; but in such cases, the donor, too, would suffer. The saint might fail to aid his monks, who might then feel compelled to respond to his tardiness in protecting them by humiliating his relics.[144] In a sense, even God was not a totally reliable party to the exchange, because those who made gifts to God's friends, the saints, were not given absolute assurances of receiving salvation.

There is nothing odd or paradoxical about the feelings of anxiety and distrust that were barely masked in exchange ceremonies. It was precisely the instability of secular, religious, and supernatural relationships that gave meaning and importance to the transactions through which knights and lords tried to control their immediate social world and their posthumous fate. The very fact that gifts to saints could not be effectively stabilized by the various means already discussed and that they were frequently disrupted by various kinds of challenges made these efforts to control social and religious relationships especially important. Whether exchanges of gifts were made between lay kin groups and monks or simply between different groups of lay people, they should not be seen as benign expressions of solidarity or as mechanisms for promoting some harmonious and politically neutral form of social and religious integration. The exchange of gifts was not simply a way of establishing contact with others or of expressing some ideal of solidarity. It constituted a way of trying to structure, manipulate, and control a treacherous social and supernatural world. Sometimes, it was also a method of checking overt hostilities. Like other medieval manifestations of reciprocity, exchanges between lay people and saints were marred by contradictions that are only obscured if the exchanges are viewed simply as a means of reinforcing a stable social order.

In one sense, the dramas initiated by exchanges between laymen and monasteries were marred because a certain sort of property played an essential role in what might otherwise have been a purely spiritual transaction. Sometimes, the lay donor's purpose was to gain a spiritual inheritance for himself from God through the continuous double mediation of a saint and some monks, while at other times the donor also hoped to procure the same sort of inheritance for dead or living kin. His claim to benefit from the intercessionary powers of both the saint and the monks was to be established by a gift of an earthly inheritance. What was problematic about this arrangement was not that many of the parties to this transaction were either dead or dying or else imaginary, or that the spiritual inheritance to be obtained was like the most contingent of contingent remainders, or that there was any lack of heavenly inheritances to be shared out among the small band of people who had enough earthly wealth to exchange for these parcels of celestial real estate. The problem was that the people who hoped to exchange their earthly inheritances for heavenly ones held from God in the kingdom of heaven lacked the power to alienate property in perpetuity and thus to make earthly and heavenly inheritances perfectly interchangeable. The lay parties had infinitely less control over their property than God had over heavenly inheritances, especially after they died. The flaw in the drama, therefore, was that as the lay gift-givers died off one by one, the worldly property they had tried to incorporate into an otherworldly transaction endured in a world where it could at any time be seized by their kin, their lords, or mere strangers, or else be pawned, sold, or given away by the monks. No matter how charitable the saints and the monastic parties to these transactions may have been, they could not fully countenance exchanges that were not, in some sense, balanced. Like all honorable and prudent lords, the saints did not regularly give away gifts for free. They could usually be counted on to intercede with God for someone who sought their friendship, provided that they had received the proper gift from the person who sought their mercy. If the benefactor's gift failed, however, intercession might cease, even though the person who suffered from the termination of saintly favor was in no way responsible for disturbing his gift.

It is important to remember, however, that while the religious ideology animating gifts to saints constituted a framework endowing both gifts to saints and the *laudatio parentum* with certain meanings, it was incapable of resolving a fundamental contradiction that was inherent in the exchange process itself. Whereas some of the participants in exchanges and some of the items of exchange were safely located in the realm of the imaginary and could therefore be controlled through imagination and rendered predictable, other participants and other items of exchange were part of a material world in which unpredictability, change, and degeneration were inherent and unavoidable, as both monks and their benefactors recognized. Although it was considered essential to the efficacy of the exchanges that the landed property given to monks remain forever under their control, there was no way of guaranteeing that this goal would be attained. Whereas monks and lay people were relatively free to impose a particular vision of the future on the world of the supernatural and to posit that God and God's saints would behave in a particular way, the political task of imposing a particular form of action on unborn humans was riskier. Moreover, many of the ideas and customs associated with gifts to saints and the *laudatio* were no more stable than was the society in which these gifts were made. And after several centuries, some of these beliefs and practices had either lost their central position in medieval French culture or else disappeared completely, as did the *laudatio* itself. This process, however, proceeded so slowly and quietly that now, historians can barely perceive it or chart it, let alone explain it adequately or grasp its full implications.

In a curious way, therefore, the exchanges between lay people and saints that were so common in France during the eleventh and twelfth centuries and on which so many people relied were unstable and even treacherous. The people of this era imputed to saints a seemingly benevolent insistence on reciprocity in human relationships. But this principle of reciprocity could sometimes be used to justify disinheritance from a tenure in the heavenly kingdom. To these people, this state of affairs probably seemed unremarkable or at least unsurprising, for every feature of these religious dramas was replicated in their own social world. In the society of knights, it was common to incur a great lord's anger on account of a kinsman's fault, to seek that lord's forgiveness through the mediation of well-connected friends to whom deference was shown and gifts were given, to strive to acquire the inheritance to which one had a birthright, and to be accompanied and supported in this endeavor by kinsmen and kinswomen. It was equally commonplace, no doubt, for such efforts to prove fruitless or only temporarily successful. The act of exchanging gifts was not an easy way of making friends. Gifts made friends and friends made gifts. But knights and lords never knew whether friends would become enemies or whether they had really been enemies all along.

What is central to this way of interpreting gifts to saints, therefore, is not the claim that they served a truly integrative function, but the contention that the giving of gifts with the approval of kin constituted an important means by which people of a certain class tried, in association with kin, to control the world around them. While this way of viewing of gifts to saints may help to make sense of the *laudatio parentum*, it does not tell us how to interpret changes over time in the frequency with which the *laudatio* is found or in the composition of the kin groups that participated in gifts to saints. This problem will be considered in the sixth and final chapter.

Chapter 6

The Decline of the *Laudatio Parentum*

INITIALLY, THE LONG-TERM HISTORY of the *laudatio parentum* seems simple when compared with involved discussions of whether the *laudatio* had to be given, who was supposed to give it, and why it was given at all. Once certain obstacles of coding, classifying, and counting have been surmounted, it is a relatively straightforward, if laborious, task to calculate for any given period what percentage of land transfers were approved by relatives, what kinds of kin groups generally gave the *laudatio*, and how commonly approval was given by sons, brothers, wives, or other sorts of relatives. Using indices of these kinds, historians have identified several long-term trends in the history of the *laudatio*. In particular, they have found that after 1200 it became progressively less common for gifts to be made with the consent of relatives and that in cases where the *laudatio parentum* was given during the thirteenth century, consenting groups were smaller and included only the donor's close kin.

These statistical trends, however, are easier to discern than they are to interpret and explain. While it is hard enough to understand individual cases in which relatives approved alienations and harder still to make sense of cases in which they did not, difficulties of interpretation increase geometrically when historians confront the problem of first analyzing indices constructed from studies of hundreds or even thousands of different transactions and then explaining fluctuations over time in these statistics. The act of interpreting the quantitative history of the *laudatio parentum* involves several distinct but interdependent types of analysis, each of which, as we have seen in previous chapters, is problematic.

Even if we put aside vexing and imponderable questions about whether the charters of this period survive in random samples and accurately record social practice,[1] many other questions arise about the ways in which the quantitative history of the *laudatio parentum* has been constructed and interpreted. If historians can justifiably assume that the *laudatio* was required by law and was supposed to be given by all relatives of an alienor and that kin gave the *laudatio* because they had legal rights in the property being alienated, then it is relatively easy to interpret both declines in the prevalence of the *laudatio* and changes in the composition of consenting kin groups. But if, as earlier chapters have suggested, none of these assumptions is tenable, then the long-term history of the *laudatio* becomes much more difficult to explicate.

Because the charters of Marmoutier, Noyers, Saint Aubin, Saint Vincent, and La Trinité are plentiful only for the period between 1050 and 1150, they do not clearly portray the era when the *laudatio parentum* declined in prevalence and ultimately disappeared.[2] Nevertheless, arguments already presented about the *laudatio* during the period when it was a common practice can still serve, along with other evidence, as a basis for evaluating previous discussions of the history of the *laudatio*. Before treating the implications of the present study for the interpretation of statistical analyses of the *laudatio* in studies of medieval social history, we must first consider the ways in which historians since the time of Marc Bloch have constructed, interpreted, and explained the quantitative history of the *laudatio*.

Bloch published no precise statistical findings about the *laudatio parentum*. But his brief discussion of its history in *Feudal Society* treated two topics that other scholars later analyzed more carefully through the use of quantitative data: first, a decline in what he called the "economic solidarity" of the *lignage* or family, and, second, a contraction in the size of the *lignage*.[3] Bloch claimed that during a period that he never defined precisely, but that probably antedated 1100, the economic solidarity of the family was both manifested and maintained in two ways. Relying, it seems, on evidence indicating that land transfers were sometimes made jointly by several relatives, rather than by a single alienor acting with the consent of his kin, Bloch argued that among certain nobles, as well as among many peasants, there were a significant number of " 'brotherhoods' . . . consisting of several interrelated households sharing the same hearth and the same board" and controlling the same lands in common.[4] He also claimed that charters recording donations to churches almost never failed to record the *laudatio*, which seemed "so far necessary that as a rule there was no hesitation in paying for it."[5]

After 1100 or so, according to Bloch, the economic solidarity of the family became attenuated and the *laudatio* lost its earlier legal or customary force. As "changes in the economy rendered restrictions on buying and selling more irksome" and as the customary law of the earlier feudal age was gradually replaced by a system of more clearly articulated legal rules, genuine sales of land became more common, while restraints on making them became less strict and more clearly defined.[6] Alluding first to the practice sometimes known as the "*offre aux parents*"[7] and then to the so-called *retrait lignager*,[8] Bloch argued that as sales ceased to be governed by the *laudatio parentum*,

the tendency at first was to require that before every alienation [of inherited land] for value received the property should be offered first to one of the relatives . . . Finally, from about the beginning of the thirteenth century, family control [as exercised under the *retrait lignager*] was reduced to a simple recognition of the right of the relatives, within prescribed limits and according to a stipulated order, to take the place of the buyer once the sale had occurred, on repayment of the price originally paid. . . . Thus, through more attenuated forms, the economic influence of the family lived on.[9]

Related, in Bloch's view, to the decline of the *laudatio* and its replacement in cases of sale by the *retrait lignager* was a significant change in the composition of consenting kin groups. He asserted that during the period when the *laudatio* was most prevalent,

No fixed principle limited the size of the group whose consent was considered necessary, and collaterals might intervene despite the presence of direct descendants; or in the same branch [of a family] the different generations might be called on concurrently to give this approval. The idea was to obtain [what one text referred to as] the favorable opinion of "as many kinsmen as possible."[10]

According to Bloch, "the whole family felt that it had suffered damage when a property passed out of its grip."[11] In his opinion, families at this time consisted of large cognatic kin groups that could include very distant cousins and had no clear boundaries.[12] Later on, however, the composition of consenting kin groups changed in such a way as to suggest that "a sort of contraction" in the family was taking place.[13] This process, as Bloch described it, went through two main stages. In the late twelfth century, there was "a tendency to restrict to the next of kin the request for family approval."[14] Then, the *laudatio* itself was, in a sense, replaced by the *retrait lignager*, and because the latter custom distinguished acquired from inherited property and, with respect to the latter, between "possessions subject, according to their origins, to the claims of either the paternal or maternal lines, it conformed much less than [the *laudatio* had] to the conception of an almost unlimited kinship."[15] In the decline and disappearance of the *laudatio parentum* during the late twelfth and thirteenth centuries, Bloch therefore saw evidence of an important stage in the process through which "the vast kindreds of not so long before were slowly being replaced by groups much more like our small families of today."[16] Bloch's interpretation of the *laudatio* also implied that during the medieval period, land tenure passed from a collectivist to a somewhat more individualistic stage.[17]

Although Bloch's views on the *laudatio* presumably influenced later scholars, they were soon modified significantly in a study of the Mâconnais by Georges Duby.[18] Although Duby's innovative argument about the *laudatio* has since been slightly modified by the author himself,[19] it has had a profound influence on all subsequent discussions of this topic, including the present one. By constructing a quantitative index showing how prevalent the *laudatio* was in one small region of France during different segments of the period between 900 and 1300, Duby demonstrated that in the Mâconnais the history of the *laudatio* could be divided into three main stages and not two, as Bloch had suggested.[20] In the tenth century, Duby found, less than 5 percent of all alienations were made with the consent of one or more relatives.[21] But during the next hundred years, the *laudatio* gradually became much more common, so that between 1050 and 1100, it appeared in two out of every three charters recording land transactions.[22]

In the twelfth century, the practice of alienating land with the consent of relatives remained common in the Mâconnais, as no one, according to Duby, could alienate inherited or even acquired property by himself or herself.[23] But after 1210, more and more alienations were made without the *laudatio*, and between 1250 and 1300, the practice disappeared almost completely.[24] At the same time, Duby, like Bloch, gave special attention to cases in which property was jointly alienated by two or more relatives, because he believed, as Bloch had, that land conveyed in this way was held collectively. Unlike Bloch, however, Duby suggested that at least in the Mâconnais, fraternities (or *frèrèches*) did not simply become steadily less common as the medieval period progressed; instead they followed a developmental course similar to that of the *laudatio*. Relatively rare in the tenth century, this form of tenure became more common between 1000 and 1100 and less prevalent after 1210.[25]

Duby also demonstrated that between 900 and 1300, major changes occurred in the composition both of consenting kin groups and of groups, such as *frèrèches*, that controlled undivided estates collectively. In the tenth-century Mâconnais, wives and sons made up a third of the total group of familial *laudatores*. Brothers approved alienations only when the donor had no descendants. Approval by distant kin was almost unknown.[26] During the same period, communal landholding was common only within the conjugal family; *frèrèches* constituted only a third of the groups holding undivided inheritances and almost always broke up as soon as one or more members married and had children.[27] During the eleventh century, however, as the *laudatio* became more common, it was given by larger and larger groups composed of more types, and more distant types, of kin. Between 1000 and 1050, "sons, now accompanied by daughters and sons-in-law, regularly gave their consent" to alienations.[28] "Brothers, uncles and nephews joined with them and sometimes even more distant kin designated by the vague term *proximi*."[29] In one case out of six, consent was given by uncles, nephews, or *proximi*, even in cases where the gift was also approved by children and brothers.[30] Between 1050 and 1100, the trend toward large consenting kin groups evidently continued.[31]

At the same time, as it became more common for groups of brothers to live on undivided inheritances, fraternities sometimes prolonged their existence, even when some of their members entered monasteries or married and had children. As a result, uncles, nephews, and cousins would remain united in the same "economic solidarity," and groups sharing a single estate grew as the family increased in size and structural complexity.[32] Between 1050 and 1100, the *laudatio* was given by relatives from the most remote branches of the family.[33] By the beginning of the thirteenth century, however, this expansion in the size and complexity of consenting kin groups had stopped. Indeed, the groups that gave the *laudatio* were growing smaller. "After 1210, distant kin, uncles and cousins were no longer consulted [about alienations], and more and more, a man did without the authorization of his brothers and sons."[34]

Because Duby's analysis of the *laudatio* was closely integrated into a complex argument about the development of an entire regional community over several centuries, his interpretation of the quantitative history of the *laudatio* cannot be fully summarized here. But several features of it demand attention. First and foremost, his finding that the *laudatio* became much more common after 1000 and much less so after 1210 and his discovery that consenting kin groups first expanded in the eleventh century and then contracted in the thirteenth allowed him to challenge the conventional hypothesis, espoused by Bloch, that the history of the medieval family was a relatively simple story about how large and cohesive clans of the early Middle Ages gradually broke down into smaller family groups whose members were less closely bound to each other.[35] Instead, Duby argued, there were segments of the medieval period—notably the eleventh century—when families became larger, more complex in structure, and more cohesive.

The tenth-century family seemed to Duby to have consisted of nothing more than a conjugal unit of parents and children.[36] Its individual members were only tenuously tied to each other and were free from collective constraints on the disposition of their property, which was held individually and not communally.[37] During the eleventh century, however, the family expanded in size and became more structurally complex. Individual members of large extended family groups were united in "the same economic solidarity" and were tightly bound to their kin by close, constraining ties.[38] In particular, each of them held legal rights in what was considered collective family property, which could be alienated only with the approval of all family members.[39] After prevailing in the Mâconnais for well over a century, this form of family organization changed dramatically after 1210, as the family contracted and as rights in land became individualized and less communal.[40] Even though Duby did not contend that this shift in family involved anything as simple as a return to the conditions of the tenth century,[41] his analysis of the *laudatio* and associated practices in the Mâconnais between 900 and 1300 focused on a cyclical movement in the composition of families and on a movement in land-holding practices from individualism to collectivism and then back to individualism.

According to Duby, the underlying causes of these long-term changes were mainly political and not, as Bloch had suggested, economic.[42] Duby maintained that the family was the main "refuge" in which individuals sought shelter during periods of weak state power. But when the state grew in authority to the point where it could give people adequate protection, he argued, they broke free from familial constraints, so that kinship ties grew weaker. "L'histoire du lignage," he concluded, "est une succession de contractions et de détentes, dont le rythme suit les modifications de l'ordre politique."[43] To support this broad hypothesis, Duby demonstrated that periods such as the eleventh and early twelfth centuries when the *laudatio* was common and was often given by large kin groups corresponded with periods of weak public power[44] and that in the tenth and thirteenth centuries, when the state had more authority, the *laudatio* was given, if at all, only by small family groups.[45] Between 1000 and 1200, property was held communally.[46] But in the tenth and thirteenth centuries, more individualistic conceptions of property prevailed.[47]

Although Duby himself later placed the quantitative history of the *laudatio parentum* in a slightly different analytical context,[48] the arguments set forth in his early book on the Mâconnais were largely accepted by his successors in this field. In a major study of Picardy, Robert Fossier examined the *laudatio* from a somewhat different perspective and explained its history in a more elaborate way.[49] But he concurred with Duby's claims that the history of the *laudatio* and of the family did not follow a unilineal path of development[50] and that political factors played a major role in determining family organization.[51] Using statistics more elaborate than the ones presented by Duby and organizing them in a different way, Fossier provided for his particular region a more precise version of the quantitative history of the *laudatio* and focused more closely than Duby had on the role of married couples in alienating land.

After locating 11,358 usable transactions from Picardy for the period between 800 and 1300, Fossier divided them into three categories: first, "individual acts" carried out by a single person who acted alone or with an eldest son and whose act was not even witnessed by kin; second, "conjugal acts" in which a man acted together with his wife or alienated land with her approval; and, third, "collective acts" carried out by a person acting either with one relative other than a spouse or eldest son or with two or more types of kin. Fossier also placed examples of familial challenges in the third category and divided his total data base into five subsets, each containing acts from a different part of Picardy. Along with graphs indicating how common each of the three types of transactions was in each of the five regions during half- or sometimes quarter-century intervals from 800 to 1300, he constructed an index showing the prevalence of acts that were either individual or conjugal.[52]

From these statistics, Fossier concluded that in Picardy, the quantitative history of the *laudatio* was even more complex than it was, according to Duby, in the Mâconnais. Individual acts, Fossier found, were particularly prevalent in three different periods—the tenth century, the late eleventh, and the thirteenth—and relatively rare during three others—the ninth century, the early eleventh, and the twelfth.[53] As a result, although his figures supposedly provided evidence of what he called "the defeat of the large family," he still supported Duby's view that the history of the family did not follow a unilineal path.[54] Fossier also justified his rejection of any simple evolutionary schema by noting that the

history of the *laudatio* followed somewhat different paths in different parts of Picardy.[55] Whereas his statistical findings were more
complex than Duby's, he supported his predecessor by arguing
that "upsurges of individualism in the family" could have resulted
from increased political security. On the one hand, "a man who
would not hope to receive protection from declining public institutions and who had no refuge in professional bodies drew nearer
to his own people and willingly submitted himself to the demands
of the group." On the other hand, "the reestablishment of order
substituted public control for private constraints and pushed the
individual to escape from the protection of the family."[56]

Nevertheless, after showing how changes in the political organization of various regions of Picardy could help to explain why
individual acts were common in some periods and rare in others,
Fossier claimed that this political explanation did not account for
everything and should be supplemented by a social one.[57] To explain the growth of individualism in the thirteenth century, he
noted that at this time, more and more transactions in his sample
involved peasants and townspeople, for whom, he claimed,
strong feelings of family identity were less "natural" than they
were for the representatives of older, richer noble kin groups.[58]
Fossier also noted, however, that earlier increases in individualism
during the tenth and later eleventh centuries could hardly be attributed to increases in alienations by peasants or townspeople.[59]
To supplement political and social explanations for the earlier history of the *laudatio* in Picardy, he therefore argued that economi-
cally motivated reorganizations of estates had led, at least during
the eleventh century if not during the tenth, to the *"dissociation"* of
the family and had continued to exert pressure in this direction
down to the thirteenth century, when, he claimed, an entirely new
family structure took shape.[60] With the break of the older forms of
family, the conjugal cell came to constitute the core of this new
family structure.[61]

After citing the role of churchmen in elevating the status of marriage in such a way as to promote the married couple to a central
position in every medieval family,[62] Fossier concluded by arguing
that "the family was deprived of its constraining power" to the
benefit of the married couple, not the individual.[63] To round out
his complicated theory of family evolution, in which economic,

religious, and political factors contributed to fundamental changes in family organization, he also cited population increases as a force tending to dissolve the family organization of the earlier medieval period.[64] In these ways, Fossier, like Duby, relied heavily on the quantitative history of the *laudatio parentum* in his efforts to trace and explain a broad evolutionary movement in the history of the medieval family.

Shortly after Fossier advanced this involved argument about the significance of the quantitative history of the *laudatio parentum*, Duby restated his own earlier findings about the *laudatio* in a study on "Lineage, nobility and knighthood" in the Mâconnais.[65] Here and in other later writings, he placed the history of this practice and of the aristocratic *lignage* in what was in some ways a novel argumentative context by linking them more closely than he had previously done with the more general problem of class formation within a newly constituted seigneurial mode of production.[66] While continuing to treat the growing prevalence of the *laudatio* during the eleventh and early twelfth centuries as a sign of "a greater cohesion of the family group,"[67] Duby also emphasized that family members did not all benefit equally from this "increase in the solidarity of blood relations centered on the inheritance."[68] Instead, as "the rights of sons and brothers [grew] at the expense of those of their sisters,"[69] the "gradual acceptance of male primacy" created within the nobility

> a society where the succession concerned only men and where women had only subsidiary rights, where unmarried sisters remained under the tutelage of their brothers and received at most, as a gift for their funeral alms, a small share in the joint inheritance, usually a part of the property brought into the family by their mother, where the married daughters finally left the household with their small dowry, without being able from then on to claim anything from the family allodial holdings.[70]

At the same time, according to Duby, the elevation of eldest sons to a more privileged familial position led to "a narrowing and a tightening of the family around the male line, from which emerged a dynastic spirit that was probably more noticeable amongst the owners of castles, but was nonetheless quite common throughout the aristocracy."[71]

In a later study, Duby argued that these transformations in family organization inevitably generated intense intrafamilial conflict, as rules of succession were modified and as power was concentrated "in the hands of heads of families."[72] The sons of the *caput generis*, he asserted,

> felt frustrated and, as soon as they came of age, gave voice to their claims and grabbed by force what they could when they could. Equally bitter were the husbands of their sisters and aunts, who saw what they had hoped to inherit absorbed into one estate. At the same time the man responsible for a family's honor would try to preserve its prestige by exercising stricter control over the marriages of the young men and women subject to his authority. He would hand over the women quite willingly but would allow only *some* of the men to contract lawful marriages, thus forcing most of the knights to remain bachelors, which only increased their resentment and unruliness.[73]

In these ways, Duby associated the rise of the *laudatio parentum* after 1000 not only with an increase in family solidarity, but also with other important changes in aristocratic family organization.[74] Moreover, the context in which he considered the *laudatio* was all the more complex, because he associated the establishment of a new kind of noble kin group with the formation of a seigneurial mode of production.[75] All these developments, including the growing prevalence of the *laudatio*, resulted in "the rearrangement of kinship ties [among nobles] into the framework of a strictly masculine line and the appearance of a truly lineal structure."[76] In an earlier period, whose chronological boundaries varied, depending on the political status of the person considered, a noble regarded his family as "a horizontal grouping, spread out in the present, with no precise or fixed limits, made up as much of *propinqui* as of *consanguinei*, of men and women whose bonds were as much the result of marriage alliances as of blood."[77] Later, however,

> an individual felt himself . . . to be part of a family group with a much more rigid structure, centered on agnatic consanguinity and its vertical links. He felt himself to be a member of a lineage, of a race whose inheritance was transmitted

from father to son, in which the eldest son took over the direction of the household and whose history could be displayed in the form of a tree rooted in the person of the founding father from whom came all power and glory of the race.[78]

Because this shift in family structure and familial consciousness could only have occurred through a process that subordinated the interests of certain family members, notably women and younger sons, Duby implicitly treated the kin groups of this era not only as "refuges" from disorders external to the family,[79] but also as centers of intense and embittered conflicts about how the family should be organized and defined and how family interests should be defined and pursued. Moreover, in emphasizing the fact that the head of a noble *lignage* could only establish his own power and that of his race by enriching himself from "the profits of 'exactions' raised from peasants" and by assuming a position of leadership over "local *militia*,"[80] Duby further elaborated upon the picture of the noble family as a "refuge" from disorder. The aristocratic *lignage* therefore appears as a center of conflict, a repressive agency through which an elder male dominated and controlled his kin, and an organization through which nobles dominated the countryside.[81] Moreover, by linking the history of the *laudatio parentum* to the history of aristocratic kinship structures, which he linked, in turn, to the establishment of a seigneurial regime, Duby, in effect, dissolved the arbitrary division between the social history of the family and the history of politics.[82]

In briefer analyses of medieval family organization, other scholars have merely used quantitative methods similar to the ones first developed by Duby and later extended by Fossier.[83] Of these writings, the ones most relevant to the present discussion are those of Robert Hajdu.[84] In an article dealing with the *laudatio* in both Poitou and Picardy from 1100 to 1300, Hajdu found evidence confirming the view that "wives replaced the husband's male relatives as consenters to transactions during the course of the twelfth century."[85] Whereas charters between 1100 and 1300 mention wives less and less frequently as "consenters" to alienations, they also indicate that women acted more and more often as "co-actors" with their husbands.[86] In another study, Hajdu showed that in Picardy between 1100 and 1300, the *laudatio* steadily became less prevalent, as the percentage of acts mentioning it declined from 67 percent to 23 percent.[87] From this evidence and from the finding that brothers, younger sons, and even eldest sons approved alienations with declining frequency between 1100 and 1300, he maintained that during these two centuries, "the family contracted drastically as a basic unit of society."[88]

On the basis of further quantitative data about references in charters to different kinds of living or dead kin,[89] Hajdu argued that this period saw "a fundamental shift in family size, structure, participation, and loyalties."[90] At the beginning of the twelfth century, "family sentiment may be understood as a composite of two opposing tendencies." On the one hand, "A sense of lineage, of a noble past, demanded an undivided inheritance, and the monopolization of all advantages in the marriage market in one child, in order that one descendant might carry on the family name and tradition in all its glory." On the other hand, "Equal division of holdings or at least significant endowment of all children and assurance of a socially acceptable future for all through suitable marriages was demanded by more prosaic family sentiment."[91] Building on certain aspects of Duby's more recent work on the noble *lignage*,[92] Hajdu asserted that at this time, there existed in Poitou a "conflict" between a "vertical" model of the family, expressed in the first set of sentiments, and a "horizontal" model, expressed in the second. After contending that during the twelfth century a "brilliant compromise" between the two opposing views was reached,[93] he concluded that "this vertical-horizontal balance of the twelfth century . . . was upset during the first half of the thirteenth century and replaced by a clearly vertical orientation during the next fifty years. After 1200 the conjugal family took over as the active social unit. It cultivated a warm memory of direct ancestors, it bequeathed its holdings to its eldest male offspring, and made only minimal provisions for other children."[94] This broad conclusion was based largely on the quantitative history of the *laudatio parentum*.

From the preceding summaries of earlier scholarship it is clear, first, that numerous methodological problems are involved in the process of creating, interpreting, and explaining the quantitative history of the *laudatio* and, second, that the assumptions and hypotheses central to previous interpretations of that history differ in several respects from the ones adopted in the present study. To determine how best to interpret the history of the *laudatio* in the light of the arguments advanced in previous chapters, we first need to ask how accurately and meaningfully the quantitative indices constructed by previous scholars represent its decline and disappearance. Next, following the order of our earlier discussion of the *laudatio* in chapters 3, 4, and 5, we can consider what the quantitative history of the *laudatio* may reveal about modifications in norms or legal rules governing land transfers, about the development of medieval kinship and family life, about the changing role of individuals and kin groups in controlling landed property, and about the importance of family solidarity and individualism in different periods of medieval French history. Finally, we can try to determine how best to explain the legal and social changes that are directly or indirectly reflected in the quantitative history of the *laudatio*. At each stage of the following argument, readers should keep in mind that because the present analysis of the long-term history of the *laudatio parentum* is based largely on secondary works whose authors treat several different regions of France from various perspectives, it is highly provisional and provides only some general hypotheses about how to view the decline and disappearance of the *laudatio*.

In constructing a statistical index indicating how frequently the *laudatio parentum* was given during different segments of long periods ending in 1300, each of the studies summarized above used a data base that included various types of land transfers. Fossier, for example, chose to ignore differences between different kinds of alienations, because, he claimed, they had only juridical significance and revealed nothing about actual social practice. He also included in his category of "collective acts" transactions that became the subjects of familial challenges.[95] Although this method enabled him to provide precise quantitative measurements of broad trends in the history of land transfers and to improve significantly on earlier, impressionistic histories of the *laudatio*,[96] the indices that he and other scholars have constructed are not fully adequate for a study concerned with the participation of kin in gifts to saints, as opposed to land transfers in general, because they obscure significant differences between thirteenth-century land transfers and earlier ones and sometimes fail to distinguish between different forms of familial participation in alienations.

By 1200 if not earlier, the overall profile of land transfers recorded in surviving documents was changing in several ways. As Fossier noted, for example, his own indices did not reveal that during the thirteenth century, the proportion of alienations made by nobles was declining, as more land transfers were made by members of other social classes.[97] This finding implies that previously published figures indicating how often the *laudatio* was given in different periods would change for the period after 1200, if they were based on a sample of thirteenth-century alienations that was identical, in terms of the social status of alienors, with samples drawn from eleventh- and twelfth-century charters. In addition, if familial challenges began to decline in prevalence after 1150 or 1200, there must be significant differences between thirteenth- and eleventh-century samples of conveyances made with or without the *laudatio*.

Standard indices, moreover, may conceal other noteworthy changes during the same period in the nature of land transactions, in the identity of alienees, in the timing of alienations, in the form of documents recording alienations, and in the legal context in which land was transferred. Because genuine sales—as Bloch observed and as other historians have since confirmed[98]—became more common after 1150 or 1200, samples of thirteenth-century charters must include a smaller percentage of gifts to saints than do samples of earlier alienations. The purely proprietary dimension of land transfers in these samples, therefore, must have assumed more importance as alienations of land were less likely to be integrally associated with the establishment or reaffirmation of enduring social ties. After 1100, there was also a change in the kinds of religious houses that received most of the property alienated in alms by lay people. During the twelfth century, the rate of giving to Benedictine monasteries slowed appreciably, while more and more alienations were made to Cistercians and regular canons and to other new religious groups.[99]

This last change is particularly important to this study because the benefactors of new orders sometimes differed, in terms of wealth and class identity, from the patrons of older Benedictine abbeys. Moreover, the benefactors of new orders established relationships with their religious beneficiaries that differed from the ones that existed between Benedictines and their patrons.[100] As attitudes toward monastic burial were modified during the twelfth century,[101] and as the practice of admitting child oblates into monasteries came under increasing criticism until it was ultimately banned in 1215,[102] significant changes presumably occurred in the timing of gifts to abbeys and in the general social context in which such gifts were made. It has also been recently argued that during the twelfth century, there were important modifications both in the kinds of prayers that nobles procured for themselves and their kin[103] and in the relationships that they established with religious communities.[104]

Even when nobles gave lands to religious houses in return for prayers, their donations increasingly took on the character of commercial transactions, in which carefully enumerated services were procured in return for properties of clearly established monetary value and which did not necessarily establish ongoing ties between donor and donee.[105] Moreover, it has been shown that at least in the region around Chartres, nobles became more likely to procure prayers from several different religious communities, so that their relationships with any one of these houses were bound to be less intimate.[106] Finally, there are grounds for thinking that during the later twelfth century, noteworthy changes were occurring in attitudes toward burial[107] and prayers for the dead.[108] For all the reasons just cited, it seems evident that the cultural significance of land transfers to monasteries underwent pronounced changes during the twelfth and thirteenth centuries. In particular, transactions that can be properly termed gifts to saints became increasingly rare, as other types of land transfers grew more prevalent, not only among the laity, but also between lay people and religious communities.

In addition, because thirteenth-century charters do not routinely mention the restraints on alienation that were legally recognized at this time, they do not have the same evidentiary value as earlier documents have for studies of family interests in land. Whereas eleventh-century scribes carefully recorded the *laudatio*, their thirteenth-century counterparts neither routinely alluded to the rights of the seller's kin under the *retrait lignager*[109] nor indicated that under the *réserve coutumière*, donors could legally alienate only a limited part of their land away from their kin, who could challenge alienations that were too large.[110] Under the *retrait lignager*, a seller's kin could take the buyer's place and constrain him to transfer the alienated land to them, provided that they acted within a specified time period and reimbursed the original buyer for his payment to the seller.[111] At the same time, under the so-called *réserve coutumière* (or *lignagère*), a certain portion of a landholder's inherited real property, which often consisted of a fifth, a quarter, or a third, could not be alienated at all and had to pass to the landholder's heirs.[112] Taking no account of these two practices, statistics indicating how often gifts were made with the *laudatio* may minimize the interests of relatives in thirteenth-century land transfers. Moreover, in cases where the *laudatio* is found in transactions from this period, it did not necessarily have the same function that it had had in earlier periods. After the development of the *réserve coutumière*, the *laudatio* was used in a new way in cases where an alienation of inherited property exceeded the limits established under the *réserve*.[113] In indices showing the prevalence of the *laudatio* in different periods, however, this change in function is not clearly signaled.

Furthermore, when considering statistics of this kind, we should remember that the decline of the *laudatio* during the thirteenth century coincided with important modifications in the form of charters recording land transfers and in the legal context in which such transfers were made. During the preceding century, moreover, the form of the *laudatio parentum* itself was changing in many regions, as increasing importance was attached to the consent of the donor's heir. Whereas earlier medieval charters were usually drafted by the scribes of monastic beneficiaries, thirteenth-century charters often took the form of notices issued by the alienors themselves, by their lords, or by bishops, deacons, and *officiales*.[114] The later texts differed from the earlier ones by virtue of their substantive provisions, as well as their stylistic features. The rambling, yet informative narratives of eleventh-century charters were replaced in later documents by passages constructed almost exclusively out of increasingly conventionalized and opaque legal formulae.[115] Earlier, scribes tried to legitimate and stabilize the transactions they recorded by including biblically inspired preambles, fearsome malediction clauses, and long lists of witnesses and/or signatories.[116] Later, these diplomatic features disappeared, as charters were often authenticated by the seal of the alienor or his lord and usually listed few if any witnesses.[117]

Thirteenth-century charters included with increasing frequency a kind of clause that did not figure in eleventh- or early twelfth-century documents. In texts from the later period, the alienor or his lord stipulated that he had obligated not only himself but also his heirs to warrant, defend, or abstain from disturbing the recorded transaction.[118] After 1230 or so, for example, such stipulations were made by people alienating land to La Trinité of Vendôme,[119] and during the next half century, similar clauses appear in charters recording transfers of land to Marmoutier.[120] Even though promises of this kind sometimes appear alongside references to the *laudatio parentum*,[121] their growing prevalence in thirteenth-century documents suggests that alienors at this time were acquiring powers of alienation that would render the consent of their relatives redundant. For if a landholder, acting alone, could legally bind his kin to observe his alienation and even to support it in court, then there was no longer any *legal* rationale for the *laudatio parentum*:[122] Although it seems clear, therefore, that the decline of the *laudatio* was related to the development of the law of warranty, this connection, whose nature is problematic, is not signaled in graphs that merely plot out the first of these two interrelated developments.

Statistical tables showing the frequency with which land transfers were made by individuals with the consent of kin also fail to indicate that during the eleventh century, not all forms of the *laudatio* were identical and that during the twelfth, when the *laudatio* was still prevalent in many areas, the form of the approval given to land transfers was changing in ways that may foreshadow the later development of warranty clauses binding the alienor's heirs as well as the alienor.[123] As we saw in chapter 4, the kin who gave the *laudatio* were not always selected on the same basis and did not all necessarily play the same role in alienations. After 1100, if not before, an alienor's heir was increasingly likely to play a uniquely prominent role in land transactions, not only in cases where he alone gave the *laudatio*, but also in instances where the role of other kin in giving it was less important than that of the heir.[124] Whereas eleventh-century charters do not necessarily specify clearly the capacity in which a donor's son or other relative was acting when he or she gave the *laudatio*, documents from the next century often suggest that the people who approved their kinsman's gift were doing so in their capacity as heirs or prospective heirs.[125] Even if no parallel change had been occurring at this time in the composition of consenting kin groups, the increasing prominence of the donor's heir in approving alienations suggests that during the twelfth century, the nature of the *laudatio* was changing in ways that are not always clearly reflected in the quantitative history of this practice.[126] Moreover, if alienations were made with only the consent of the alienor's son and heir, this may imply that other kin were bound by the heir's consent. If so, we are only one step away from a warranty binding all the donor's heirs.

Finally, although late twelfth- and thirteenth-century charters clearly reveal that land transfers from this period were sometimes made with the *laudatio*, their references to this practice differ from those often found in earlier texts.[127] Eleventh-century scribes frequently indicate that the people who gave the *laudatio* were participants in a complex process of exchange, in which they not only approved an alienation, but also received material and spiritual countergifts. By contrast, thirteenth-century charters do not normally indicate that an alienor's relatives did anything more than approve an alienation.[128] If this change does not merely involve a change in scribal practice, it shows that the act of giving the *laudatio* had been transformed from a process of participation in a social exchange to a mere act of approving a conveyance. If this is so, then the decline in the prevalence of the *laudatio parentum* must have involved more than a mere change in conveyancing practices.

Although the arguments just presented do nothing to undermine the conventional view that the *laudatio* declined and ultimately disappeared during the thirteenth century, they strongly suggest that this development did not involve anything remotely resembling a reversal of earlier trends or a return to conditions prevailing in the period before the *laudatio* became a common practice.[129] Even though statistics compiled for the thirteenth century resemble those compiled for the tenth, the decline and disappearance of the *laudatio* after 1200 can be seen, from one perspective, as a continuation of a trend that Duby treated as being characteristic of the intervening period: the growing dominance of the heads of families and their heirs over other family members.[130] In addition, our analysis of the quantitative history of the *laudatio* suggests that the decline of the *laudatio* was associated not only with the rise in state power and changes in family organization, but also with other important trends that will be more fully discussed below.[131]

If we now examine the second main question raised above about what the decline of the *laudatio* may reveal about changes in norms concerning land transfers, we will again find that the quantitative history of the *laudatio* is even more difficult to interpret than previous studies have sometimes suggested. Statistics showing that the *laudatio* was common during the eleventh and twelfth centuries but rare thereafter do not show simply that a legal rule barring individuals from alienating land without the consent of their kin disappeared after 1200. As Bloch pointed out, the legal context in which land transfers were made was itself changing during the very period when the *laudatio* was dying out.[132] As we saw in chapter 3, it is misleading to represent the normative status of the *laudatio* during the period of its greatest prevalence by stating that a legal rule barred landholders from alienating land without the consent of their kin. Instead, we can best represent the normative status of the *laudatio* by arguing that although a general norm stipulated that gifts should be made with the consent of kin, it lacked authoritative legal status and did not form part of a system of real property law. As this custom gradually lost its force during the thirteenth century, new rules governing land transfers were being established, so that thirteenth-century alienors were in some ways restricted in their power of alienation by the *retrait lignager* and the *réserve coutumière*, while they also possessed a kind of freedom that their ancestors had lacked.[133] Even more important in the present context is the fact that customs governing land transfers acquired during the thirteenth century a kind of precision and legal authority that was unknown in the period when the *laudatio* became prevalent. In particular, a distinction between gifts and sales that had previously been almost unthinkable was now clearly established.[134]

During the first half of the thirteenth century, landholders in most parts of northern France, including the regions where the five abbeys were located, gradually established a legal right to give away a third of their inherited property without the consent of their kin. In the late 1240s the *réserve coutumière* was mentioned in a custumal drawn up for the Touraine and Anjou and was also in force in Maine.[135] The same custumal also referred to the *retrait lignager*,[136] which, like the *réserve*, was an established custom by this time throughout northern France.[137] These two customs had a kind of legal force that the *laudatio parentum* had previously lacked. Both were associated with specific legal rules that governed the alienation of land, that were clearly distinguished from religious or customary norms, and that were applied by courts to particular cases.[138] Because the institutional, political, and intellectual developments presupposed by the appearance of rules of this kind must have been in progress for decades before the formal establishment of the two new customs, it is also clear that in the century or so before the *laudatio* died out completely, a change was occurring in the juridical context in which this practice was observed.

If the quantitative history of the *laudatio parentum* does not signal a simple change in the rules of real property law, neither does it provide clear evidence of a contraction in the medieval French family. This conclusion is not clearly supported by statistics indicating that consenting kin groups first grew smaller during the late twelfth and early thirteenth centuries and then ceased to approve most land transfers. The study of these groups, as Duby has noted, only reveals how kin groups were constituted on just one of the occasions when relatives gathered[139] and does not reveal how kin groups organized themselves at other times for other purposes.[140] As developed in chapter 4, this way of looking at consenting kin groups has several implications for the interpretation of the history of the *laudatio parentum*.[141] First, the disappearance of a certain kind of relative from consenting groups does not show that relatives of this type were no longer recognized as kin for any purpose. It merely reveals that these sorts of relatives no longer participated actively and formally in land transfers. The fact that cousins, for example, stopped giving the *laudatio* hardly indicates that people ceased to recognize the offspring of their father's or mother's siblings or never engaged in collective action with them.[142] Moreover, the fact that thirteenth-century landholders often alienated land without the *laudatio* does not show that they had no relatives at all or normally acted as isolated individuals.[143] Instead, it reveals that they had acquired the power to alienate some of their land by themselves and that their kin had no interest in approving or participating in their alienations. Finally, the fact that the wives of thirteenth-century alienors assumed a more prominent position, relative to that of other kin, in the alienation of landed property does not necessarily imply that the conjugal family was the dominant form of kinship group at this time. The prominence of wives is perfectly compatible with the hypothesis that for certain purposes other than the alienation of land, other kinds of kin groups had important social roles.

The discovery that fewer relatives and fewer types of relatives gave the *laudatio* does not show that "the family" was contracting. Instead, the history of the *laudatio* and of the kin groups that gave it can be read in a different way that is consistent with our earlier analysis of consenting kin groups, with Duby's views about the development of aristocratic kin groups, and with studies of the *réserve coutumière* and *retrait lignager*. Under this interpretation, the contraction of consenting groups that began before or after 1200 reveals that the power to control landed property was increasingly concentrated in the hands of individual landholders and, in some cases, their wives or heirs. When viewed in this way, both the contraction in consenting kin groups and even the complete disappearance of the *laudatio* itself mark the culmination of a long process that had begun as early as the eleventh century, when, as Duby has argued, the power of elder males grew at the expense of the proprietary interests of female and younger male children.[144] Whereas an eleventh-century monastic benefactor was sometimes expected to make gifts to saints in association with numerous kin and could not count on his relatives to assume the obligation of maintaining and defending his gift after he died,[145] a man who gave or sold some of his land during the thirteenth century could act either alone or with only his wife or heir and gradually gained the power to impose on his heirs the obligation to warrant his alienation. Between c. 1050 and c. 1250, therefore, what had changed was not necessarily the actual composition of any kin group other than the one that participated in land transfers, but rather the way in which power over property was distributed within upper-class kin groups.

If the history of the *laudatio parentum*, at least when considered in isolation, does not support the claim that the family was contracting during the late twelfth or thirteenth centuries, there are also grounds for questioning the view that the gradual disappearance of the *laudatio parentum* signals a major shift from communitarian to individualistic forms of land tenure, as well as the claim that whereas increases in the prevalence of the *laudatio* reflect increases in family solidarity, declines reveal a rise in individualism. Even though the *laudatio* disappeared during the thirteenth century, this period did not, in fact, see the development of a system of property law in which individual property holders had full powers of alienation or in which familial claims on property had no legal force. Because the property interests of an alienor's *lignage* were recognized and given some measure of protection under the *retrait lignager* and the *réserve coutumière*,[146] the period in which the *laudatio parentum* disappeared should not be seen as one of proprietary individualism. As Bloch noted, "the economic influence of the family," though "attenuated," lived on through these two customs until well after 1200.[147]

The significance of this fact can be brought out by comparing northern French legal developments with contemporaneous English ones. In England, the disappearance of so-called familial restraints on alienations of feudal property by around 1200 left a tenant in fee legally free to alienate his entire fief in perpetuity by himself and thus to ignore what could now be viewed as the moral, as opposed to legal, claims of his heirs, whom the tenant could now disinherit at will. Tenants in fee tail generally lacked such extensive powers of alienation. But in thirteenth-century England, the principle that feoffments to a man "and his heirs" gave nothing to the heirs and that knights' fees were thus freely alienable was apparently well established.[148] In France, however, the legal position of tenants in fee was different.[149] The French tenant could not completely ignore the interests of his kin, to whom the *retrait lignager* and the *réserve coutumière* accorded certain legal rights to his property. The members of a potential alienor's *lignage* therefore had legal interests in at least part of his property. What they lacked, or were gradually losing, was the privilege and expectation, sanctioned by established custom, of participating in certain transactions that involved, among other things, the alienation of their kinsman's land. What was dying out in this period, therefore, was not "family solidarity" in general or even familial control over land, but a special sort of familial activity that was centered on the exchange of land but that also involved the establishment or reaffirmation of enduring social ties.

In this period, as in earlier ones, moreover, even alienations made by individuals should not necessarily be used to show that ties between kin were becoming weaker. In some of these cases, donors were acting on their own but not simply on their own behalf. When in 1223, for example, Andreas de Aleia acted alone in giving some property in alms to the monks of La Trinité, he did so for the souls of his *amici* as well as his own.[150] More than sixty years later, when Count Jean de Vendôme gave the same abbey some property, he acted not only for his own soul, but also for the souls of his father and their common ancestors.[151] When individuals made gifts without the *laudatio*, but procured spiritual benefits for their relatives, they were not engaging in individualistic behavior. Yet in statistical studies of the *laudatio*, transactions of this kind are assigned the same value as alienations made by individuals for their own individual benefit.

If gifts to saints by individuals sometimes provide evidence of the force of kinship ties, it is also true that individual, as opposed to group, interests were sometimes supported by implicit or explicit appeals to the norm that land should be alienated only with the *laudatio parentum*. One of the paradoxical implications of what is usually seen as the collectivist principle that gifts should be made with the *laudatio* was that a gift that had been approved by several of the donor's kin could be challenged by a single kinsman who had not approved it. This is precisely what happened in the case of Hugo, son of Burchardus, and in scores of other cases from the eleventh and twelfth centuries.[152] These cases show that a custom calling for collective action by relatives in making gifts to saints could be invoked by single individuals to challenge the acts of several kin.[153]

As the preceding argument indicates, the form of family solidarity that was both expressed and reinforced by the *laudatio parentum* was ephemeral. In the absence of legal representation under which an heir would assume his ancestor's obligations as well as that ancestor's rights, the living members of a kin group could not ensure that future generations would defend or even respect their gifts. Integrally associated with the *laudatio*, therefore, were attitudes toward property, kinship, and social obligation that allowed for and even encouraged intergenerational strife between monastic benefactors and their kin, notably their sons and sons-in-law, and between different descendants of benefactors. In fact, the apparent cohesiveness of upper-class kin groups during the period when the *laudatio* was most prevalent was regularly compromised and undermined by several contradictions in the familial practices of knights and lords. Out of a limited stock of resources, a knight, for example, had to allocate property in such a way as to provide for the material support of his wife and kin and for the spiritual needs of himself, his dead relatives, and possibly his living kin as well. As a result, the possibilities for intragroup conflict over the form that this allocation took were virtually endless, and as the evidence of familial challenges indicates, possibilities for conflict often became realities.

Evidence about the structure of consenting kin groups can also be interpreted in such a way as to undermine efforts to treat the *laudatio parentum* as an unambiguous sign of family solidarity. For this evidence, as set out in chapter 4, shows that what characterized kin groups participating in gifts to saints was not some generalized form of solidarity uniting donors with all of those people whom they recognized as kin, but a form of group cohesion that brought certain *selected* kin together, while separating them from other relatives. Precisely the same point can be made about the groups of dead and living kin who received spiritual countergifts, because the act of selecting some kin for inclusion in these groups entailed the exclusion of others.

The mere fact that a gift or other kind of alienation was made with the *laudatio* does not show that it either reflected or reinforced a generalized form of family solidarity. In eleventh- or early twelfth-century cases, when eldest sons were given precedence over their male siblings or where daughters were evidently excluded from consenting groups, we can see clearly that the inter-

ests of certain relatives were being compromised or totally undermined. What these cases reveal is that only one of several possible
definitions of a kin group's interest was being acted upon. This
line of argument indicates that the distinction commonly made
between individual and family interests needs to be scrutinized
closely and that instead of talking generally of "family solidarity,"
we need to determine precisely how a kin group's interests were
being defined in any particular transaction. We should also consider the possibility that alienations made by individuals were not
necessarily individualistic acts, not only because they were sometimes made in return for countergifts benefiting the alienor's kin,
but also because newly developed warranty clauses indicate that
alienors were controlling their descendants, rather than acting independently of them.

If the early history of the *laudatio parentum* is viewed in this way,
then the later history of this practice cannot be viewed as involving nothing more than a return to earlier conditions. The fact that
fraternities in some regions became less common during the 1200s
than they had been one or two centuries earlier shows that estates
were being divided more frequently and that one form of familial
control over land was becoming less prevalent.[154] But if thirteenth-
century landholders were less closely linked to their siblings and
collaterals than their eleventh-century predecessors had been,
they had also assumed more direct control over their lineal descendants. Although limited by the *retrait lignager* and the *réserve
coutumière* and by the proprietary claims of their wives, male
heads of kin groups were acquiring more power to control their
property and their lineal descendants. They had gained the
power, never securely possessed by their eleventh-century counterparts, to impose legal obligations on unborn descendants. Fore-
shadowings of this new proprietary and familial regime can be
seen prior to the thirteenth century in the growing prevalence of
the practice by which a donor's eldest son took a preeminent place
in the making of gifts and the receiving of countergifts. Underlying this practice was the belief that the consent of this one kinsman, rather than the consent of the donor's relatives generally,
was crucial. The real establishment of the new regime, however, is
signaled by the development of a new way of stabilizing perpetual

alienations: a legally enforceable promise by the donor that he *and his heirs* would warrant and defend his gift forever.

The construction of this new type of warranty clause out of words traditionally used since the eleventh century must have been the work of scribes and lawyers.[155] But words alone could not have had their desired effect, if an important change had not occurred in generally shared ideas about property, kinship, and obligations. Since the early Middle Ages, monks and their benefactors had repeatedly expressed concern that the gifts made to saints in return for spiritual benefits might be disturbed by familial challenges. But traditional methods of stabilizing gifts could not reach very far into the future. It was only with the development of warranty in the thirteenth century that an effective means of cutting off familial claims came into being.

The working out of the ideas implicit in the fully developed warranty clauses of the thirteenth century must have been a complex process in which legal logic, the demands of a bureaucratic state, and the exigencies of a growing land market surely played a part. But the emergence of the notion that an heir could be bound by his ancestor's promises and should therefore assume at least some of his ancestor's obligations may also have been associated with the process by which nobles became more prone to see themselves as members of a certain kind of *lignage*. Implicit in the new warranty clauses was the notion that a noble's family also extended forward in time so as to include his unborn heirs. Under the proprietary regime of the thirteenth century, a man's heir had a sort of birthright, just as his eleventh-century counterpart had had. But the former was more strictly bound than the latter had been by the obligations assumed by his ancestor.

The emergence of the notion that a *lignage* extended into the future as well as into the past and an enhanced sense of patrilineal descent are not consistent with a real decline in family solidarity or a rise in social individualism. Instead, they provide evidence of the crystallization of a new form of family solidarity that bound together not just the living and dead members of a *lignage*, but their unborn descendants as well. In other words, the decline in the participation of kin in gifts to saints, as manifested in the quantitative history of the *laudatio parentum*, can be read as a sign

that a further stage had been reached in the process that had begun, according to Duby, in the eleventh century or even earlier:
the process by which aristocratic control over property and political power was strengthened through the adoption of a more structured and more authoritarian form of family organization.

If conventional methods of interpreting the quantitative history
of the *laudatio parentum* are in some ways misleading, then associated methods of explaining trends supposedly reflected in that
history obviously require modification. Instead of trying to account for a change in legal rules governing land transfers, a contraction in the medieval family, a decline in family solidarity, and
the waning of communitarian forms of land tenure, we need to
consider the interrelationships between an even larger number of
interlocking trends. In previous sections of the present chapter the
decline and ultimate disappearance of the *laudatio parentum* have
been associated in one way or another with the following developments: the establishment of a more systematically organized legal
order in which legal rules were more clearly distinguished from
other sorts of norms than they had been previously and in which
distinctions between different kinds of land transfers were clearly
articulated; the growth in the power of a state whose functionaries
not only maintained a certain sort of social order, but also provided bureaucratic mechanisms through which disputes over
property could, at least in theory, be resolved through the systematic application of rules to facts; the appearance of the *retrait lignager* and *réserve coutumière* and the development of an alienor's
power to bind his heirs to warrant his alienation; the growing
prevalence of land sales and a correlative decline in the frequency
with which alienations of land can be considered as elements in
"total" exchanges; the decline of an older style of monasticism in
which monastic communities and their lay benefactors were
bound together by enduring social ties and associated changes in
religious attitudes, notably those relating to death and prayers for
the dead; and, finally, changes in the internal organization of kin
groups that resulted in the concentration of more and more power
in the hands of the heads of families and, in some cases, their
heirs and wives.

By building on the preceding analysis and on the explanatory theories of previous scholars, notably Duby, it is possible to sketch out some of the main reasons why the *laudatio parentum* disappeared. If we think of the *laudatio* during the earlier phases of its history as being, among other things, a means by which at least some of a landholder's kin asserted or tried to assert their claims to his landed property and to prevent the fragmentation of what they considered their own inheritances, then we can see that when these functions were performed with even greater effectiveness by the *retrait lignager* and the *réserve coutumière*, the *laudatio* lost its reason for being, except in cases where more than the allowable portion, under the *réserve*, was being alienated. While landholders could do as they wished with a strictly limited portion of landed wealth, most of their land could not legally be alienated to the detriment of their kin, who also had the option of purchasing for themselves any land that was sold to people who did not belong to the *lignage*. At the same time, if we also view the *laudatio* as a mechanism used by alienors and alienees to stabilize land transactions by associating and implicating potential familial challengers in conveyances and by doing as much as was then possible to bar their claims, then we can see that in this respect, the *laudatio* became redundant during the period when the stability of land transfers was maintained by seals, warranty clauses, and various kinds of confirmations, and by officials associated with well-established courts.

The development of the *retrait*, the *réserve*, and new forms of warranty, however, would have been impossible, had it not been for other important changes in political institutions and in prevailing conceptions of kinship. The development of state institutions provided bureaucratized methods of adjudicating disputes and fostered a new kind of legal culture, in which laws were distinguished from other sorts of norms and in which increasingly well articulated distinctions could be made between different kinds of land, such as inheritances and aquisitions, and between different kinds of alienations, such as gifts and sales. Of the changes in medieval kinship that had the greatest bearing on the history of the *laudatio*, the most important, as Duby has argued, was the development of a sense of *lignage* that was not so universally operative in all spheres of aristocratic life as to drain cognatic (i.e. bilateral) kinship of all importance, but that had a profound impact on such matters as the control of land.[156] By strictly subordinating female kin, younger sons, and collateral kin to the interests of the head of the family and his heir, this change in upper-class kinship undercut the proprietary claims of many kinds of relatives who had once given the *laudatio parentum*. In addition, increasing acceptance of the idea that the *lignage* stretched back to the dead ancestor who had founded it and extended forward to include unborn heirs served, along with the concentration of authority in the hands of the *caput generis*, to legitimate the efforts of the head of the family to control the destiny of some of his land, even after he died, by making alienations on his own and by imposing an obligation to warrant on his unborn descendants. Once this position was reached, it made little legal sense, in most cases, for the *laudatio* to be procured.

While giving some indication as to why, by the later thirteenth century, if not earlier, the *laudatio* no longer served any obvious legal or practical function, the arguments just outlined do not explain why the participation of kin in the transfer of land was eventually seen to have no importance at all. For there was nothing to prevent an alienor's kin from joining in his conveyance, if they felt it important to do so. Although relatives may have given the *laudatio* without their approval or participation being recorded by scribes who knew it had no legal significance and were increasingly disposed to record only what was legally significant, it seems much more likely that over time, the interest of an alienor's relatives in participating in his alienations waned to the point where such participation seemed meaningless and therefore pointless.

Why should this have been so? By some point after the year 1200, the act of transferring land no longer possessed the kind of social significance and cultural meaning that it had once had. As increasing percentages of alienations took the form of sales, in which land was merely sold for money, it must have been rarer and rarer for land transfers to be the subject of intense interest on the part of the seller's kin, especially when they had the option of buying it back from the buyer. At the same time, the decline in the appeal of old-style Benedictine monasticism and in the significance of relationships between lay kin and monastic communities led to a situation in which even eleemosynary gifts of land were no longer necessarily associated as regularly as they had been before with important moments in the life of a kin group. As land was increasingly treated by nobles as a source of feudal rent, the process of alienating it lost much of its cultural import and became transformed into a more routinized activity, governed by technical, enforceable legal rules and endowed with less ceremony and cultural resonance.

To provide a more vivid, if inevitably impressionistic, sense of the legal, social, and cultural distance separating earlier and later land transfers by lay people to monastic communities, we can conclude this study of the participation of relatives in gifts to saints by comparing two documents recording land transfers made by lay people to the abbey of Marmoutier in two widely separated periods. Sometime around 1040, Salomon de Lavardin founded a priory of Marmoutier at Lavardin and, along with his wife, Adela, and with the consent of their two daughters, gave extensive rights in land to it.[157] More than two centuries later, in 1264, Johannes de Chenevelle and his wife, Ysabellis, conveyed to the same abbey some property in Villeau near Voves that formed part of the latter's inheritance.[158] The differences between these two transactions are striking.

In recording the eleventh-century transaction, a scribe of Marmoutier began in what was then a conventional way by explaining the religious basis of the gift made by Salomon and his wife:

How great and how very benign is the beneficence of God toward the human race, no mortal person can either imagine in his heart or express in words. For He invites us to return to him after the many sins we have committed, saying: "Come to me all you who labor and are burdened and I shall restore you." And in another place, the Evangelist urges us to acquire a heavenly and eternal dwelling from earthly and fleeting inheritances, saying: "Make unto you friends of the mammon of iniquity; that when you shall fail, they may receive you into everlasting dwellings."[159]

In 1264, the land transfer of Ysabellis was prefaced with a different, far more standardized formula, as the official of Chartres first greeted all those who would later inspect the document and then recorded a transaction carried out in his presence by the married couple just mentioned.[160]

More than two hundred years earlier, Salomon and his wife

Adela, acting with the approval of their daughters Matilda and Avelina, were supposedly mindful of the multitude of their sins, sorely afraid of the day of the last judgment, and desirous of being reckoned among those of the faithful to whom God on that day would say: "Come, ye blessed of my father, and possess the kingdom prepared for you."[161] Unlike the earlier scribe, the later one showed no interest in representing the motives that had led Johannis and Ysabellis to sell some land to a religious community. He only took care to note, using what were then established legal formulae, that Ysabellis, whose inherited property was being alienated, was acting "willingly, without compulsion" and had not been influenced in this matter by force or deceit.[162]

According to the earlier writer, it was for the salvation of their souls that Salomon and Adela gave to "the place of the most blessed Martin and to the monks serving Christ there" some land to be held in perpetuity. More specifically, Salomon and Adela made their gift with the understanding that the monks of Saint Martin would always commemorate them in prayer and would entreat God to show clemency for their sins, so that when they died, the destructive enemy would not rejoice in the possession of their souls and that instead, through the intercession of Saint Martin, the mercy of Christ would snatch them both from the hand of the devil and the punishment of hell and convey them to the joys of paradise.[163] In contrast to Salomon and Adela, Johannis and Ysabellis received no spiritual benefits of any sort from their monastic alienee and were merely given sixteen pounds of silver.[164] Moreover, whereas Johannis and Ysabellis apparently had no other contacts with Marmoutier, Salomon and various relatives of his and his wife's were involved in other transactions with the monks of Saint Martin.[165]

To guard against the troubling prospect that their gift would later be disturbed in a way that would doubtless have jeopardized the spiritual benefits that they hoped to receive, Salomon and Adela, according to the Marmoutier scribe, made the following stipulation, which was probably read publicly when this transaction was formalized. If any of their brothers and sisters, or *nepotes*, or other kin challenged the gift of this couple or if any other man or woman did so without quickly making humble satisfaction, he or she should incur the anger of almighty God, the Virgin Mary,

Saint Peter, Martin the glorious confessor of Christ, and all the elect of God and, with the traitor Judas and Simon Magus and with all enemies of the holy church of God, should descend into hell and burn there forever. On the soul of such a challenger all forms of hellish punishments should descend and his challenge should come to nothing. To make the gift even firmer and more stable, the charter recording it was marked with crosses by Salomon, Adela, Matilda, Avelina, and one son-in-law of Salomon and Adela's. Also listed as signatories were seventeen laymen; the abbot of Marmoutier and three of his monks; and, at the very top of the list, the bishop of Angers, who excommunicated in advance anyone who disturbed the gift.

The measures taken in 1264 to stabilize the sale to Marmoutier by Johannis and Ysabellis were very different. In addition to carrying out this transaction in the presence of an ecclesiastical functionary, who routinely handled such matters, the two vendors undertook to warrant and defend the alienated property against all men and women, and in the presence of the official, they obligated themselves and all their heirs to maintain, fulfill, and faithfully observe the transaction. Instead of being witnessed by monks and important lay people and instead of being approved by relatives of Johannis and Ysabellis, the sale was simply recorded in a document to which the official of Chartres affixed his seal. In this transaction, there was no place for the *laudatio parentum* or for any of the other ceremonial acts that had once figured prominently in exchanges between lay people and monastic communities.

Appendix

TABLE 3-1A: The *Laudatio Parentum*—Saint Aubin

	1000–1024	1025–49	1050–74	1075–99	1100–1124
Gifts					
Main Donor and					
Consenting	0%	36.3%	65.5%	62.2%	58.9%
Kin	0	4	19	56	43
Joint Gift	0%	0%	6.8%	7.7%	2.7%
	0	0	2	7	2
Laudatio	0%	36.3%	72.4%	70%	61.6%
Parentum	0	4	21	63	45
Total Gifts	1	11	29	90	73
Quitclaims					
Main Claimant					
and Consent-	—	0%	37.5%	50%	60%
ing Kin	0	0	6	17	18
Joint Quitclaim	—	0%	12.5%	8.8%	6.6%
	0	0	2	3	2
Laudatio	—	0%	50%	58.8%	66.6%
Parentum	0	0	8	20	20
Total Quitclaims	0	3	16	34	30
Transfers					
(Gifts and Quitclaims)					
Main Transferrer					
and Consent-	0%	28.5%	55.5%	58.8%	59.2%
ing Kin	0	4	25	73	61
Joint Transfer	0%	0%	8.8%	8%	3.8%
	0	0	4	10	4
Laudatio	0%	28.5%	64.4%	66.9%	63.1%
Parentum	0	4	29	83	65
Total Transfers	1	14	45	124	103

125–49	1150–74	1175–99	Undated	Total
71.8%	60%	60%	54.7%	60.1%
23	24	6	29	204
6.2%	7.5%	10%	11.3%	6.7%
2	3	1	6	23
78.1%	67.5%	70%	66%	66.9%
25	27	7	35	227
32	40	10	53	339
40%	33.3%	40%	18.1%	44%
4	3	2	2	52
20%	11.1%	0%	18.1%	10.1%
2	1	0	2	12
60%	44.4%	40%	36.3%	54.2%
6	4	2	4	64
10	9	5	11	118
64.2%	55.1%	53.3%	48.4%	56%
27	27	8	31	256
9.5%	8.1%	6.6%	12.5%	7.6%
4	4	1	8	35
73.8%	63.2%	60%	60.9%	63.6%
31	31	9	39	291
42	49	15	64	457

TABLE 3-1B: The *Laudatio Parentum*—Marmoutier

	1000–1024	1025–49	1050–74	1075–99
Gifts				
Main Donor	0%	56.7%	53.1%	54.4%
and Consenting Kin	0	21	76	55
Joint Gift	50%	13.5%	13.9%	12.8%
	1	5	20	13
Laudatio Parentum	50%	70.2%	67.1%	67.3%
	1	26	96	68
Total Gifts	2	37	143	101
Quitclaims				
Main Claimant	—	33.3%	37.1%	54.8%
and Consenting Kin	0	2	29	17
Joint Quitclaim	—	0%	15.3%	3.2%
	0	0	12	1
Laudatio Parentum	—	33.3%	52.5%	58%
	0	2	41	18
Total Quitclaims	0	6	78	31
Transfers				
(Gifts and Quitclaims)				
Main Transferrer	0%	53.4%	47.5%	54.5%
and Consenting Kin	0	23	105	72
Joint Transfer	50%	11.6%	14.4%	10.6%
	1	5	32	14
Laudatio Parentum	50%	65.1%	61.9%	60.5%
	1	28	137	86
Total Transfers	2	43	221	132

1100–1124	1125–49	1150–74	1175–99	Total
46.1%	71.4%	75%	82.6%	55.5%
24	10	6	19	211
17.3%	0%	0%	4.3%	12.8%
9	0	0	1	49
63.4%	71.4%	75%	86.9%	68.4%
33	10	6	20	260
52	14	8	23	380
56.4%	60%	100%	33.3%	45.8%
22	3	2	3	78
7.6%	0%	0%	11.1%	10%
3	0	0	1	17
64.1%	60%	100%	44.4%	55.8%
25	3	2	4	95
39	5	2	9	170
50.5%	68.4%	80%	68.7%	52.5%
46	13	8	22	289
13.1%	0%	0%	6.2%	12%
12	0	0	2	66
63.7%	68.4%	80%	75%	64.5%
58	13	8	24	355
91	19	10	32	550

TABLE 3-1C: The *Laudatio Parentum*—Noyers

	1000–1024	1025–49	1050–74	1075–99
Gifts				
Main Donor		45.4%	59.2%	54%
and Consenting Kin	—	5	32	128
Joint Gifts		36.3%	5.5%	13%
	—	4	3	31
Laudatio Parentum		81.8%	64.8%	67%
	—	9	35	159
Total Gifts	—	11	54	237
Quitclaims				
Main Claimant		—	66.6%	17.1%
and Consenting Kin	—	0	4	6
Joint Quitclaim		—	0%	34.2%
	—	0	0	12
Laudatio Parentum		—	66.6%	51.4%
	—	0	4	18
Total Quitclaims	—	0	6	35
Transfers				
(Gifts and Quitclaims)				
Main Transferrer		45.4%	60%	49.2%
and Consenting Kin	—	5	36	134
Joint Transfer		36.3%	5%	15.8%
	—	4	3	43
Laudatio Parentum		81.8%	65%	65%
	—	9	39	177
Total Transfers	—	11	60	272

1100–1124	1125–49	1150–74	1175–99	Total
55.5%	61.1%	66.6%	63.3%	56.7%
80	41	20	19	325
11.1%	10.4%	10%	26.6%	12.6%
16	7	3	8	72
66.6%	71.6%	76.6%	90%	69.2%
96	48	23	27	397
144	67	30	30	573
31.4%	52.1%	50%	80%	36.6%
11	12	4	4	41
22.8%	8.6%	12.5%	0%	20.5%
8	2	1	0	23
54.2%	60.8%	62.5%	80%	57.1%
19	14	5	4	64
35	23	8	5	112
50.8%	58.8%	63.1%	65.7%	53.4%
91	53	24	23	366
13.4%	10%	10.5%	22.8%	13.8%
24	9	4	8	95
64.2%	68.8%	73.6%	88.5%	67.2%
115	62	28	31	461
179	90	38	35	685

TABLE 3-1D: The *Laudatio Parentum*—La Trinité

	1000–1024	1025–49	1050–74	1075–99
Gifts				
Main Donor and		51.2%	32.3%	45.9%
Consenting Kin	—	20	22	28
Joint Gift		5.1%	19.1%	11.4%
	—	2	13	7
Laudatio Parentum		56.4%	51.4%	57.3%
	—	22	35	35
Total Gifts	—	39	68	61
Quitclaims				
Main Claimant		0%	25%	31.5%
and Consenting Kin	—	0	3	6
Joint Quitclaim		14.2%	16.6%	0%
	—	1	2	0
Laudatio Parentum		14.2%	41.6%	31.5%
	—	1	5	6
Total Quitclaims	—	7	12	19
Transfers				
(Gifts and Quitclaims)				
Main Transferrer and		43.4%	31.2%	42.5%
Consenting Kin	—	20	25	34
Joint Transfer		6.5%	18.7%	8.7%
	—	3	15	7
Laudatio Parentum		50%	50%	51.2%
	—	23	40	41
Total Transfers	—	46	80	80

1100–1124	1125–49	1150–74	1175–99	Total
73.3%	85.7%	57.1%	63.3%	50.9%
11	18	12	19	130
13.3%	4.7%	14.2%	10%	12.1%
2	1	3	3	31
86.6%	90.4%	71.4%	73.3%	63.1%
13	19	15	22	161
15	21	21	30	255
50%	60%	53.8%	55.5%	40%
5	6	7	5	32
10%	0%	23%	22.2%	11.2%
1	0	3	2	9
60%	60%	76.9%	77.7%	51.2%
6	6	10	7	41
10	10	13	9	80
64%	77.4%	55.8%	61.5%	48.3%
16	24	19	24	162
12%	3.2%	17.6%	12.8%	11.9%
3	1	6	5	40
76%	80.6%	73.5%	74.3%	60.2%
19	25	25	29	202
25	31	34	39	335

TABLE 3-1E: The *Laudatio Parentum*—Saint Vincent

	1000–1024	1025–49	1050–74	1075–99
Gifts				
Main Donor	0%	75%	30.8%	49.8%
and Consenting Kin	0	3	25	152
Joint Gift	100%	25%	14.8%	13.1%
	1	1	12	40
Laudatio Parentum	100%	100%	45.6%	62.9%
	1	4	37	192
Total Gifts	1	4	81	305
Quitclaims				
Main Claimant	—	—	26.6%	38.7%
and Consenting Kin	0	0	4	36
Joint Quitclaim	—	—	53.3%	12.9%
	0	0	8	12
Laudatio Parentum	—	—	80%	51.6%
	0	0	12	48
Total Quitclaims	0	0	15	93
Transfers				
(Gifts and Quitclaims)				
Main Transferrer	0%	75%	30.2%	47.2%
and Consenting Kin	0	3	29	188
Joint Transfer	100%	25%	20.8%	13%
	1	1	20	52
Laudatio Parentum	100%	100%	51%	60%
	1	4	49	240
Total Transfers	1	4	96	398

1100–1124	1125–49	1150–74	1175–99	Total
49.6%	40%	42.8%	33.3%	46.7%
69	2	3	1	255
11.5%	0%	14.2%	0%	13%
16	0	1	0	71
61.1%	40%	57.1%	33.3%	59.8%
85	2	4	1	326
139	5	7	3	545
44%	0%	66.6%	0%	39%
22	0	2	0	64
6%	0%	0%	0%	14%
3	0	0	0	23
50%	0%	66.6%	0%	53%
25	0	2	0	87
50	2	3	1	164
48.1%	28.5%	50%	25%	44.9%
91	2	5	1	319
10%	0%	10%	0%	13.2%
19	0	1	0	94
58.2%	28.5%	60%	25%	58.2%
110	2	6	1	413
189	7	10	4	709

TABLE 3-2A: The *Laudatio Domini*—Saint Aubin

	1000–1024	1025–49	1050–74	1075–99	1100–1124
Gifts					
Lord's Consent	0%	18.1%	27.5%	20%	21.9%
	0	2	8	18	16
Total Gifts	1	11	29	90	73
Quitclaims					
Lord's Consent	—	0%	12.5%	2.9%	10%
	0	0	2	1	3
Total Quitclaims	0	3	16	34	30
Transfers					
Lord's Consent	0%	14.2%	22.2%	15.3%	18.4%
	0	2	10	19	19
Total Transfers	1	14	45	124	103
Lord's Consent with Consenting Kin	—	100%	40%	34.6%	36%
	0	2	4	7	9
Total Lord's Consent	0	2	10	26	25

TABLE 3-2B: The *Laudatio Domini*—Marmoutier

	1000–1024	1025–49	1050–74	1075–99
Gifts				
Lord's Consent	50%	22%	37%	37%
	1	8	53	37
Total Gifts	2	37	143	101
Quitclaims				
Lord's Consent		0%	4%	3%
	—	0	3	1
Total Quitclaims	0	6	78	31
Transfers				
Lord's Consent	50%	19%	25%	28.7%
	1	8	56	38
Total Transfers	2	43	221	132
Lord's Consent with Consenting Kin	50%	19%	39%	48%
	1	2	32	29
Total Lord's Consent	2	12	83	60

1125–49	1150–74	1175–99	Undated	Total
21.8%	27.5%	20%	15%	21.2%
7	11	2	8	72
32	40	10	53	339
0%	0%	20%	0%	6.5%
0	0	1	0	7
10	9	5	11	118
16.6%	22.4%	20%	12.5%	17.2%
7	11	3	8	79
42	49	15	64	457
42.8%	36.3%	33.3%	31.2%	35%
3	4	1	5	35
7	11	3	16	100

1100–1124	1125–49	1150–74	1175–99	Total
35%	38%	50%	9%	34%
18	5	4	2	128
52	14	8	23	380
10%	20%	0%	0%	5%
4	1	0	0	9
39	5	2	9	170
24%	32%	40%	6%	25%
22	6	4	2	137
91	19	10	32	550
64%	43%	33%	100%	43%
16	3	1	1	85
25	7	3	1	200

TABLE 3-2C: The *Laudatio Domini*—Noyers

	1000–1024	1025–49	1050–74	1075–99
Gifts				
Lord's Consent		18.1%	31.4%	22.7%
	—	2	17	54
Total Gifts	0	11	54	237
Quitclaims				
Lord's Consent	—	—	0%	2.8%
			0	1
Total Quitclaims	0	0	6	35
Transfers				
Lord's Consent	—	18.1%	28.3%	20.2%
		2	17	55
Total Transfers	0	11	60	272
Lord's Consent with		50%	50%	34%
Consenting Kin	—	1	12	33
Total Lord's Consent	0	2	24	97

TABLE 3-2D: The *Laudatio Domini*—La Trinité

	1000–1024	1025–49	1050–74	1075–99
Gifts				
Lord's Consent		15.3%	11.7%	26.2%
	—	6	8	16
Total Gifts	—	39	68	61
Quitclaims				
Lord's Consent		14.2%	0%	10.5%
	—	1	0	2
Total Quitclaims	—	7	12	19
Transfers				
Lord's Consent		15.2%	10%	22.5%
	—	7	8	18
Total Transfers	—	46	80	80
Lord's Consent with		57.1%	30.7%	36.8%
Consenting Kin	—	4	4	7
Total Lord's Consent	—	7	13	19

1100–1124	1125–49	1150–74	1175–99	Total
24.3%	22.3%	23.3%	20%	23.7%
35	15	7	6	136
144	67	30	30	573
0%	0%	0%	0%	1%
0	0	0	0	1
35	23	8	5	112
19.5%	16.6%	18.4%	17.1%	20%
35	15	7	6	137
179	90	38	35	685
61.3%	66.6%	55.5%	66.6%	47.5%
27	12	5	8	98
44	18	9	12	206

1100–1124	1125–49	1150–74	1175–99	Total
0%	19%	14.2%	23.3%	17.2%
0	4	3	7	44
15	21	21	30	255
0%	10%	15.3%	0%	7.5%
0	1	2	0	6
10	10	13	9	80
0%	16.1%	14.7%	17.9%	14.9%
0	5	5	7	50
25	31	34	39	335
0%	20%	60%	57.1%	41%
0	1	3	4	23
0	5	5	7	56

TABLE 3-2E: The *Laudatio Domini*—Saint Vincent

	1000–1024	1025–49	1050–74	1075–99
Gifts				
Lord's Consent	0%	25%	41.9%	17.7%
	0	1	34	54
Total Gifts	1	4	81	305
Quitclaims				
Lord's Consent			0%	8.6%
	—	—	0	8
Total Quitclaims	0	0	15	93
Transfers				
Lord's Consent	0%	25%	35.4%	15.5%
	0	1	34	62
Total Transfers	1	4	96	398
Lord's Consent with		100%	26.6%	44.3%
Consenting Kin	—	1	12	35
Total Lord's Consent	0	1	45	79

1100–1124	1125–49	1150–74	1175–99	Total
23%	20%	14.2%	0%	22.5%
32	1	1	0	123
139	5	7	3	545
8%	0%	0%	0%	7.3%
4	0	0	0	12
50	2	3	1	164
19%	14.2%	10%	0%	19%
36	1	1	0	135
89	7	10	4	709
60.5%	0%	0%	—	43.2%
23	0	0	0	71
38	1	1	0	165

TABLE 3-3: Types of Familial Challengers, 1040–1099

	Saint Aubin	Marmoutier	Noyers	La Trinité	Saint Vincent	Total
S	34.4%	24.4%	20%	23.5%	46.1%	31.3%
	10	11	4	4	18	47
DH	20.6%	26.6%	30%	11.6%	10.2%	20%
	6	12	6	2	4	30
Nepos	13.7%	15.5%	15%		10.2%	12%
	4	7	3	0	4	18
B	6.8%	13.3%	25%	17.6%	5.1%	12%
	2	6	5	3	2	18
D	17.2%	2.2%		5.8%	5.1%	6%
	5	1	0	1	2	9
W	3.4%		5%	5.8%	12.8%	5.3%
	1	0	1	1	5	8
ZH		4.4%				1.3%
	0	2	0	0	0	2
Z		2.2%		11.6%		2%
	0	1	0	2	0	3
WH		2.2%				.6%
	0	1	0	0	0	1
Bast. Son		2.2%				.6%
	0	1	0	0	0	1
SS or DS		2.2%				.6%
	0	1	0	0	0	1
WB				5.8%		.6%
	0	0	0	1	0	1
F				5.8%		.6%
	0	0	0	1	0	1
WS			5%		2.5%	1.3%
	0	0	1	0	1	2
M				5.8%		.6%
	0	0	0	1	0	1
Other	3.4%	4.4%		5.8%	7.6%	4.6%
	1	2	0	1	3	7
Totals	29	45	20	17	39	150

TABLE 4-1: Types of Consenting Kin

	Saint Aubin	Marmoutier	Noyers	La Trinité	Saint Vincent	Total
F	.1% 1	.1% 2	.3% 6	.3% 3	.1% 2	.2% 14
FB	.1% 1	.3% 4	.1% 2	.5% 2	0% 0	.1% 9
M	3.7% 21	2.1% 26	2.7% 41	3% 16	3% 37	2.8% 141
MB	0% 0	0% 0	.06% 1	0% 0	.4% 5	.1% 6
MZ	.1% 1	0% 0	0% 0	0% 0	0% 0	.02% 1
MH	0% 0	0% 0	.06% 1	0% 0	.08% 1	.04% 2
FB or MB	.7% 4	.6% 7	0% 0	.7% 4	.2% 3	.3% 18
B	16.8% 93	12.5% 152	14.5% 218	14.5% 75	12.1% 148	13.7% 686
Bast. B	.1% 1	.06% 1	0% 0	0% 0	.08% 1	.06% 3
BW	.1% 1	0% 0	.4% 7	.5% 3	.3% 4	.3% 15
BS	.1% 1	0% 0	.3% 6	.7% 4	.3% 4	.3% 15
BD	0% 0	.4% 5	.5% 8	0% 0	0% 0	.2% 13
BS or BD	0% 0	.1% 2	.2% 4	0% 0	.1% 2	.1% 8
BDD	0% 0	.06% 1	0% 0	0% 0	0% 0	.02% 1
Z	4.1% 23	3.1% 38	3.7% 57	2.5% 13	2.4% 30	3.2% 161
ZH	1.6% 12	.4% 5	.5% 8	.8% 4	.9% 11	.8% 40
ZS	.1% 1	1.3% 16	1.3% 21	.5% 3	.1% 2	.8% 43

TABLE 4-1 *continued*

	Saint Aubin	Marmoutier	Noyers	La Trinité	Saint Vincent	Total
	.1%	0%	.06%	0%	.08%	.06%
ZSW	1	0	1	0	1	3
	.1%	.6%	.5%	0%	.08%	.3%
ZD	1	8	9	0	1	19
	0%	0%	.06%	0%	0%	.04%
ZDH	0	0	1	0	1	2
	0%	0%	.1%	0%	0%	.04%
ZS OR ZD	0	0	2	0	0	2
	33%	36.5%	30.8%	36%	35.9%	33.7%
S	183	442	464	187	437	1686
	0%	0%	0%	0%	.08%	.02%
Bast. S	0	0	0	0	1	1
	.5%	.3%	.7%	.7%	.1%	4.8%
SW	3	4	11	4	2	24
	0%	.1%	.4%	0%	.2%	.2%
SS	0	2	7	0	3	12
	0%	0%	.06%	0%	0%	.02%
SD	0	0	1	0	0	1
	0%	0%	0%	0%	.08%	.02%
SDS	0	0	0	0	1	1
	0%	0%	0%	0%	.08%	.02%
S Nepos	0	0	0	0	1	1
	5.2%	11%	9.1%	9%	5.7%	8.3%
D	29	134	138	47	70	418
	1.9%	.7%	.4%	.3%	1.4%	.9%
DH	11	9	7	2	17	46
	0%	.2%	.3%	0%	.08%	.1%
DS	0	3	5	0	1	9
	0%	0%	0%	0%	.3%	.08%
DS or DD	0	0	0	0	4	4
	0%	0%	.06%	0%	0%	.02%
DHM	0	0	1	0	0	1
	.5%	0%	.06%	0%	0%	.08%
DD	3	0	1	0	0	4

TABLE 4-1 *continued*

	Saint Aubin	Marmoutier	Noyers	La Trinité	Saint Vincent	Total
D or S	2.8%	.9%	3%	2.3%	4.1%	2.7%
	16	12	46	12	50	136
W	20%	18.2%	17.3%	18%	19%	18.3%
	111	221	260	93	231	916
WF	.5%	.06%	.13%	0%	.4%	.2%
	3	1	2	0	5	11
WM	0%	.06%	.2%	0%	0%	.08%
	0	1	3	0	0	4
WMB or WFB	.1%	.06%	0%	0%	.3%	.1%
	1	1	0	0	4	6
WB	.3%	.06%	0%	.5%	.9%	.3%
	2	1	0	3	11	17
W Bast. B	0%	0%	0%	0%	.08%	.02%
	0	0	0	0	1	1
WZ	0%	0%	.2%	0%	.2%	.1%
	0	0	4	0	3	7
WZH	0%	0%	.2%	0%	0%	.06%
	0	0	3	0	0	3
WZD	0%	0%	.06%	0%	0%	.02%
	0	0	1	0	0	1
WS	.7%	.2%	.3%	.3%	.7%	.4%
	4	3	5	2	9	23
WSW	0%	0%	0%	0%	.08%	.02%
	0	0	0	0	1	1
WD	0%	0%	.13%	.3%	.1%	.1%
	0	0	2	2	2	6
WDS	0%	0%	0%	0%	.08%	.02%
	0	0	0	0	1	1
WDD	0%	0%	.06%	0%	0%	.02%
	0	0	1	0	0	1
WBDH or WZDH	0%	.06%	0%	0%	0%	.02%
	0	1	0	0	0	1
WBD or WZD	0%	.06%	0%	0%	.2%	.08%
	0	1	0	0	3	4

TABLE 4-1 *continued*

	Saint Aubin	Marmoutier	Noyers	La Trinité	Saint Vincent	Total
Nepos	7.2%	2.4%	2.3%	3.3%	1.9%	2.9%
	40	30	36	17	23	146
Nepos W	.1%	0%	.06%	0%	0%	.04%
	1	0	1	0	0	2
Nepos D	0%	0%	.13%	0%	0%	.04%
	0	0	2	0	0	2
Neptis	0%	0%	.4%	0%	.1%	.1%
	0	0	6	0	2	8
Neptis H	0%	0%	.13%	0%	.08%	.06%
	0	0	2	0	1	3
Neptis S	0%	0%	.13%	0%	0%	.04%
	0	0	2	0	0	2
Neptis D	0%	0%	.13%	0%	0%	.04%
	0	0	2	0	0	2
Neptis HB	0%	0%	0%	0%	.08%	.02%
	0	0	0	0	1	1
Other	5.6%	2.4%	6.3%	3.3%	4.4%	4.5%
	31	30	96	17	54	228
Total Relatives	553	1208	1502	514	1214	4991
Total Male	306	707	857	303	707	2880
Total Female	195	447	557	178	387	1764
Total Relatives of Unidentified Sex	52	54	88	33	120	347
Total Transactions	262	426	685	212	466	2051
Average Consenting Group	2.11	2.835	2.192	2.42	2.605	2.433

TABLE 4-2: *Laudatio* by Sons and Daughters[a]

	Total Gifts[b]	Sons[c]	Daughters[d]	Sons and Daughters[e]	Sex Ratio[f]
Saint Vincent					
		89%	0%	10.7%	
1050–74	28	25	0	3	5:4
		71%	5%	23.6%	
1075–99	148	105	8	35	77:46
		62%	9%	28%	
1100–1124	74	46	7	21	48:34
		70.4%	6%	23.6%	1.54:1
Total	250	176	15	59	130:84
Saint Aubin					
		100%	0%	0%	
1050–74	12	12	0	0	—
		78%	9%	12%	
1075–99	32	25	3	4	10:6
		77%	11.4%	11.4%	
1100–1124	35	27	4	4	7:5
		81%	9%	10.1%	1.54:1
Total	79	64	7	8	17:11
La Trinité					
		76.9%	0%	23%	
1050–74	13	10	0	3	7:4
		64.7%	5.8%	29.4%	
1075–99	17	11	1	5	7:7
		90%	0%	10%	
1100–1124	10	9	0	1	2:1
		75%	5%	22.5%	1.33:1
Total	40	30	1	9	16:12

a. The total number of sons or daughters who approved gifts to Saint Vincent, Saint Aubin, or La Trinité during the periods 1050–74, 1075–99, and 1100–1124 is given in Table 3-1E, 3-1A, or 3-1D.

b. Total number of gifts in which *laudatio* is given by one or more sons, one or more daughters, or one or more sons and one or more daughters.

c. Number of cases and percentage of total cases in which *laudatio* was given by one or more sons and no daughters.

TABLE 4-2 *continued*

d. Number of cases and percentage of total cases in which *laudatio* was given by one or more daughters and no sons.

e. Number of cases and percentage of total cases in which *laudatio* was given by one or more sons and one or more daughters.

f. Total number of sons and total number of daughters who gave the *laudatio* in cases (given in Column IV) in which *laudatio* was given by one or more sons and by one or more daughters.

Notes

The following abbreviations are used in the notes:

A   *Cartulaire de l'abbaye de Saint-Aubin d'Angers.* 3 vols. Edited by Bertrand de Broussillon. Paris, 1903.

MB   *Marmoutier: Cartulaire blésois.* Edited by Charles Métais. Blois, 1889–91.

MD   *Cartulaire de Marmoutier pour le Dunois.* Edited by Emile Mabille. Châteaudun, 1874.

MM   *Cartulaire manceau de Marmoutier.* 2 vols. Edited by E. Laurain. Laval, 1911–40.

MP   *Cartulaire de Marmoutier pour le Perche.* Edited by Philibert Barret. Mortagne, 1894.

MV   *Cartulaire de Marmoutier pour le Vendômois.* Edited by de Trémault. Vendôme, 1893.

N   *Cartulaire de l'abbaye de Noyers.* Edited by C. Chevalier. Mémoires de la Société archéologique de Touraine, vol. 22. Tours, 1872.

T   *Cartulaire de l'abbaye cardinale de la Trinité de Vendôme.* 5 vols. Edited by Charles Métais. Paris, 1893–1904.

V   *Cartulaire de l'abbaye de Saint-Vincent du Mans.* Edited by R. Charles and Menjot d'Elbenne. Mamers, 1886–1913.

CHAPTER 1

1. MB 29, 52, 8, and 55.
2. In certain French charters scribes used the verb *laudare* to indicate that a donor's kin had approved his gift (Laplanche, *La réserve coutumière*, pp. 67–68 and p. 68 n. 1). In the charters considered in the present work scribes generally made the same point either by using verbs such as *annuere, auctorizare,* or *concedere,* or by indicating that the gift had been made with the *assensus, auctoramentum,* or *consensus* of the donor's relatives.
3. In a detailed analysis of Norman transfers of property during the eleventh century, Tabuteau distinguishes "permanent alienations"

from "conditional, temporary and posthumous alienations." In the first category, she places gifts, sales, and exchanges ("Transfers of Property," pp. 32–124). In the second, she includes conditional gifts, post-obit gifts, mortgages, rentals, grants for a purpose or a term of years, and grants of life estates ("Transfers of Property," pp. 125–247). Although it is therefore possible to distinguish several different kinds of alienations, it is dangerous, as Cheyette points out, to attach very much significance to the different terms that scribes sometimes used to describe land transactions, because what they wrote "may have corresponded only distantly to the actual relations between the parties involved" (Cheyette, "Invention of the State," p. 153).

4. See Brissaud, *History of French Private Law*, pp. 435–37; Chénon, *Histoire générale*, 1:457 and 2:272–78; Olivier-Martin, *Histoire du droit français*, p. 271; Ourliac and Malafosse *Histoire du droit privé*, 2:423–24; Ourliac and Gazzaniga, *Histoire du droit privé*, pp. 211, 245, 336.

5. See Auffroy, *Evolution du testament*, pp. 466–79; Olivier-Martin, *Histoire de la coutume*, 2:151–59, 379–81; Falletti, *Le retrait lignager*, pp. 12–53; Laplanche, *La réserve coutumière*, esp. pp. 66–116; Fontette, *Recherches*, pp. 64–68; Floren, *La vente immobilière*, pp. 122–25; Tabuteau, "Transfers of Property," esp. pp. 743–57. For a valuable review of earlier legal literature on the *laudatio*, along with discussion of work on similar practices outside France, see Partsch, *Das Mitwirkungsrecht*, pp. 1–18. For a brief note that places the *laudatio* in a broader context, see Dawson, *Gifts and Promises*, esp. pp. 29–35.

6. Duby, *La société*, esp. pp. 221–24, 366–68; Duby, "Lineage, Nobility, and Knighthood," pp. 69–71; Fossier, *La terre*, 1:262–73.

7. See Duby, *The Knight*, pp. 110–14; Bouchard, "The Structure of a Twelfth-Century French Family"; Donahue, "What Causes Fundamental Legal Ideas?"; Fossier, "Les structures de la famille"; Gold, *The Lady and the Virgin*, pp. 116–44; Hajdu, "Family and Feudal Ties"; Hajdu, "The Position of Noblewomen"; Herlihy, "Land, Family and Women"; Wemple, *Women in Frankish Society*, pp. 106–23.

8. Bloch, *Feudal Society*, pp. 130–41; Fossier, *Histoire sociale*, esp. p. 151; Fossier, *Enfance de l'Europe*, 1:101, 155, 318–20, 338–41; 2:906–19; Poly and Bournazel, *La mutation féodale*, pp. 184–92.

9. On the consent of heirs to the alienations of English feudal tenants, see Pollock and Maitland, *History*, 2:13–14, 251, 309, 311; Thorne, "English Feudalism"; Milsom, *Legal Framework*, pp. 109 n. 6, 122, 123, 132 and n. 3, 137–38; White, "Succession to Fiefs." On familial restraints on alienation in medieval Italy, see Calisse, *History of Italian Law*, pp. 534, 662–63; Becker, *Medieval Italy*, p. 21.

10. See, for example, Lewis, *Social Anthropology*, pp. 181, 188; Biebuyck, "Land Tenure," pp. 565–66.

11. For an argument in which medieval European kinship and land tenure are placed in a broad comparative context, see Goody, *The Development of the Family and Marriage*, where the *laudatio* and similar prac-

tices are discussed in chap. 6, esp. pp. 105, 107, 111, 120–125, 141–142.

12. For regional studies, see above, n. 6. Most of the works cited above in nn. 4 and 5 treat the *laudatio* throughout much, if not all, of France.

13. Evans-Pritchard, Introduction, p. vii. See also Mauss, *The Gift*, p. 1.

14. On Weber's distinction between "status" contracts and "purposive" contracts, see Kronman, *Max Weber*, pp. 96–117.

15. For a recent discussion of gift-exchange, together with a lengthy bibliography on this topic, see Gregory, *Gifts and Commodities*.

16. For examples of work by historians of medieval Europe who have utilized anthropological discussions of gift-exchange, see Duby, *Early Growth of the European Economy*, pp. 48–57; Gurevic, "Wealth and Gift-Bestowal"; Gurevic, "Représentations et attitudes"; Gurevic, *Les catégories de la culture*, pp. 219–41; Rosenthal, *The Purchase of Paradise*, p. 10 and passim; Little, *Religious Poverty*, pp. 3–8, 61–69; Geary, "Echanges et relations." See also the forthcoming work of Natalie Zemon Davis on gift-exchange in sixteenth-century France.

17. See the works cited above in nn. 4 and 5.

18. See for example, Olivier-Martin, *Histoire du droit français*, p. 272; Falletti, *Le retrait lignager*, p. 17.

19. Olivier-Martin, *Histoire du droit français*, pp. 272–73; Laplanche, *La réserve coutumière*, pp. 66–116 passim.

20. These scholars recognized, however, that true sales were very rare until the late twelfth century (see Olivier-Martin, *Histoire du droit français*, p. 272; Falletti, *Le retrait lignager*, pp. 16–17; Fontette, *Recherches*, pp. 13-29; Floren, *La vente immobilière*, p. 39). In addition, to deal with transactions that could not be easily classified as either gifts or sales, Fontette, for example, created a third category of "mixed acts" (see *Recherches*, pp. 19–28). Floren speaks of a confusion between sales and donations (see *La vente immobilière*, pp. 40–43). For a discussion of "mixed gifts" in later periods, see Dawson, *Gifts and Promises*, pp. 102–13. On donations and sales, see also Chevrier, "Evolution de la notion de donation"; and Chevrier, "Remarques sur la distinction."

21. For reviews of various different stages of this debate, see, for example, Dopsch, *Economic and Social Foundations*, pp. 1–29; Geiger, *The Theory of the Land Question*, pp. 103–75; Schlatter, *Private Property*, pp. 261–77; Beer, "Communism"; Latouche, "Fustel de Coulanges." On discussions of "primitive communism" by anthropologists, see Leacock, Introduction, pp. 18–25. Old debates about the origins of private property in land have recently been revived in Macfarlane, *Origins of English Individualism*. For a critique of Macfarlane's work, see White and Vann, "The Invention of English Individualism."

22. See, for example, Falletti, *Le retrait lignager*, pp. 8, 48.

23. See the works cited above in n. 6.

24. On the *retrait lignager*, see Falletti, *Le retrait lignager*; Génestal, "Le
retrait lignager"; Ourliac, "Le retrait lignager"; Cailteaux, "Note sur
le delai"; Cailteaux, "La solidarité familiale"; Brissaud, *History of
French Private Law*, pp. 433–44; Olivier–Martin, *Histoire de la coutume*,
2:319–30; Olivier–Martin, *Histoire du droit français*, pp. 272–73;
Fontette, *Recherches*, p. 66; Floren, *La vente immobilière*, pp. 121–40;
Ourliac and Malafosse, *Histoire du droit privé*, 2:421–39; Ourliac and
Gazzaniga, *Histoire du droit privé*, pp. 425–29. On the relationship be-
tween the *laudatio* and the *retrait lignager*, see, above all, Falletti, *Le
retrait lignager*; and, for a different view, Ourliac, "Le retrait lignager,"
p. 217. On the *réserve coutumière*, see Laplanche, *La réserve coutumière*;
Olivier–Martin, *Histoire de la coutume*, 2:304–18, 426; Olivier–Martin,
Histoire du droit français, pp. 272–73; Fontette, *Recherches*, pp. 69–70;
Ourliac and Malafosse, *Histoire du droit privé*, 2:422–39; Ourliac and
Gazzaniga, *Histoire du droit privé*, pp. 335–38.
25. See, in particular, Duby, *La société*; Duby, "Lineage, Nobility, and
Knighthood"; Duby, *The Three Orders*; Duby, *The Knight*.
26. In one form or another, these broad questions are addressed in
Bloch, *Feudal Society*; Duby, *La société*; Fossier, *Histoire sociale*; Fossier,
Enfance de l'Europe; and Poly and Bournazel, *La mutation féodale*.
27. Trends in debates on this issue have been discussed in Herlihy,
"Family Solidarity"; and Thirsk, "The Family."
28. Statistical analyses of the *laudatio* are presented in most of the works
cited above in nn. 6–8. On statistical analyses of data contained in
medieval documents, see Herlihy, "Numerical and Formal Analysis."
On the indices constructed by writers on the *laudatio parentum*, see
below, chap. 6.
29. Bloch, *Feudal Society*, p. 139. For comments on Bloch's view, see below, chap. 6.
30. See, above all, Duby, "Lineage, Nobility, and Knighthood." For other
statements of his position on the history of *lignages*, see Duby, "The
Structure of Kinship and Nobility"; "French Genealogical Literature";
"Structures familiales aristocratique"; and *The Knight*, pp. 87–106. For
some useful comments on the way in which Duby and others use the
term *lignage*, see Goody, *The Development of the Family and Marriage*,
app. 1 (pp. 222–39). On Duby's views on the long–term history of the
laudatio, see below, chap. 6.
31. Fossier, *La terre*, 1:262–73. On Fossier's views on the long–term history of the *laudatio*, see below, chap. 6.
32. Bloch, *Feudal Society*, pp. 130–33.
33. See, above all, Duby, "Lineage, Nobility, and Knighthood."
34. Fossier, for example, treats increases in the percentage of acts carried
out by individuals as evidence of "poussées d'individualisme dans la
famille" (*La terre*, 1:267), while Bloch treated the prevalence of the
laudatio as an index of the "economic solidarity" of the family (*Feudal
Society*, pp. 130–33). In both instances, evidence about the preva-

lence of a particular kind of action is transformed into evidence about pervasive features of society. This procedure is reminiscent of the one used by Durkheim in analyzing the more general concept of "social solidarity." In analyzing Durkheim's practice, Anthony Giddens points out that because "social solidarity is, according to Durkheim— as is the case of every moral phenomenon—not directly measurable, it follows that in order to chart the changing form of moral solidarity 'we must substitute for the internal fact which escapes us an external index (*fait extérieur*) which symbolises it.' Such an index can be found in legal codes" (*Capitalism and Modern Social Theory*, p. 74). On solidarity and/or individualism, see also ibid., esp. pp. 74–81; Lukes, *Individualism*, esp. pp. 3–16; and Harris, *The Rise of Anthropological Theory*, pp. 466–69, 500–501, 510, 515–16. The implications of this way of using quantitative evidence merit further analysis. On the similarities between Durkheim's views about the history of the family and the views of several writers on the history of the *laudatio*, see below, chap. 6.

35. See, for example, Laplanche, *La réserve coutumière*, pp. 102–14.

36. On the specific ways in which historians have linked the history of the *laudatio* with more general trends in medieval history, see below, chap. 6.

37. According to Fossier, for example, "le consentement des parents. . . a été nécessaire pour donner un acte juridique sa pleine valeur" (*La terre*, 1:262).

38. According to Auffroy, for example, it was a delicate matter to decide whether "l'intervention familiale était-elle de nécessité juridique, ou simplement d'usage et de convenance" (*Evolution du testament*, p. 468). According to Tabuteau, "it is . . . impossible to know whether the consent of relatives was legally necessary or merely desirable in practice" ("Transfers of Property," p. 744). See also Falletti, *Le retrait lignager*, pp. 47–48; Ourliac and Malafosse, *Histoire du droit privé*, 2:423–24.

39. Although writers on the *laudatio* have been reluctant to indicate what kinds of kin were supposed to give the *laudatio*, they have often shown little or no hesitation in characterizing the kin groups that gave it as "families." See, for example, Olivier–Martin, *Histoire du droit français*, p. 271.

40. For this argument, see below, chap. 4.

41. See, for example, Ourliac and Malafosse, *Histoire du droit privé*, 2:424; and below, chap. 5.

42. See, for example, Falletti, *Le retrait lignager*, p. 47.

43. Whereas Duby's writings on the *laudatio* (cited above in n. 6) focus on the Mâconnais, Fossier's main discussion (*La terre*) deals with Picardy. The work of Hajdu (cited above in n. 7) deals mainly with Poitou, while that of Gold (also cited above in n. 7) discusses Anjou. Among legal historians, Olivier–Martin (in *Histoire de la coutume*) and Fontette

(*Recherches*) base their remarks on studies of the Isle–de–France. Tabuteau treats Normandy ("Transfers of Property"), while Falletti (*Le retrait lignager*) and Laplanche (*La réserve coutumière*) consider all of northern France.

44. On several distinctive features of Fossier's method of constructing the quantitative history of the *laudatio*, see below, chap. 6, text accompanying nn. 49–64.
45. See Tabuteau, "Transfers of Property," pp. 22–26.
46. See Geertz, "Thick Description," where it is acknowledged, however, that what anthropologists call "our data are really our own constructions of other people's constructions of what they and their compatriots are up to" (p. 9).
47. It is hard to believe that a complex transaction involving many different people was not open to different interpretations by different people, especially after the fact. On the gap that must have existed between lay understandings of such ceremonies and what can be called "the official ideology," see Gurevic, "Représentations et attitudes," p. 524.
48. See Bloch, *Feudal Society*, pp. 75–77; Gurevic, "Représentations et attitudes," p. 525 and passim; Duby, *The Three Orders*, pp. 147–50.
49. See Cheyette, "The Invention of the State."
50. On the role of anthropology and, by implication, anthropological theory in historical writings about medieval gift–exchange, see above, n. 16. On the possible influence of Durkheim on discussions of "solidarity" by medievalists, see above, n. 34. On the influence of Marxism on the ideas of one major writer on the *laudatio parentum*, see Duby and Lardreau, *Dialogues*, pp. 117–20.
51. On rules, see, for example, Roberts, *Order and Dispute*; Comaroff and Roberts, *Rules and Processes*; Comaroff and Roberts, "The Invocation of Norms"; the essays collected in Collett, ed., *Social Rules*; Humphreys, "Law as Discourse," esp. pp. 243–44 and the works cited there; and Bourdieu, *Outline*, esp. pp. 1–71.
52. See below, chap. 3.
53. On some of these problems, see, for example, Barnard and Good, *Research Practices*, esp. pp. 161–89; Bourdieu, *Outline*, esp. pp. 1–71; Fox, *Kinship and Marriage*; Keesing, *Kin Groups*; Geertz and Geertz, *Kinship in Bali*, esp. pp. 153–69; and Schneider, *A Critique*.
54. On these problems, as they relate to the discussion of medieval French kinship, see below, chap. 4.
55. See below, chap. 5.
56. On this debate, see the works cited above in n. 21.
57. See below, passim, esp. chaps. 2, 3, and 5.
58. See below, chap. 6.
59. See below, chap. 6.
60. For the period 1000–1199 the cartulary referred to as A records 457 usable transactions, most of them concentrated in the period 1050–1174. See app., table 3–1A.

61. For the period 1000–1199 the cartularies referred to as MB, MD, MM, MP, and MV record 550 usable transactions, most of them concentrated in the period 1025–1124. See app., table 3–1B.

62. For the period 1000–1199 the cartulary referred to as N records 685 usable transactions, most of them concentrated in the period 1050–1149. See app., table 3–1C.

63. For the period 1000–1199 the cartulary referred to as T records 335 usable transactions, most of them concentrated in the period 1025–1150. See app., table 3–1D.

64. For the period 1000–1199 the cartulary referred to as V records 709 usable transactions, most of them concentrated in the period 1050–1124. See app., table 3–1E.

65. On the history of the *laudatio* during the late twelfth and thirteenth centuries, see below, chap. 6.

66. For outlines of the histories of these abbeys, see below, chap. 2.

67. On the history of these regions during the eleventh and earlier twelfth centuries, see, above all, Guillot, *Le comte d'Anjou*; Halphen, *Le comté d'Anjou*; Chartrou, *Anjou*; Boussard, *Le comté d'Anjou*; Boussard, "La vie dans le comté d'Anjou"; Boussard, "L'origine des familles seigneuriales"; Bur, *La formation du comté de Champagne*; Chédeville, *Chartres et ses compagnes*; Latouche, *Histoire du comté du Maine*. For brief, recent general accounts with useful bibliographical references, see Dunbabin, *France in the Making*, pp. 184–96, 310–12, 333–40; and Hallam, *Capetian France*, pp. 52–54.

68. See Yver, *Egalité entre héritiers*, pp. 110–21 and map appended to this work; Yver, "Les caractères originaux du groupe de coutumes de l'Ouest." Although some of the charters in MB concern areas not governed, according to Yver, by customs belonging to what he calls "le groupe tourangeau–angévin," others relate to the Vendômois, which was governed by these customs. Because the present study is concerned primarily with the relationships between lay kin groups and particular monastic communities during the eleventh and early twelfth centuries, rather than with the social and legal organization of particular regions, it seems best not to exclude evidence that illuminates the first of these two topics, even when it is partly concerned with territories that were, at least at a later time, governed by different customs.

CHAPTER 2

1. According to Duby, it was during "the five or six decades overlapping the year 1000" that lay gifts to churches were particularly large and numerous. This "enormous transfer of landed property—of which the Benedictine abbeys were the greatest beneficiaries, with episcopal churches in second place—was the most dynamic change affecting the European economy at this time" (*Early Growth of the Eu-*

ropean Economy, p. 15). For an estimate of the percentage of land held by ecclesiastical institutions at this time, see Herlihy, "Church Property."

2. See Little, *Religious Poverty*, p. 64. For a reference to precious objects that Robert the Pious gave to the cathedral of Sainte-Croix d'Orleans for his own soul and the souls of his sons, see Helgaud, *Vie de Robert le Pieux*, pp. 86, 87. For a reference to movable property given to one of the five abbeys considered in this study, see V 476.

3. In a small sample of transactions involving Saint Vincent of Le Mans, donors made their gifts to God and Saint Vincent (V 49); God, Saint Vincent, and Saint Lawrence (V 16); God, Saint Vincent, Saint Lawrence, and the monks serving God (V 23); God and the monks of Saint Vincent (V 35); Saint Vincent and Saint Lawrence (V 24, 31); the church of Saint Vincent and Saint Lawrence (V 39); Saint Vincent (V 15); Saint Vincent, the abbot, and the monks (V 36); the monks of Saint Vincent (V 30, 34). Similarly, gifts to the abbey of Saint Mary of Noyers were represented as being made to Saint Mary and the brothers serving God under her *patrocinium* (N 28, 30); Saint Mary, the abbot, and the monks serving God (N 29); God, Saint Mary, and the monks of Noyers (N 14); God and the monks of Saint Mary of Noyers (N 15); the monks of Saint Mary of Noyers (N 17). Because there seems to be no clear rationale for these variations in scribal usage at Saint Vincent or Noyers, it seems reasonable to assume that all of the donees mentioned in charters of a particular abbey at one time or another were generally considered to be parties to gifts to this religious establishment. On the significance of the fact that gifts to monasteries were represented as being made in these ways, see below, chap. 5.

4. On the different types of property given to three of the abbeys considered in this study, see Chédeville, "Notice historique," pp. 50–70; Gantier, "Recherches"; and Johnson, *Prayer*, pp. 56–61. On the kinds of properties given to medieval monasteries generally, see Lesne, *Les églises et les monastères*. On one kind of property commonly given to religious houses, see Constable, *Monastic Tithes*.

5. Grants of this kind were often made after at least some of the customs in question had been the subject of a dispute. See, for example, MB 28, 40, 42, 49, 74, 86, 93, 96; MD 1, 4, 13, 48, 61, 126; MV 30, 32, 87, 174. Of the many studies treating seigneurial exactions of this kind, see, for example, Lemarignier, "La dislocation du 'pagus' "; and Magnou-Noirtier, "Les mauvaises coutumes."

6. Outright gifts of serfs to monasteries were often made with the *laudatio parentum*. See Falletti, *Le retrait lignager*, pp. 19–20; Laplanche, *La réserve coutumière*, p. 85 n. 2. For examples of such gifts, see *Livre des serfs*, passim.

7. Chédeville, "Avant-Propos," pp. 9–10. On the history of this abbey, see also Chédeville, "Les restitutions des églises"; and works cited in *Liber Controversiarum*, at pp. v–vii.

8. Chédeville, "Avant-Propos," p. 10.
9. Ibid., pp. 10–11.
10. Ibid., p. 11.
11. See Chédeville, "Notice Historique," p. 36.
12. For a detailed picture of the lands held by this abbey in the late twelfth and thirteenth centuries, when the distribution of properties did not differ greatly from the distribution in earlier periods, see the map in *Liber Controversiarum*.
13. Chédeville, "Avant-Propos," p. 11.
14. See app., table 3-1E, which indicates that most transactions recorded in V date from the period 1050 to 1124. Although the second cartulary of Saint Vincent contains 355 documents for the period between c. 1100 and c. 1230 (see *Liber Controversiarum*, pp. 369–75), most of them come from the late twelfth or early thirteenth centuries and do not record many very valuable donations (Chédeville, "Avant-Propos," p. 11).
15. Chédeville, "Avant-Propos," p. 11.
16. On Marmoutier see Gantier, "Recherches"; Guillot, *Le comte d'Anjou*, 1:175–93; Oury, "La reconstruction monastique"; Martène, *Histoire de Marmoutier*.
17. Gantier, "Recherches," 53:95.
18. Ibid., 93; Guillot, *Le comte d'Anjou*, 1:173–74.
19. See Gantier, "Recherches," 53:93–94.
20. Ibid., pp. 94, 100.
21. See the map in Gantier, "Recherches," at 53:101.
22. On these benefactors, see below, chap. 3, text accompanying nn. 111–55.
23. Ibid., p. 93.
24. Ibid., p. 100. See also app., table 3-1B, which indicates that transactions recorded in the texts on which the present study, as well as Gantier's (see "Recherches," 53:94), is based became much less common after 1125.
25. See the map cited above in n. 21.
26. On the abbey of La Trinité de Vendôme, see Johnson, *Prayer*, which contains a useful bibliography. On the connection between La Trinité and Marmoutier, see below, n. 32 and accompanying text.
27. See Johnson, *Prayer*, pp. 8–23.
28. See ibid., pp. 8–23, 76–98. On some of the benefactors of La Trinité, see below, chap. 3.
29. Ibid., pp. 85–87.
30. See the table in ibid., at p. 87.
31. Ibid., p. 86.
32. On the connections between La Trinité and Marmoutier, see ibid., pp. 15, 30, 37, 61, 77, 88–89, 111–15, 123, 172–73.
33. On several lay people who had dealings with both abbeys, see below, chap. 3, text accompanying nn. 111–29.
34. On the abbey of Saint Aubin of Angers, see Guillot, *Le comte d'Anjou*,

1:129–62; and the works cited in Poirier-Coutansais and Souchon, *Guide des archives de Maine-et-Loire*, p. 173.

35. Guillot, *Le comte d'Anjou*, 1:138–65.
36. Ibid., 129–62 passim.
37. A rough picture of the abbey's holdings can be formed by locating the main priories, as listed in A.
38. On the relationship between the abbey and the counts of Anjou, see Guillot, *Le comte d'Anjou*, 1:129–62.
39. See app., table 3-1A, which suggests that there was a decline in benefactions after 1125.
40. On the abbey of Saint Mary of Noyers, see Chevalier, *Histoire de l'abbaye de Noyers*; and White, "Feuding and Peace-Making."
41. On the early history of the abbey, see N 1, 3; Chevalier, *Histoire de l'abbaye de Noyers*, pp. iv–vii.
42. On the site of Noyers, see Chevalier, *Histoire de l'abbaye de Noyers*, p. ix.
43. On Rainerius, see ibid., pp. xxxiii–xl; on Stephanus, see ibid., pp. xl–civ.
44. See White, "Feuding and Peace-Making."
45. On Evrardus, Andreas, and Gaufridus, see Chevalier, *Histoire de l'abbaye de Noyers*, pp. iv–xxxii.
46. See White, "Feuding and Peace-Making."
47. See app., table 3-1C, which suggests that donations to Noyers began to decline after 1150.
48. For gifts by bishops, see, for example, V 12, 28–29, 472. For gifts by priests, see T 91, 265; V 275, 302, 452, 468, 474, 508, 822; N 41, 60, 165; A 758; MV 22; MD 12. For gifts by canons, see T 137, 195, 570; V 83, 392; N 12; MV 58. Gifts made by these sorts of people have not been systematically considered in this study.
49. The following kinds of people, for example, made gifts to one or another of our monasteries: burgenses (A 336, 572); blacksmiths (T 47, V 287, MD 19); bakers (V 30, 133, 150); carpenters (T 60, V 111, 513); pelterers (T 168, A 127); famuli (T 156, V 82, 97); rustici (T 200, A 246, 258). Like gifts by clerics (see above, n. 48), gifts by the sorts of lay people just mentioned have been excluded from the sample of data on which the statistical tables in this study are based.
50. See, for example, Southern, *Western Society and the Church*, pp. 214–30.
51. Duby, *Age of the Cathedrals*, p. 69.
52. On the social class of benefactors of La Trinité, see Johnson, *Prayer*, pp. 85–98 and the table on p. 87. On the class status of monastic benefactors generally, see Southern, *Western Society and the Church*, pp. 214–50; Lawrence, *Monasticism*, pp. 60–65, 116–18; Lynch, *Simoniacal Entry*, pp. 3–18; Little, *Religious Poverty*, pp. 61–69; Duby, *Age of the Cathedrals*, pp. 54–73; Vauchez, *La spiritualité*, pp. 37–38; Rosenwein and Little, "Social Meaning," pp. 12–13.

53. Gifts and quitclaims in which women were the principal figures were relatively rare in the sample of transactions used for this study and are not systematically considered here. Gifts by women, acting as the principal donors, to one or another of the five abbeys, make up less than five percent of the total sample of gifts. On the role of women in making gifts to abbeys, see the works by Gold, Herlihy, and Hajdu cited above in chap. 1, n. 7.

54. For discussions of the main kinds of spiritual countergifts made to monastic benefactors and others they designated, see Berlière, "Les confraternités monastiques"; Berlière, "Les confréries bénédictines"; Constable, "The *Liber Memorialis* of Remiremont"; Cowdrey, *Cluniacs*, pp. 121–56; Cowdrey, "Unions and Confraternity"; Duby, *La société*, p. 222; Huyghebaert, *Les documents nécrologiques*; Johnson, *Prayer*, chaps. 1 and 3; Lawrence, *Monasticism*, pp. 60–65, 116–18; Little, *Religious Poverty*, pp. 61–69; Lynch, *Simoniacal Entry*; Southern, *Western Society and the Church*, pp. 214–30; Schmid and Wollasch, "Die Gemeinschaft"; and Wollasch, "Les obituaires." For a text indicating that material countergifts of money and goods were supposed to be valued less highly than the more intangible gifts of spiritual benefits, see A 269.

55. For examples of specific grants of anniversary masses, see V 75, 102, 366, 451, 538, 609; T 625; MV app. 32, 38. In these cases, the relatives for whom anniversaries were to be provided included the donor's father, mother, father's father, father's brother, brother, wife, and son.

56. See, for example, N 63, 78, 98, 115, 116; T 123. See also Johnson, *Prayer*, p. 91.

57. See, for example, N 115. See also Johnson, *Prayer*, p. 91.

58. Ibid., pp. 91, 159.

59. See V 261, 281, 288, 423, 791, 823; T 261.

60. For examples of grants of "society and benefit," see V 19, 32, 39, 49, 67, 73, 82, 93, 95, 105, 115, 128, 130, 148, 149, 150; MV 3, 19, 35, 38, 39, 41, 42, 43, 44, 45, 51, 55, 70. On the question of which relatives received this kind of countergift, see below, chap. 4, nn. 99–120 and accompanying text.

61. On grants of burial rights, see McLaughlin, "Consorting with Saints," pp. 49, 65; Johnson, *Prayer*, pp. 90, 163. For examples of such grants, see below, chap. 5, n. 123.

62. V 576.

63. See Johnson, *Prayer*, pp. 37–39, 41–43; Lynch, *Simoniacal Entry*, pp. 25–50. For examples, see N 55, 56, 75, 77, 79, 81, 82, 93, 115; and below, chap. 5, n. 129.

64. See MV 52, which records a dispute that arose when a benefactor did not get the kind of hospitality to which he thought he was entitled. See also MV 23, where it was stipulated by the donor that failures by the monks to provide him with adequate hospitality would not lead him to attack the abbey.

65. The monks of Saint Vincent gave the following kinds of goods to benefactors and/or consenting kin: grain of various kinds (V 108, 259, 397, 415, 426, 485, 491, 574, 617, 637, 678, 681, 686, 709, 816, 824); wine (V 347, 542, 642, 729); bread (V 79, 102, 644); nuts (V 745); horses (*caballus, equus,* or *palefredus*) (V 47, 142, 201, 264, 428, 438, 453, 617, 659, 670, 679, 739, 779–780); bulls (V 168); cows (V 234–35, 659); calves (234–35, 659); tunics (V 142, 201, 661); shoes (V 210, 404, 547, 591, 637, 691, 762, 806, 839); animal skins (V 367, 542); spurs (V 271, 404, 637); knives (V 637, 745); sheathes (V 745); saddles (V 419); armor (V 393); missals (V 202); gold by the ounce (V 303). At Saint Aubin, as at Saint Vincent, it was particularly common for horses to be used as countergifts (see A 241, 345, 637, 692, 771, 852, 869, 899). At this abbey, the following goods were also used as countergifts: shoes (A 245); stockings (A 350); wine (A 667, 671, 779); a fur coat (A 742); a mule (A 742).

   For examples of monetary countergifts to donors and/or consenting kin, see V 20, 50, 57, 58, 60, 79, 104, 121, 125, 126, 190, 196, 217, 223, 241, 277, 306, 322, 330, 338, 347, 349, 352, 372, 375, 403, 475, 495, 511, 524, 554, 568, 570, 578, 596, 599, 638, 641, 660, 675, 676, 692, 702, 708, 742, 749, 752, 784, 794. On countergifts consisting of goods or money, see below, chaps. 3, 4, and 5. See also Fontette, *Recherches,* pp. 20–28; Bloch, *Feudal Society,* p. 132; Duby, *La société,* p. 221 n. 15; and, for a particularly full discussion, Tabuteau, "Transfers of Property," pp. 497–511.

66. Other ways of looking at these transactions are provided in anthropological studies of gift-exchange, including Mauss, *The Gift;* Sahlins, "On the Sociology of Primitive Exchange"; Bourdieu, *Outline,* esp. pp. 4–6, 171–83; and Gregory, *Gifts and Commodities,* which contains a useful bibliography. On the use of anthropological approaches to the study of medieval European gift-exchange, see above, chap. 1, n. 16 and accompanying text.

67. See below, chap. 5.

68. See below, chaps. 5 and 6.

69. On the history of the view that the exchange of landed wealth for a place in a religious community constituted simony, see Lynch, *Simoniacal Entry.*

70. Gifts to Marmoutier, for example, were often made not only for the soul of the main donor, but also for the soul or souls of one or more of the following people linked to the donor: F (MV 17, 41, 62, 74, 124, 184); M (MV 17, 41, 62, 74, 107, 124, 187); B (MV 46, 116 *ter,* 183); W (MV 14, 17, 72, 130, 167, 187); S (MV 14, 62, 130, 167); D (MV 62); *parentes* (MV 72, 123, 167, 183, 187); *antecessores* (MV 185). For further discussion of the granting of spiritual benefits to a donor's kin, see below, chap. 4. For cases in which a donor's lord received spiritual benefits in return for the donor's gift, see A 174, 880; V 276. For gifts in return for which the donor's knight or man received these bene-

fits, see T 374, 526; V 773. For gifts that donors made for the souls of those whom they and/or their kin had killed, see V 224, 281, 350, 275; N 67, 157, 168, 199, 310, 320, 341, 355, 482, 564. On gifts of this last kind, see White, "Feuding and Peace-Making."

71. See MV 100; V 101, 224. Sometimes, we are told that a donor had been advised to make a gift by a particular person or persons, such as his father (V 528), his *fideles* (V 834), or an abbot (V 27, 706). Certain donors apparently made gifts in order to atone for a specific sin (see V 753–54; MV app. 40).

72. On biblical passages in which people were enjoined to give alms, see below, chap. 5, nn. 74–85 and accompanying text.

73. Luke, 16:9. On this passage, see Cowdrey, "Unions and Confraternity"; Little, *Religious Poverty*, p. 94; and below, chap. 5 at n. 85.

74. See MB 68, where this doctrine is clearly articulated; and Little, *Religious Poverty*, pp. 94–95.

75. For clear expressions of the view that saints were "friends" of God, see, for example, *Prayers and Meditations of Saint Anselm*, p. 127 (lines 19, 27, and 133) (Prayer to St. John the Baptist); p. 149 (line 280) (Prayer to St. Paul); p. 157 (line 22) (Prayer to St. John the Evangelist); p. 174 (line 23) (Prayer to St. Stephen); p. 184 (line 26) (Prayer to St. Nicholas); p. 199 (line 100) (Prayer to St. Benedict); p. 202 (line 50) (Prayer to St. Mary Magdelene); p. 207 (line 3) (Prayer by a Bishop or Abbot to the Patron Saint of his Church). On saints as intermediaries, see, for example, Brown, *The Cult of the Saints*; and Brown, "The Rise and Function of the Holy Man," pp. 143–52. On the use of familial imagery in representations of spiritual relationships, see below, chap. 5, nn. 103–106 and accompanying text.

76. On the propensity of monks at this time to represent salvation in terms that were identical with the ones used in representing landholding among the nobility, see Duby, *Age of the Cathedrals*, pp. 44, 45, 59.

77. This argument draws on Geary's discussion of saints in *Furta Sacra*, pp. 21–25. See also the works of Brown cited above in n. 75.

78. On the political and social benefits that lay nobles could hope to gain by patronizing two of the abbeys considered in this study, see Johnson, *Prayer*, chaps. 1 and 3; and White, "Feuding and Peace-Making."

79. Johnson, *Prayer*, chap. 1.

80. On the role of preexisting ties between Noyers and their noble neighbors in providing a framework for at least temporary settlements of feuds, see White, "Feuding and Peace-Making."

81. See above, n. 63, and below, chap. 5, n. 129.

82. See above, n. 61, and below, chap. 5, n. 123.

83. On the practice of admitting to monasteries men who were old and/or afflicted with mortal illness and wished to die as monks (generally known as monks *ad succurrendum*), see Johnson, *Prayer*, pp. 41–43; Lynch, *Simoniacal Entry*, pp. 27–36; and the works cited in Consta-

ble, *Medieval Monasticism*, p. 125. On the close association between many gifts to monasteries and death, see below, chap. 5.

84. On the visits of Hugo de Sainte-Maure to Noyers, where two of his sons were buried, see N 155, 307, 308. On the close relationship between this lord and the monks of Saint Mary, see White, "Feuding and Peace-Making," n. 165 and accompanying text.

85. On "symbolic capital" see Bourdieu, *Outline*, esp. pp. 171–83. In certain kinds of societies, he argues, "symbolic capital, which in the form of the prestige and reknown attached to a family and a name is readily convertible back into economic capital, is *perhaps the most valuable form of accumulation*" (*Outline*, p. 179; author's italics). "In its full definition," Bourdieu contends, "the patrimony of a family or lineage includes not only their land and instruments of production but also their kin and their clientele . . . , the network of alliances, or, more broadly, relationships, to be kept up and regularly maintained, representing a heritage of commitments and debts of honour, a capital of rights and duties built up in the course of successive generations and providing an additional source of strength which can be called upon when extra-ordinary situations break in upon the daily routine" (*Outline*, p. 178).

86. See Little, *Religious Poverty*, pp. 66–67; Duby, *Age of the Cathedrals*, pp. 30–53.

87. On the varied forms of influence exercised by the abbeys of Saint Aubin and Marmoutier, for example, see Guillot, *Le comte d'Anjou*, 1:129–62, 175–93.

88. According to Lynch, "religious houses were seigneuries, similar in many ways to their lay counterparts" (*Simoniacal Entry*, p. 4).

89. On the kinds of properties held by abbeys, see the works cited above in n. 4.

90. On disputes in which the monks of La Trinité were involved, see Johnson, *Prayer*, pp. 91–97. On litigation of Marmoutier, see White, "Pactum." For a brief note on disputes involving the abbey of Saint Vincent, see Chédeville, "Notice historique," pp. 36–37. On disputes involving religious communities in this period, see also Weinberger, "Les conflits"; Beitscher, " 'As the Twig is Bent' "; Geary, "Vivre en conflit"; White, "Claims to Inheritances" and the works cited in n. 7.

91. For a discussion of the ways in which gifts to saints supposedly provided men and women with a means to gain salvation, see below, chap. 5. For an interesting hypothesis that support for one major monastery, namely Cluny, constituted "a socially constructive response to anomie," see Rosenwein, *Rhinoceros Bound*, p. 106 and passim.

92. See, generally, Duby, *The Three Orders*.

93. On deathbed gifts, see below, chap. 5 at n. 122. For a gift supposedly made by a young knight as he died in battle, see below, chap. 4, text accompanying n. 189. For a gift that the lord of Marmande made to

Noyers shortly after committing what he supposedly recognized as a terrible sin, see N 67. For a gift that a knight made to Saint Vincent after plundering the abbey and taking one hundred pigs, see V 753 and 754. For a gift that the count of Vendôme made to Marmoutier after damaging the abbey's priory at Lavardin, see MV app. 40. On gifts that slayers and/or their kin made for the souls of homicide victims, see White, "Feuding and Peace-Making." Even in most of the cases just cited, it is not clear that gifts were made on the spur of the moment.

94. Before making a gift to an abbey, a donor sometimes discussed it with other people, such as his kin, his lord, his men, or monks from the community he planned to endow. See V 69 (W); V 528 (F, now a monk); 529 (lord and lord's wife); 834 (*fideles*); 630 (abbot and monk). See above, n. 71.

95. V 397, 413, 526.

96. V 243, 402, 531.

97. V 251, 444, 456.

98. V 570. See also N 17, which concerns the conclusion of a dispute.

99. As a *memoria* of a concord, a prior of Marmoutier redeemed some property that one of his abbey's adversaries had taken from a serf (MV 11).

100. Gifts made in the chapterhouse are numerous. See, for example, V 58, 79, 80. For gifts made *in claustro*, see V 110, 844. For gifts made *in cellerario*, see V 46, 581. For gifts made *ante cellerario*, see V 300, 696. For a gift made at the tomb of the donor's father, see MV app. 26.

101. On the objects used in liveries of seisin, see Le Goff, "Le rituel symbolique," esp. pp. 370–84. For useful lists of such objects, see ibid., pp. 415–19. On the objects used for this purpose in eleventh-century Normandy, see Tabuteau, "Transfers of Property," pp. 519–21. In cases recorded in the first cartulary of Saint Vincent, gifts were made *per baculum* (staff) (V 377, 738, 748, 786): *per cartam* (charter) (V 606); *per clochear de turribulo* (censer bell) (V 302); *per cultellum* (knife) (V 90, 140, 372, 550, 734, 801); *per candalabrum* (candlestick) (V 340); *per denarium* (penny) (V 398, 595); *per furcam* (fork) (V 481); *per guagium* (gage) (V 745); *per librum* (book) (V 261, 455, 633, 637, 649, 792, 821, 844); *per malleolum* (hammer) (V 105, 130, 271, 743); *per malleum* (hammer) (V 340); *per martellum* (hammer) (V 596, 650); *per textum* (book) (V 626); *per vademonium* (gage) (V 370, 696); *per wantos* (gloves) (V 200). On some if not all occasions, the monks kept these objects (see A 84, 111; MB 71), on which the name of the donor could be inscribed (see MV 50).

102. For brief descriptions of grants of confraternity or other spiritual privileges, see A 215; V 49, 137, 166, 188, 296–97, 314, 476, 540, 626, 640, 693, 791, 825. On the important role played by the hand in exchange rituals, see Le Goff, "Le rituel symbolique," p. 374.

103. For examples of this kind of ritualized kissing, see A 99, 65, 695; V 334, 743. On the measures taken when the donor was female, see A 695.

104. For a case in which the object placed on the altar was clearly identical with the one with which the abbot had given the donor the *societas* of the abbey, see V 626.

105. V 158, 188.

106. See below, chap. 5.

107. For references to occasions when gifts were approved by people who had apparently been absent from the ceremony at the church and who therefore confirmed the gift at some later time, see below, n. 129.

108. For evidence indicating that monks, at least, located participants in gifts temporally in relation to the Fall and the Last Judgment, see below, chap. 5, nn. 69–106 and accompanying text.

109. Several sons of a dying benefactor of La Trinité requested that the monks write the name of their elder brother into the abbey's martyrology, even though he was not present when his siblings approved their father's gift (T 123).

110. See Tabuteau, "Transfers of Property," pp. 584–601.

111. See V 372, 485; MV app. 36; MV 7; T 589. For other cases in which so-called *infantes* supposedly gave their consent, see T 205, 498, 503. It was sometimes provided that children would consent when they came of age (see T 711; A 304). Relatives who had supposedly approved gifts as children sometimes argued much later that they had been too young to give valid consent (see A 168).

112. See, for example, below, n. 129.

113. For cases in which the confirmation of an old gift provided an occasion for the making of a new one, see A 760; and V 66.

114. A 308. For gifts made to Noyers after the donors or their kin had been granted burial rights, see N 18, 566.

115. For a gift made to Saint Vincent on the feast of Saint Leonard, when the abbot of Saint Vincent had gone to a church dedicated to Saint Leonard, see V 529.

116. See V 59, 69, 105, 149, 155, 164, 166, 170, 176, 204, 207, 216, 247, 261, 263, 275, 357, 377, 395, 414, 458, 466, 480, 484, 496, 523, 526, 541, 542, 544, 635, 688, 721, 728, 735, 768, 778, 783, 791, 820; A 250, 311, 409–10, 412, 748, 759, 872, 897, 929. Gifts of this kind could cause trouble later, if the donor recovered from his illness and regretted his earlier generosity and/or his decision to become a monk. See V 395; and Lynch, *Simoniacal Entry*, pp. 32–33. For a case in which an abbot was reluctant to receive as a monk a dying man whose wife was absent and might later have objected to her husband's act, see A 683.

117. See, for example, V 635, 768, 776, 820; A 748.

118. V 110 (H), 147 (Z), 155 (S), 288 (S), 368 (S), 405 (WB), 516 (F), 664

(B), 823 (W); A 309 (M), 310 (S), 777 (W), 841 (B); MV 58 (M), 96 (F), 106 (F), 118 (F); T 374 (donor's man), 476 (W), 526 (donor's *miles*), 565 (B).

119. For examples, see MV app. 29 (S), 31 (S); V 61 (*nepos*), 71 (D's *filiolus*), 140 (WF), 313 (S), 329 (B), 354 (S), 355 (S), 384 (infant S), 428 (B), 447 (S), 464 (*nepotulus*), 640 (B), 646 (S), 682 (S), 728 (lord's S), 752 (B), 841 (S), 842 (S). It was sometimes provided at the time of the gift that a relative who might or might not be specifically identified could enter the abbey later on. See MV app. 59; V 491, 520, 533, 618.

120. See A 175, 228, 305, 319, 628, 683, 749; V 36, 59, 105, 156, 285, 304, 505. For confirmations carried out at the time of the father's burial, see A 749; V 393, 777.

121. On the possible implications of the close temporal association between gifts to saints and death, see below, chap. 5.

122. Although it was during the eleventh century, according to Bynum, that one sees the beginning of "the process of locating supernatural power most centrally in the eucharist, which the priest controlled" (*Jesus as Mother*, p. 10), the process had not advanced very far before 1200. On its history see Bynum, *Holy Feast*.

123. For examples, see *Livre des serfs*, passim.

124. See above, nn. 49 and 52 and accompanying text.

125. See above, nn. 5–6 and accompanying text.

126. See V 79, 135, 733. On saints as heads of families, see Geary, *Furta Sacra*, p. 22.

127. According to prevailing attitudes, "the relics *were* the saint" (Geary, *Furta Sacra*, p. 39; author's italics).

128. On the prevalence of this practice, see below, chap. 3.

129. For cases in which a donor's relatives approved or joined in his gift after he had made it, see, for example, A 175, 228, 305, 319, 683, 692, 749; V 36, 59, 105, 156, 285, 304, 393, 540, 626, 777. In several of these instances (V 393, 540, 777; A 749), the *laudatio* was given at the time of the donor's burial. In other cases, approval was given after a marriage (V 628), after a sermon by the abbot of the monastic beneficiary (V 143), or when the consenting relative was setting out for Jerusalem (V 505). For cases in which the time of the *laudatio* is unspecified but in which relatives consented in a location other than the one where the gift was made, see, for example, A 60, 105, 117, 118, 239, 409; MV 7, 11, 19; T 516, 521; and V 20, 47, 375, 391, 475, 495, 554, 596, 659, 755.

130. On the consent of the donor's lord and lord's kin, see below, chap. 3.

131. See, for example, V 784, 175.

132. See MV app. 26.

133. See above, nn. 90–95 and accompanying text.

134. For references to deathbed gifts, see below, chap. 5, nn. 118–22. On

the practice of dying in the presence of others see Ariès, *The Hour of Our Death*, esp. pp. 18–19.

135. See, for example, V 414.

136. One phase in the making of a gift was sometimes carried out in a marketplace (V 272–273, 584, 716); in front of a church (V 453); before the whole parish (V 576, 578); and under oak or elm trees (V 432, 640).

137. For cases in which people specifically identified as relatives of the donor allegedly witnessed gifts or quitclaims, instead of approving them, see, for example, N 8, 9, 16, 35, 59, 106, 108, 144, 159, 182, 188, 197, 238, 254, 379, 618; MV 99, 126; MD 123, 149; A 112, 124, 141, 758; T 136, 276, 307, 375, 463, 580; V 245, 499, 544, 597, 656, 714, 768. Because relatives not specifically designated as such witnessed gifts and quitclaims, it is not easy to decide how to measure the prevalence of the *laudatio parentum*. On this problem, see below, chap. 3.

138. A 415.

139. V 366.

140. For a charter stating that if any doubt should arise about the gift, the witnesses could testify about it, see MP 150.

141. In cases, such as the ones cited above in n. 129, where a donor's relatives approved his gift after it had first been made, the distinction between the approval of a gift and the independent confirmation of a gift is hard to make.

142. See, for example, MB 3; A 225.

143. See, for example, MB 8; V 139, 175, 180, 186, 303, 510, 576, 605, 607, 608, 719, 782. On this sanction, see Little, "La morphologie des malédictions."

144. See, for example, V 608. For cases in which excommunication was actually imposed, see V 188, 206, 524. On excommunication generally, see Vodola, *Excommunication*.

145. On the importance ascribed to anger and hostility in the political conflicts of this era, see White, "Feuding and Peace-Making," n. 13 and accompanying text.

146. On the force of proprietary imagery in monastic thought at this time, see Duby, *Age of the Cathedrals*, pp. 44, 45, 59.

147. See MV 3, 5, 11, 56, 60; V 115, 146, 182, 199, 303, 330, 337, 367, 377, 535, 564, 579, 626, 646, 656, 714, 740, 777, 788, 802, 806–7, 810. On warranty, see below, chap. 6 at n. 118 and the works cited there.

148. See A 73, 122, 272, 276, 336, 366; MD 19, 20, 97, 101, 150, 151, 152; MP 11, 16; V 17, 19, 50, 80, 85, 86, 111, 125, 182, 328, 385, 539, 563, 576, 578, 585, 637, 647, 651, 707, 748, 750, 794, 800. On pledges (sometimes known as *fidejussores*), see Tabuteau, "Transfers of Property," pp. 709–25.

149. See above, n. 56 and accompanying text.

150. See, for example, A 84, 111; MB 71.

151. According to Gurevic, "La charte était avant tout un objet" ("Représentations et attitudes," p. 533). On the degree to which the wording of charters was bound by tradition, see Cheyette, "Invention of the State," esp. pp. 150–56. On charters as symbolic objects see also Clanchy, *From Memory to Written Record*, pp. 203–8.
152. See MV 7, 106; V 160, 245, 204.
153. For an example of investiture *per cartam*, see V 606.
154. See A 798.
155. For cases in which charters were used as evidence in disputes, see, for example, A 70, 120, 325; MV 4, 57, 128; N 100; T 470; V 481.
156. For examples of charter illustrations, see Boinet, "L'illustration du cartulaire du Mont Saint-Michel." I am indebted to Katharine Gilbert for this reference. See also Maines, "Good Works."
157. See above, n. 64.
158. On disputes of this kind, see the works cited above in n. 90.
159. On the settlement of these disputes, see White, "*Pactum*."
160. On the approval of *concordiae* or *guerpitiones* by relatives, see below, chap. 3.
161. On the frequency with which settlements broke down, see Johnson, *Prayer*, pp. 93–97; and Geary, "Vivre en conflit," p. 1123 and n. 74.

CHAPTER 3

1. Bourdieu, *Outline*, p. 27.
2. Ourliac and Malafosse, *Histoire du droit privé*, 2:424.
3. On these questions, see below, chaps. 4 and 5.
4. For this plausible hypothesis, see Fossier, *La terre*, 1:263 n. 63.
5. Because it seems likely that earlier medieval charters, as Cheyette contends, "*do not* precisely record the accepted patterns of social life as it was lived and experienced" ("Invention of the State," p. 156; author's italics) and that surviving charters do not provide us with random samples of the gifts made to particular abbeys—not to mention land transfers in general—all statistics based on the study of charters from this period should be viewed skeptically. Whereas certain gifts and quitclaims were recorded over and over again in slightly different forms, records of other transactions may have been lost or discarded when the transaction in question broke down.
6. Bloch, for example, was exaggerating the prevalence of the *laudatio* when he claimed that charters "almost never" failed to mention it (*Feudal Society*, p. 132).
7. On these studies, see below, chap. 6.
8. In the calculation of the statistics given in the text and in app., tables 3-1A to 3-1E, two kinds of transactions have been distinguished from one another: gifts and quitclaims. In addition, gifts or quitclaims made by a single person with the consent of relatives are distin-

guished from so-called "joint gifts" or "joint quitclaims" that were made by two or more donors or quitclaimers, who were linked to each other by kinship and acted as equals. In some cases, joint gifts and joint quitclaims were approved by one or more additional relatives, whose role in the transaction was somehow subordinate to that of the joint donors or joint quitclaimers. Although gifts and quitclaims approved by relatives are distinguished, for certain purposes, from joint gifts and joint quitclaims, all four types of transactions are treated as instances of the *laudatio parentum*. Because distinctions between these various types of transactions are not always easy to make, there is yet another reason, in addition to the ones mentioned above in n. 5, for not attaching too much importance to seemingly precise statistical findings about the *laudatio*.

9. See app., tables 3-1A, 3-1B, 3-1C, 3-1D, and 3-1E.
10. For examples of quitclaims, see A 81, 93, 94, 96, 99, 104, 112, 120, 134, 137, 144, 149, 156, 160, 176; MV 2–12, 23, 25, 38–39, 42, 45–47, 51, 53, 54, 55, 56, 57, 60, 71, 75, 80; N 24, 25, 43, 52, 58, 65, 70, 71, 73, 76, 77, 79, 84, 89, 93, 96, 97; T 52, 79, 84, 89, 91, 100, 101, 134, 150, 151, 166, 168, 184, 216, 224, 232; V 15, 40, 51, 55, 64, 73, 78, 84, 104, 117, 119, 121–22, 123, 132.
11. On the frequency with which gifts or quitclaims were approved by the feudal lord or lords of the donor or quitclaimer, see app., tables 3-2A, 3-2B, 3-2C, 3-2D, 3-2E. These tables also give the percentage of feudal confirmations in which the lord was joined in his or her confirmation by one or more relatives. Because transactions in which a lord, with or without one or more consenting relatives, issued a general confirmation of gifts from his fief are included in the category of "Total Lord's Consent," totals in this category may exceed totals in the category of "Lord's Consent" to "Total Transfers." For examples of confirmations by lords, see A 32, 35, 68, 86, 114, 117–18, 121, 150, 153, 155, 160, 170, 172, 176; MV 1, 12, 17, 20, 21, 50, 72, 78, 90, 115, 117, 120, 121, 126, 129, 160; MV app. 2, 17, 18, 20, 21, 24, 25, 29, 30, 32; MD 22, 29, 31, 35, 42, 46, 49, 51, 58, 62, 65; MB 14, 22, 29, 52, 57, 66; N 1, 15, 27, 36, 40, 44, 45, 48, 50, 51, 63, 77, 82, 86, 88 *bis*; T 20, 21, 28, 52, 82, 102, 116, 185, 197, 220, 250, 272, 281, 323, 324; V 74, 79, 94, 109, 128, 137, 143, 155, 171, 174, 198, 212, 234–35.
12. See app., tables 3-1A, 3-1B, 3-1C, 3-1D, 3-1E.
13. See app., tables 3-2A, 3-2B, 3-2C, 3-2D, 3-2E.
14. See MD 22; MV app. 64; V 82, 548, 550; N 17, 34, 245, 516; T 12, 15; A 663. For a case in which the scribe indicated only that a gift was approved by the donor's *parentes* and *propinqui*, see V 15. See also Falletti, *Le retrait lignager*, p. 24.
15. See A 260, 878; MD 22; T 539, 550; V 59, 470, 570, 795, 803. On the term *amicus* see, for example, Bloch, *Feudal Society*, pp. 123–25.
16. In some cases, however, the ambiguity of certain kinship terms, such as *nepos* (which can refer to a son's or daughter's son, as well as to a brother's or sister's son), and/or the difficulty in definitively identify-

ing the antecedents of pronouns make it impossible to determine conclusively which kinds of relatives were giving the *laudatio*. On medieval kinship terms, see Depoin, *Les relations de famille*.

17. N 468. On several of the people mentioned in this charter, see N 532, 533.

18. MD 197.

19. MV 69. For other long, detailed lists of consenting relatives, see MD 111, 182, 184, 197; MB 185; T 521; V 495, 554–59, 802.

20. A 347.

21. V 682.

22. T 410. See also V 158 (donor's W pregnant); MD 160 (donor's W childless); V 684 (donor's D unmarried).

23. T 123.

24. V 585.

25. T 184. See also A 55 (second S absent); V 47 (Z absent from first ceremony but not second); V 332 (eldest S absent).

26. See T 205, 494, 498, 503, 589. On the consent of children and on disputes that could arise when people who had consented as children later contended that their approval was not binding (see, for example, A 304), see above, chap. 2, n. 111 and accompanying text, and below, chap. 3.

27. See A 382, 484; T 125; V 214, 222, 266, 279, 298, 388, 420, 484, 632, 696, 726, 727, 740, 755. On these promises, known as *clauses de portefort*, see Falletti, *Le retrait lignager*, p. 27.

28. See, for example, A 73, 122, 272, 276, 336, 366; V 17, 19, 50, 80, 85, 86, 111, 125, 182, 328, 385, 539, 563, 576, 578, 579, 585, 637, 647, 651, 707, 748, 750, 794, 800; MD 19, 20, 97, 101, 150, 151, 152; MP 11, 16; MB 25, 28, 42, 58, 67, 70, 76, 169; MV 30, 53, 60, 107, 120, 129, 170, 180; MV app. 21, 64. On this practice, see above, chap. 2, n. 148 and accompanying text.

29. See V 20, 196, and the cases cited in nn. 30 and 31 below. See also the cases (cited above, chap. 2, n. 129), in which relatives consent in a location other than the one in which the main gift was made.

30. V 437.

31. V 554–59.

32. See N 377. For an even clearer example, see du Broussay, *Cartulaire d'Azé et du Géneteil*, no. 6 (1096–1108). The hypothesis that relatives normally expressed their approval orally is strengthened by passages stating that they consented freely, speedily, and/or willingly (see A 807, 919; V 104, 522).

33. A 308.

34. See A 424; T 156, 299.

35. For charters that describe the act of signing, see V 160, 204, 245. On the frequency with which relatives appear as signatories to charters in the Mâconnais, see Duby, "Lineage, Nobility, and Knighthood," p. 69.

36. For an indication of how prevalent transactions of this kind, referred

to here as joint gifts (see above, n. 8), were, see app., tables 3-1A, 3-1B, 3-1C, 3-1D, and 3-1E. For examples, see A 60, 221, 237, 242, 313, 317, 354; MB 12, 17, 18, 82, 93, 97; N 84, 96, 114, 115, 119, 135, 142; T 102, 115, 135, 140, 160, 185, 186; V 35, 46, 47, 237, 703, 776, 834. As the tables just cited also indicate, certain quitclaims were supposedly made jointly by two or more kin, rather than by a single person acting with the approval of his kin. For examples, see A 134, 189, 137, 221, 827; MV 32, 51, 89, 91, 116 *ter*, 130; N 73, 76, 89, 96, 159, 181, 212, 224; T 216, 224, 532, 552; V 40, 55, 250, 408, 612, 753, 787.

37. For examples of joint gifts taking this form—which are less common than joint gifts of the type just noted and are not distinguished in the tables from the other kinds of joint gifts—see A 316, 884; MV 8, 173, 176; N 117, 139, 184, 249; T 221, 611, 626; V 75, 243, 430, 501. In these examples, the relatives playing what may have been a less prominent role were usually the children of one of the main donors. A few quitclaims also took this form (see MB 77; MV 169; N 254, 341, 409).

38. Whereas some scholars do not distinguish transactions of this kind from transactions involving a main donor and his consenting kin (see, for example, Fossier, *La terre*, 1:262), others attach considerable importance to this distinction (see, for example, Hajdu, "Family and Feudal Ties" and "The Position of Noblewomen").

39. On the possible significance of joint gifts, see below, chap. 5, especially the text accompanying nn. 16–19.

40. On this practice, see below, chap. 4, text accompanying nn. 99–120.

41. See above, chap. 2, n. 63 and below, chap. 5, n. 129.

42. For references to examples of this practice, see above, chap. 2, n. 65. In addition to the examples of countergifts cited there, see MB 25, 69, 75; MP 10, 31, 38, 54, 79, 88, 91, 166; MV 35, 50, 177, 185; N 43, 78, 89, 93, 119, 123; T 121, 128, 250, 277. For further discussion of countergifts, see below, chaps. 4 and 5.

43. Many of the examples cited above in n. 42 and in chap. 2, n. 65 indicate that material countergifts were supposedly made *"ex caritate"* or *"caritative."*

44. On the question of whether the recipients of these countergifts were simply being paid for something of value, see below, chaps. 4 and 5.

45. See below, n. 202 and accompanying text.

46. See A 247, 424; MD 54; V 51, 97, 452.

47. A 247.

48. A 252.

49. See V 253, 419, 703, 784. Similar purposes are ascribed to monks in making material countergifts to main donors (see V 245, 276, 322, 702).

50. V 223.

51. T 526.

52. V 367.

53. A 424.

54. A 272–73. For other cases in which relatives showed unwillingness to approve a gift, see A 319; MV 19, 71; T 127; V 25.
55. MP 64.
56. MD 46.
57. MD 134.
58. MD 59.
59. Falletti, *Le retrait lignager*, p. 26.
60. MP 11.
61. T 233 (1072). For comments on this document, see Falletti, *Le retrait lignager*, pp. 18, 37–38, 55–56.
62. See, for example, A 3, 8; N 464.
63. See above, chap. 2, n. 143 and accompanying text.
64. For this argument, which is used in a discussion of early medieval English charters, see Pollock and Maitland, *History*, 2:251–52. It is also possible that these clauses were included only because they formed part of a tradition that scribes slavishly followed.
65. For references to discussions of disputes of this kind, see above, chap. 2, n. 90. On the kinds of relatives who initiated familial challenges, see below, n. 162 and accompanying text and app., table 3-4.
66. See MV 3, 79, 92, 116; MB 77; MD 33, 132; T 52, 261. There were also cases in which a claimant simply asserted that the disputed property had once pertained to a kinsman of his (see MV 47, 49, 91). In yet another group of cases, the litigant claimed either that the disputed property was part of his own patrimony (see T 79, 143, 372) or that he had some sort of right to it (see T 330).
67. MV 79.
68. MV 57.
69. T 52.
70. T 261.
71. MD 33.
72. MD 132.
73. MD 117.
74. On the prosecution of disputes of this kind, see White, *"Pactum"*; and White, "Claims to Inheritances," n. 99.
75. MV 91.
76. MV 37.
77. MV 30.
78. For references to disputes over "evil customs," see above, chap. 2, n. 5.
79. On the ways in which disputes of this kind were carried on, see, in addition to the charters cited above in nn. 75–77, MV 6, 11, 32, 42, 47, 55, 56, 57, 92, 94, 108, 116, 128, 169; MV app. 22; MB 26, 28, 34, 39, 60, 74, 86, 98.
80. Livre Blanc de Saint-Florent de Saumur, fols. 36 *bis*-37.
81. On the peace-movements, see Fossier, *Enfance de l'Europe*, 1:313–18 and Poly and Bournazel, *La mutation féodale*, pp. 234–50, both of

which contain extensive references to recent work on this topic.

82. Guibert of Nogent, *Self and Society*, p. 63. For charters from our sample in which similar sentiments are expressed, see below, chap. 5, n. 94.

83. A number of these cases are discussed in White, *"Pactum."*

84. See MV 2, 6, 7, 9, 23, 42, 53, 56, 57, 75, 87, 94, 165, 173.

85. See MV 5, 25, 30, 32, 49; MB 46, 49.

86. See above, nn. 12–13 and accompanying text. For examples of material countergifts to relatives who approved quitclaims, see MV 3, 7, 8, 11, 12, 20; N 189, 212, 308, 446, 458, 459, 478, 487, 490, 491, 502. For examples of spiritual countergifts to relatives who approved quitclaims, see MV 8, 51, 183. It seems probable that just as relatives approved quitclaims less often than they approved gifts, relatives who approved quitclaims were less likely to receive countergifts than relatives who consented to new gifts.

87. On this practice, see above, n. 11 and accompanying text. On its later history, see Fontette, *Recherches*, pp. 70–74.

88. See app., tables 3-2A, 3-2B, 3-2C, 3-2D, 3-2E. Scribes recorded the *laudatio domini* as precisely as the *laudatio parentum*.

89. For a case in which a lord was granted one hundred *solidi*, see V 745. For a case in which the lord got ten pounds, see A 170. For other examples of payments to consenting lords, see A 153, 155, 176, 207, 212; V 203, 392.

90. See MV 4, 6, 25, 94; MB 26, 39, 89; MD 10, 23, 141.

91. See app., tables 3-2A, 3-2B, 3-2C, 3-2D, 3-2E.

92. See, for example, MV 32, 38, 55.

93. On the question of why lords consented to land transfers, see below, chap. 5.

94. See Thorne, "English Feudalism"; and Hyams, "Warranty and Good Lordship."

95. For cases in which donors promised to warrant, acquit, or defend their gifts, see V 115, 199, 303, 337, 535, 646, 656, 714. For cases in which people promised to warrant their quitclaims, see MV 3, 5, 11, 56, 60; V 182, 564, 579, 740.

96. For warranties by lords, see V 337, 626, 802, 806–7. For warranties by donors' relatives, see V 367, 777.

97. On the later history of warranty, see below, chap. 6 at n. 118. On warranty during our period, see above, chap. 2, n. 147 and accompanying text.

98. See above, chap. 2, nn. 142–48 and accompanying text.

99. A few litigants lost their cases outright. But most received something of value in return for a quitclaim. On eleventh- and early twelfth-century courts, see White, *"Pactum,"* and the works cited there on p. 281 n. 1.

100. On this issue, see below, pp. 106–14.

101. See below, nn. 173–74 and accompanying text; chap. 4, nn. 188–89

and accompanying text; and chap. 5, nn. 20–21 and accompanying text.

102. Cheyette argues brilliantly for the view that "rules were not expressed, and therefore not thought of, in the same way before the twelfth century as they were from that time on" ("Invention of the State," p. 158). This claim, which is generally consistent with the position taken here, does not completely rule out the possibility that norms were vaguely articulated in the form of general adages, or else were *implicitly* invoked.

103. See, for example, MV 32.

104. See Falletti, *Le retrait lignager*, pp. 20–23.

105. See MV 32.

106. See app., tables 3-1A, 3-1B, 3-1C, 3-1D, 3-1E.

107. On genealogical consciousness among the nobility during our period, see Duby, "The Structure of Kinship" and "French Genealogical Literature."

108. According to Poly and Bournazel, "il est peu probable . . . que ceux qui nous apparaissent dans les donations ou les ventes au Xe siècle comme disposant de leurs biens à titre individuel aient vécu en dehors de toute solidarité" (*La mutation féodale*, p. 187). This observation is applicable to later periods, including the ones in which the *laudatio* was very common.

109. For example, Hainricus de Vendôme, who made a gift to Marmoutier between 1037 and 1060 (MV 77), had a brother named Odo decanus, who witnessed one transaction involving the same abbey in c. 1050 (MV 30) and another dated 1037–62 (MV 83).

110. For example, Hugo Duplex I, who made a quitclaim to Marmoutier by himself in 1052–63 (MV 2), had numerous kin, some of whose gifts are discussed below, at nn. 130–55.

111. For some of his kinship connections, see figure 3-1. On Salomon and his kin, see MV 13, 87, 114; MV app. 11, 12, 13, 14, 17, 26, 27; MB 8–10, 101, 104, 105, 106; T 2, 21, 44 n. 1, 52, 53, 62, 63, 68, 100, 100 n. 1, 101, 182 n. 1, 263 n. 1. See also T 35, 36, 38, 40, 52, 62, 64, 77, 84, 89, 91, 94, 95, 107; and Johnson, *Prayer*, pp. 21, 112.

112. MV app. 11, 12.

113. MB 8, 9.

114. MV app. 14; MB 10; T 100, 101.

115. On Haimericus, see MV app. 26, 32. On Lancelinus, see MV 30, 31, 126.

116. On Odo Rufus and his kinship connections, see figure 3-2. See also MB 30; MV 121, 128; T 116, 118, 196, 197. On Odo, see also Johnson, *Prayer*, pp. 21, 89, 93.

117. MB 30.

118. MV 128.

119. T 196.

120. T 197.

121. MV 121; T 116, 118.
122. On Archembaldus, see figure 3-3. See also MV 17–19, 31, 40, 45, 50, 82, 91, 117; T 8, 52, 53, 58, 95, 104, 109. See also Johnson, *Prayer*, p. 12; Guillot, *Le comte d'Anjou*, 1:407–9.
123. MV 17, 19, 40, 45, 50; T 89, 104, 120.
124. T 52.
125. T 52.
126. T 53.
127. On Tetbaldus and his kin, see figure 3-4, which is based on MV 7–12; and T 100, 116.
128. T 100, 116.
129. MV 7–12.
130. The figure has been constructed from a large number of charters from MV and T.
131. MV 130, 167.
132. MV 105.
133. Gauscelinus, who probably died young; Adela I, who married Hugo Duplex I and bore at least ten children; Agnes, who married Gelduinus de Malliaco; and a second Adela (Adela II), who married Rogerius de Turre and was the mother of Fulcherius de Turre. See figure 3-5.
134. MV 30, 31.
135. MV 61; MV app. 58.
136. MB 94.
137. MV 111; MV app. 34.
138. MV 59.
139. MV 100.
140. MV 62. This gift, like Hugo's other conveyances and like the gift made by his wife, Adela I, was not approved by their daughter Emelina.
141. T 21.
142. MV 72; T 118.
143. T 143.
144. MV 23, 24.
145. MV 30, 31.
146. On this Gislibertus, see MV 6, 30, 31, 32, 62.
147. On the question of when matrilateral kin were most likely to approve gifts, see below, chap. 4, text accompanying nn. 179–89.
148. T 359.
149. T 280.
150. MV 186.
151. See MV 176.
152. MV 176.
153. MV 84.
154. Johnson, *Prayer*, p. 89. On Ingebaldus, see ibid., pp. 21, 89–90, 93; for his genealogy, see ibid. p. 193.

155. Ibid., p. 89; and MV 129.
156. For a case in which a monastic scribe openly acknowledged that a litigant had proved the rightfulness of his claim, see MV 25 (c. 1060). In this instance, however, the litigant in question was only contending that as the lord of the fief from which property had been given to Marmoutier, he should have authorized the gift and been paid for his approval. Because it is inconceivable that monasteries never lost a case outright, we must conclude that surviving samples of disputes involving abbeys are anything but random. See above, n. 5.
157. On payments to familial challengers, see above, nn. 83–86 and accompanying text.
158. See, for example, MV 47, 60, 91, 92, 116, 166, 172.
159. See, for example, MV 73, 177; MD 55.
160. See, for example, MV 16; MD 23, 24, 32, 114, 117. In yet another class of cases, lay litigants either asserted that a relative of theirs had held the disputed property sometime previously (see MV 47, 49, 91, 166), or made claims *"jure hereditario"* (V 615), *"jure propinquitatis"* (A 191), *"per lignagium"* (A 297), or *"per parentagium"* (A 388).
161. For a different view, see Falletti, *Le retrait lignager*, p. 26.
162. See app., table 3-2, which also lists the other types of relatives who initiated familial challenges.
163. See above, chap. 1, n. 38 and accompanying text.
164. For familial challenges that may have been founded on lies or misstatements of fact, see the cases cited above in n. 158.
165. On societies in which these requirements are not met, see, for example, Roberts, *Order and Dispute*, pp. 25–27 and passim; Ungar, *Law in Modern Society*, pp. 49–50; and Bourdieu, *Outline*, esp. pp. 22–30, 38–43.
166. See, for example, Bongert, *Recherches*, chaps. 1 and 2; Lemarignier, *La France*, pp. 99–160; Duby, "The Middle Ages," pp. 32–58.
167. See Cheyette, "The Invention of the State."
168. On these criteria, see Roberts, *Order and Dispute*, pp. 17–29.
169. See Cheyette, "Suum Cuique Tribuere"; Cheyette, "The Invention of the State"; Cheyette, "Custom"; Duby, "Evolution of Judicial Institutions"; Hyams, "The Common Law"; Hyams, "Trial by Ordeal"; Hyams, "Henry II and Ganelon"; Reynolds, *Kingdoms and Communities*, chap. 1; White, *"Pactum"*; and White, "Claims to Inheritances." On the legal order antedating the period in which a centralized, bureaucratized, and professionalized system of law developed in England, see Milsom, "Law and Fact"; Milsom, *The Legal Framework*; Milsom, *Historical Foundations*; and Palmer, "The Origins of Property."
170. Bourdieu, *Outline*, p. 17.
171. Ungar, *Law in Modern Society*, p. 49.

172. See White, "*Pactum*."
173. See ibid.
174. See Falletti, *Le retrait lignager*, pp. 20–23.
175. On this type of argument, see Roberts, *Order and Dispute*, p. 171.
176. For familial challenges of this type, see MV 3, 79, 92, 116; MD 33, 117, 132; T 52, 261.
177. See MV 3. For a case in which a man made a similar argument on behalf of his wife, see MV 57.
178. For somewhat similar arguments, see the works by Cheyette and Milsom, cited above in n. 169.
179. Bourdieu, *Outline*, p. 40.
180. See the works by Milsom, cited above in n. 169. On ordeals see Baldwin, "The Intellectual Preparation for the Canon of 1215"; Bartlett, *Trial by Fire and Water*; Brown, "Society and the Supernatural"; Colman, "Reason and Unreason"; Hyams, "Trial by Ordeal"; Morris, "*Judicium Dei*"; and Radding, "Superstition to Science."
181. See White, "Claims to Inheritances."
182. See Colman, "Reason and Unreason."
183. See Cheyette, "Suum Cuique Tribuere"; Duby, "The Evolution of Judicial Institutions"; Reynolds, "Law and Communities"; Reynolds, *Kingdoms and Communities*, chap. 1; White, "*Pactum*"; White, "Claims to Inheritances."
184. S. II-II, Q. 60, A. 6; translated in *The Political Ideas of St. Thomas Aquinas*, p. xvi.
185. *Statesman's Book*, IV.2; trans. Dickinson, p. 6.
186. Cheyette, "Suum Cuique Tribuere," p. 292.
187. See Bourdieu, *Outline*, p. 17.
188. This theme is explored, to take only the most obvious and best-known example, in *Raoul de Cambrai*.
189. Bourdieu, *Outline*, p. 17.
190. On the biblical injunctions to give alms that were cited in charter preambles, see below, chap. 5, nn. 74–85 and accompanying text.
191. On the central place of generosity or largess in the ideology of secular nobles during the earlier medieval period, see, for example, Duby, *The Early Growth*, pp. 45, 51–53, 56, 57, 66, 68–69, 108, 168, 201, 230, 232–33, 259, 270.
192. See Bloch, *Feudal Society*, p. 133; Falletti, *Le retrait lignager*, pp. 49–50. See also T 8 (1032–34).
193. On these passages, see below, chap. 5, nn. 74–85 and accompanying text.
194. On these clauses, see above, chap. 2. For a paraphrase of one such clause, see below, chap. 6.
195. See above, chap. 2, n. 145.
196. In a charter dated c. 1145, Roger de Valognes was recorded as stating that Archbishop Theobald of Canterbury "showed me by most reasonable and unanswerable arguments that a noble gentleman

who has the fee of six knights should give not only the third part of
a knight's land to God and holy church for the soul's health of himself and his kin, but the whole of a knight's land or more than that,
adding also that if this man's heir should try to take away the alms
which is interposed as a bridge between his father and Paradise, by
which his father may be able to pass over, the heir, so far as he may,
is disinheriting his father from the kingdom of heaven, and therefore should not obtain the inheritance which remains, since he who
has killed his father has proved himself no son" (Stenton, *The First
Century*, p. 39).

197. This story comes from a Life of Saint Hildeburg (*Cartulaire de l'abbaye
de Saint-Martin de Pontoise*, pp. 50–53). According to the story, when
Ascelinus, the eldest son of Saint Hildeburg, took back after his
mother's death some property that he had previously granted at her
request to the monks of Pontoise for her soul and the souls of other
kin of hers, she appears to him in a dream. When she sees him,
as she washes the feet of three paupers, she angrily asks him why
he has usurped the alms that she had given to the servants of God.
Attacking him with a knife, she warns him that unless he gives back
her inheritance, he will die. He gives back the land.

198. T 168. This case involves a pelterer. But it resembles another case involving a person of noble status (T 386).

199. See below, chap. 5, n. 61 and accompanying text.

200. *Garin le Loherain*, pp. 3–4. *Hervis de Metz* contains a similar opening:
"Today when a man falls ill, and lies down to die, he does not think
of his sons or his nephews or cousins; he summons the Black
Monks of St Benedict, and gives them all his lands, his revenues,
his ovens, and his mills. The men of this age are impoverished and
the clerks are daily becoming richer" (quoted in translation by
Goody, *The Development of the Family and Marriage*, p. 105).

201. V 481.

202. Dhuoda, *Manuel*, VIII.14:318–21. On the implications of this passage see Geary, "Echanges et relations."

203. See ibid.

204. On "symbolic capital," as explained by Bourdieu, see above, chap.
2, n. 85.

205. On familial challenges of these kinds, see Falletti, *Le retrait lignager*,
pp. 27–28.

206. On this kind of familial challenge, see above, n. 160.

207. On this development, see Lemarignier, *La France*, pp. 231–47;
Ourliac and Gazzaniga, *Histoire du droit privé*, pp. 50–80. Bongert,
Recherches; Lemarignier, "Les institutions ecclésiastiques," esp.
pp. 257–78.

208. These trends, which I hope to treat in a future study, are illustrated,
in one way or another, by the following charters from three of the
abbeys discussed here: A 473 (c. 1155), 866 (1151–89), 657 (1167), 664

(1167), 851 (1160–80), 475 (c. 1156), 913 (1157–89), 808 (1165–89), 923 (1178), 557 (ante 1180), 558 (1180), 675 (1195), 814 (1198), 570 (1199), 877 (1200); MD 189 (1178), 208 (1200), 209 (1201), 222 (1212); MB 167 (1157), 170 (1163), 175 (1178), 176 (1178), 187 (1190), 200 (late 12th or early 13th century); *Liber Controversiarum*, 267 (1148), 156 (1151–57), 251 (1151–57), 158 (1151–61), 13 (1161), 269 (1160–63), 76 (1145–87), 266 (1160–78), 61 (1176), 151 (1180–81), 38 (1180–87), 44 (1180–87), 138 (1184), 306 (1186), 65 (1180–87), 66 (1181–87), 67 (1181–87), 115 (1190), 146 (1191), 150 (1186–1200), 256 (1186–1200), 56 (post 1188 or 1198), 85 (1188–1203), 301 (1188–1201), 295 (1196), 337 (1196), 339 (1191–1202), 275 (1194–1200), 254 (1195–1201), 128 (1198–99), 130 (1199), 57 (1200).

209. *Glanvill* (c. 1189) and *Le très ancien coutumier* (very late 12th century).
210. See Lemarignier, *La France*, pp. 242–43; Ourliac and Gazzaniga, *Histoire du droit privé*, pp. 99–104.
211. On the decline and ultimate disappearance of the *laudatio*, see below, chap. 6.
212. Cheyette, "Suum Cuique Tribuere."

CHAPTER 4

1. Were gifts approved only by the donor's very close kin, such as his wife, siblings, and children? Or was the *laudatio* also given by more distant relatives, such as the donor's father's brother's children or matrilateral uncles? If more distant kin approved gifts to saints, did they do so as frequently as close kin did? Or was their involvement in these transactions unusual? Are there other ways of distinguishing between relatives who often gave the *laudatio* and those who did not?
2. When historians assert that a man's gift was normally approved by his relatives, are they indicating that he was normally joined by a large, cognatic kindred, by a coherent group of patrilineal kin, by a group that included his affines, or by a conjugal family made up of his wife and children? If all of these groups are mentioned in charters, which ones appeared most frequently?
3. See Bloch, *Feudal Society*, p. 132.
4. See above, chap. 1, nn. 5–7.
5. See app., table 4-1.
6. For similar lists constructed on the basis of other documents, see Laplanche, *La réserve coutumière*, pp. 77–85; Falletti, *Le retrait lignager*, pp. 23–24; Fontette, *Recherches*, pp. 65–66; Tabuteau, "Transfers of Property," p. 747. See also Partsch, *Das Mitwirkungsrecht*, pp. 19–22.
7. For these terms, see Herlihy, "Mapping Households," p. 12. On the problems involved in distinguishing and describing different sorts of kin groups, see, in addition to the article of Herlihy's just cited, Laslett, Introduction, esp. pp. 28–34. It should be noted, however, that unlike the present study, the articles by Laslett and Herlihy are

concerned, largely if not exclusively, with coresidential kin groups.

8. V 391, 455, 25. For other examples of complex consenting groups, see, in addition to the twelve other kin groups pictured in figure 4-1, A 105, 266, 350, 745, 897; MB 58, 65, 144, 185, 194; MD 26, 111, 133, 197; MV 69, 122; MV app. 21, 36; N 105, 130, 192, 242, 368, 458, 468, 638.

9. See above, chap. 3, nn. 109–55 and accompanying text.

10. The main sources used in constructing figure 4-2 are N 14, 17, 18, 27, 31, 36, 37, 40, 65, 75, 87, 88 *bis*, 90, 103, 114, 115, 119, 130, 137, 138, 156, 157, 158, 159, 173, 176, 181, 186, 196, 197, 201, 203, 246, 263, 375, 377, 378, 447.

11. N 14.

12. N 18.

13. N 27.

14. N 31.

15. N 17.

16. N 37.

17. N 176.

18. N 40.

19. N 137.

20. N 186.

21. N 181.

22. N 36.

23. N 90.

24. N 75. This gift was also witnessed by Hubertus's grandson (*nepos*) Petrus, who was probably a son of Aldeburgis and Simon.

25. N 132.

26. N 87.

27. N 138.

28. N 114.

29. N 115.

30. N 115.

31. N 196.

32. N 156.

33. N 265.

34. N 114.

35. N 159.

36. N 119.

37. N 130.

38. N 67. On the unusual circumstances surrounding this gift, see White, "Feuding and Peace-Making," case 1.

39. N 88 *bis*, 103, 157, 173, 246.

40. N 378. For references to Acharias's son Goffridus Medla, see N 263, 377, 447. For references to Acharias's other son, Burchardus, see N 377, 378.

41. N 375, 377.

42. N 377.

43. N 377, 378.
44. N 87, 114, 115, 130, 138, 156, 159, 176.
45. N 114.
46. N 197.
47. N 158, 203.
48. N 201.
49. See above, chap. 3, nn. 109–55 and accompanying text.
50. See above, chap. 3, nn. 30–31 and accompanying text.
51. On some of these problems, see above, chap. 3, nn. 5, 8, 16, 38.
52. The list presented in app., table 4-1 differs from the lists cited above in n. 6. Instead of using modern English, French, or German kinship terms, it employs a notation that distinguishes between different kinds of cousins, uncles, and so forth.
53. Among affines, WB appears most often. See app., table 4-1.
54. Relatives who witnessed a gift should probably be distinguished from relatives who approved it or joined in it, because the former may have participated in the transaction less actively than the latter. This distinction, however, remains problematic.
55. Because certain gifts, however, were approved by people designated in charters as *consanguinei, parentes,* or *amici* and because others were made with the consent of people who were said to be members of the donor's *parentela* or *genus,* it is possible that relatives more distant than first cousins occasionally gave the *laudatio.*
56. See figure 4-3, which represents a factitious kin group made up of all types of kin that ever gave the *laudatio* in at least one instance.
57. See below, n. 63 and accompanying text.
58. In order to show how frequently relatives of a given type gave the *laudatio,* some historians give a percentage arrived at by dividing the number of transactions for a given period in which one or more relatives of that type gave the *laudatio* by the total number of transactions for that period (see, for example, Duby, "Lineage, Nobility, and Knighthood," pp. 69–71). The method used in app., table 4-1 is to present a percentage arrived at by dividing the total number of relatives of that type who gave the *laudatio* in transactions during a given period by the total number of relatives who gave the *laudatio* during that same period.
59. Although figures arrived at through the second method described above in n. 58 undoubtedly exaggerate the role of those relatives, such as sons, who often approved gifts in large numbers, they have the virtue of giving some weight to the fact that in particular cases, relatives of one kind often gave the *laudatio* in greater numbers than relatives of another kind.
60. In recorded cases at Saint Aubin, brothers and *nepotes* gave the *laudatio* more often than they did at other abbeys. See app., table 4-1. It should be noted, however, that because it is not always possible to identify consenting uncles or cousins as matrilateral uncles or cous-

ins, the figures given in the text and in app., table 4-1 are even more suspect than such figures usually are.

61. See app., table 4-1.

62. See above, n. 57 and accompanying text.

63. The ratio of male to female kin types would be even higher if we were to include in the calculation given in the text those types of kin that are represented in our sources by general or ambiguous Latin terms, such as *amicus* (N 155, 499; V 609); *cognatus* (A 352, 818; MB 144; MV 162; N 306; V 616); *consanguineus* (MB 194; N 599); *consobrinus* (A 56, 646; T 52; V 94, 596, 694, 726); *propinquus* (V 15); *heres* (A 571; MB 181; MV app. 40; V 292); *parens* (MB 82; N 17, 79, 454, 474; T 125–29; V 15, 40). When used in the singular, the first five of these terms always refer to male kin, and given the masculine bias of consenting kin groups, it seems reasonable to suppose that groups of *cognati, consanguinei, propinqui, parentes,* or *amici* were composed mainly of males. It is often possible to determine whether the ambiguous term *sororius* (A 127; MV 183; N 467; T 444, 589; V 375, 690) refers to a sister's husband or a wife's brother. In samples from individual abbeys, the numbers of male and female types of kin vary. But the pattern identified in the text still holds.

64. See above, nn. 11–47 and accompanying text; and chap. 3, nn. 109–55 and accompanying text.

65. A 45, 137, 143, 174, 279, 314, 342, 254, 919.

66. A 317, 170, 374, 768, 888.

67. A 55, 165, 170, 172, 237, 242, 270, 311, 313, 317, 342, 354.

68. A 329.

69. A 101, 228, 243, 381, 391, 749, 770, 920.

70. A 302, 383, 637, 742, 907.

71. A 270, 276.

72. A 878.

73. A 311, 378.

74. A 122, 239, 340, 409–10, 827, 899, 902, 903.

75. A 60.

76. A 901.

77. A 828.

78. A 280.

79. A 221, 245, 655, 848, 900.

80. A 59, 141, 667.

81. A 652.

82. A 826.

83. A 56.

84. V 40, 44, 55, 115, 175, 229, 234–35, 237, 245, 250, 304, 385, 394, 408, 432, 476, 480, 484, 535, 548, 549, 570, 609, 612, 640, 651, 661, 698, 703, 704, 752, 753, 783, 787, 791, 834, 35, 46, 303, 776, 47, 391.

85. V 35, 46, 303, 776.

86. V 47, 391.

87. In the Saint Aubin sample, for example, sons make up 31 percent of the total group of *laudatores*, while the figures for wives, brothers, daughters, and sisters are, respectively, 21, 18, 5, and 3 percent. In the Saint Vincent sample, sons make up 35 percent of the total group of *laudatores*, while the figures for wives, brothers, daughters, and sisters are, respectively, 19, 10, 4, and 4 percent.

88. See the essays in Goody, *The Developmental Cycle*. See also Herlihy, "Mapping Households."

89. See above, chap. 3, nn. 122–26 and accompanying text.

90. See above, chap. 3, nn. 116–21 and accompanying text.

91. See above, chap. 3, nn. 127–29 and accompanying text.

92. See above, chap. 3, nn. 111–15 and accompanying text.

93. In charters of La Trinité, for example, only 5 out of 23 consenting groups that included wives also included one or more siblings of the main donor.

94. See above, chap. 3, nn. 106–8 and accompanying text.

95. For cases in which the *laudatio* was given in a location other than the one in which the gift in question was made, see A 60, 105, 117, 118, 212, 239, 409–10; MV 7, 11, 19; T 516, 521; V 20, 47, 121–22, 136, 342, 375, 391, 392, 475, 495, 513, 547, 554–59, 596, 621, 635, 637, 641, 659, 660, 738, 742, 755, 811, 825.

96. See the story about the gift of Odo Donkey Neck in chap. 3, n. 31 and accompanying text.

97. See above, chap. 3, nn. 51–54 and accompanying text.

98. See above, chap. 3, nn. 65–86 and accompanying text.

99. For the period 1075–99, see V 94, 150, 183, 196, 331, 351, 437, 479, 514, 551, 760; A 239, 637, 765, 899.

100. See, for example, V 480, 483, 484, 573, 607, 640.

101. On monastic prayers for the dead, see McLaughlin, "Consorting With Saints," esp. chaps. 3–5.

102. See Duby, "French Genealogical Literature" and "The Structure of Kinship"; and Génicot, *Les généalogies*.

103. In forty-two cases in which "society and benefit" was granted to at least one person linked to the donor by kinship or marriage, wives were included fourteen times; sons, mothers, and brothers thirteen times each; sisters five times; and daughters three times.

104. See V 280, 340, 495, 528, 596.

105. The fact that daughters appeared much less often than sons and that sisters did so much less often than brothers suggests that groups of spiritual beneficiaries, like consenting groups, manifested a clear masculine bias. The same finding may also indicate that the responsibility for securing prayers for a woman rested mainly with the kin group into which she married, rather than with the one into which she was born.

106. The same privilege was also granted to a sister, a sister's husband, a daughter, and a *nepos*.

107. MV 17.
108. MV 19.
109. MV 184.
110. MV 59.
111. MV 62.
112. MV 84.
113. MV 126.
114. MV app. 12, 26, 27, 32.
115. Between 1075 and 1099, the average size of groups receiving "society and benefit" from Saint Vincent was 2.07, whereas the average size of the groups that approved gifts or quitclaims to the same abbey during the eleventh and twelfth centuries was 2.6 (see app., table 4-1).
116. See, for example, V 148 (W); V 39 (M); V 150 (B); V 475 (S); V 208 (W, S); V 224 (M, B); V 689 (W, S, F); V 662 (M, F, B, Z).
117. V 528, 552, 596, 606.
118. See V 19, where a grant of "society and benefit" was made to all the donor's *parentes*, both living and dead.
119. Aside from donors themselves, the usual recipients of burial rights were spouses (see V 267, 350) and sons (V 550, 572). This finding indicates that in cases where men or women did not procure burial rights for themselves, the people most likely to assume this duty were their husbands in the case of women, or their parents (usually fathers) in the case of men.
120. Along with donors themselves, the main recipients of this privilege were the sons of donors. It may have been rare for people to procure this privilege for their brothers, for example.
121. On material countergifts, see above, chap. 2, n. 65 and accompanying text and chap. 3, nn. 40–49 and accompanying text. See also below, chap. 5.
122. MD 70.
123. MV 50.
124. MV 177.
125. MV 11.
126. N 242. For other instances in which different amounts of money were given to different consenting kin, see V 20, 47, 51, 57, 58, 72, 79, 121–22, 125, 126, 139, 146, 158, 190, 196, 203, 220, 224, 228, 241, 287, 290, 306, 337, 347, 349, 372, 375, 392, 431, 449, 475, 495; MD 31, 38, 54, 88, 91, 166; MV 185; MB 25, 69, 75.
127. For references to countergifts of these kinds, see above, chap. 2, n. 65.
128. MB 100.
129. V 745. This interpretation of the countergifts is conjectural. On the problems involved in reading medieval symbols, see Bynum, "The Body of Christ."
130. MD 66, 166.

131. MB 75; MD 38; MV 35.
132. MV 185.
133. MD 88, 177.
134. MV 50.
135. MD 54.
136. MV 177.
137. MD 154.
138. MB 25.
139. The figures might be higher if certain charters specified kin more precisely.
140. At Noyers between 1050 and 1074, not one of the forty-six consenting groups whose composition is clearly described included more than three types of relatives. In documents from this abbey for the period from 1025 to 1199, only 40 out of the 556 well-documented consenting groups (or 7.1 percent) included more than three types of kin.
141. See app., table 4-1.
142. See Laslett, Introduction, p. 58.
143. See app., table 4-1.
144. See app., table 4-1.
145. No examples of this kind can be found in the charters of Noyers.
146. See app., table 4-1.
147. Because the origin of donated property is so rarely specified, there is no point in trying to provide quantitative evidence on this issue.
148. See Gold, *The Lady and the Virgin*, pp. 125–30.
149. V 202.
150. V 675.
151. A 276.
152. A 350. Several charters from Marmoutier and La Trinité also suggest that affines were especially likely to approve gifts of other kinds of property in which their kinswoman had an interest. When Warinus and his wife Mainburgis gave La Trinité some property pertaining to the latter's *patrimonium*, provision was made for the possibility that her brother would not approve the gift (T 205). When Isembardus Peregrinus, acting on behalf of his wife Gundrada, challenged a gift that Gundrada's first husband had previously made to Marmoutier, he did so expressly on the grounds that the disputed property was Gundrada's *dotalicium* and had been alienated without her approval (MV 44).

It is noteworthy, however, that wives either gave the *laudatio* or made gifts jointly with their husbands much more often than their own kin did. Even though wives, like affines, were especially likely to approve gifts of the kind just discussed, it is virtually certain either that they did so much more often than affines did or that they approved many gifts of property in which their interests were less obvious than they were in the cases already mentioned. This implies that a married woman, while remaining linked to her own kin in certain ways, became incorporated, at least for the purpose of making gifts to abbeys, into the kin group(s) of her husband. The rarity with which married sisters and daughters gave the *laudatio* (see app., table 4-1) implies that a married woman was much more likely to approve gifts made for the souls of her new kin group than she was to consent to gifts in return for spiritual benefits accorded to members of her own natal kin group.

153. V 108.
154. T 327.
155. On the parties in this case, see figure 3-5.
156. MV 32.
157. See above, chap. 3, n. 61 and accompanying text.
158. See above, n. 93 and accompanying text.
159. On fraternities, see below, chap. 6.
160. For examples, see above, figure 4-2.
161. See app., table 4-1.
162. See above, nn. 54–55 and accompanying text.
163. See above, chap. 3, nn. 30–31 and accompanying text.
164. See above, chap. 3, n. 61.
165. See app., tables 3-2A, 3-2B, 3-2C, 3-2D, 3-2E.
166. It was very rare for a group of this kind to include anyone other than the lord's wife and/or son(s).
167. See Falletti, *Le retrait lignager*, pp. 20–23.
168. For reasons already given above in n. 147, statistical analyses of this problem would be bootless.
169. See above, nn. 65–83 and accompanying text.
170. See the preceding discussions of gifts by people represented on figures 3-1 to 3-5 and 4-2.
171. See app., table 4-2.
172. See below, chap. 6, n. 16 and accompanying text.
173. On the process through which the position of daughters and younger sons was progressively weakened during the eleventh and twelfth centuries, see the arguments of Duby, which are discussed below in chap. 6 in the text accompanying nn. 65–82.
174. See the preceding discussions of gifts by people represented on figures 3-1 to 3-5 and 4-2.
175. This practice may foreshadow the later custom known as the *réserve coutumière*, on which see below, chap. 6.
176. See above, chap. 3, nn. 52–54.
177. On intrafamilial conflict in this period, see below, chap. 6.
178. See above, chap. 3, n. 202.
179. MV 126.
180. MM, Château-du-Loir, no. 11.
181. V 67.
182. V 823.

183. V 419.
184. N 130.
185. V 175.
186. MV app. 57.
187. T 541.
188. V 502.
189. N 139.
190. Bloch, *Feudal Society*, pp. 136–39.
191. For studies of household size and composition in later periods of European history and in other regions, see, for example, the essays in Laslett, *Household and Family*.
192. For a critique of these efforts, see Goody, *The Development of the Family and Marriage*, esp. pp. 222–39.
193. Bloch, *Feudal Society*, p. 138.
194. T 548 (*omnis parentela*); A 209 (*genus omne*); N 621 (*omnes de genere*). See also Falletti, *Le retrait lignager*, p. 21.
195. See, for example, the passages from Old English law codes, which are discussed in Lancaster, "Kinship"; and Loyn, "Kinship in Anglo-Saxon England."
196. For a recent discussion of this topic, see Duby, *The Knight*.
197. See White, "Feuding and Peace-Making" and the literature cited in n. 1.
198. See Duby, "The Structure of Kinship" and "French Genealogical Literature"; and Génicot, *Les généalogies*.
199. Boissevain, *Friends of Friends*, p. 9. For a critique of this view, see ibid., pp. 3–23.
200. Geertz and Geertz, *Kinship in Bali*, p. 154, where this view is criticized.
201. Bourdieu, *Outline*, p. 27 and passim.
202. On this distinction, see Keesing, *Kin Groups*, pp. 9–11.
203. Geertz and Geertz, *Kinship in Bali*, p. 154.
204. On Bourdieu's concept of "symbolic capital," see above, chap. 2, n. 85. On "rules" of kinship as idioms in which claims of various kinds are made, see Humphreys, "Law as Discourse," pp. 243–44 and the literature cited there.
205. On the distinction between "practical" and "official" kinship, see Bourdieu, *Outline*, pp. 33–38. For the view that medieval kinship groups could assume different forms at different times, see Bullough, "Early Medieval Social Groupings"; Charles-Edwards, "Kinship"; Leyser, "Maternal Kin"; Meinhard, "The Patrilineal Principle"; and, above all, Goody, *The Development of Marriage and the Family*.
206. See, above all, Duby, "French Genealogical Literature" and "Structures familiales."
207. In many *chansons de geste*, for example, it is clear that noblemen were supported by both matrilateral and patrilateral kin. See Bloch, *Feudal Society*, pp. 133–43.

208. See, generally, Duby, *Medieval Marriage*.

209. See White, "Feuding and Peace-Making."

CHAPTER 5

1. See MD 165, 166. According to A 275, a donor secured the consent of various relatives to guard against the possibility that a relative or successor of his would challenge his gift.

2. See app., tables 3-1A, 3-1B, 3-1C, 3-1D, 3-1E.

3. For a case in which a gift was delayed because of the donor's son's refusal to approve it, see above, chap. 3, n. 52 and accompanying text.

4. See app., tables 3-1A, 3-1B, 3-1C, 3-1D, 3-1E.

5. See, for example, Falletti, *Le retrait lignager*, pp. 9–10, 14, 22, 53; and Ourliac and Malafosse, *Histoire du droit privé*, 2:423. Falletti attributes the lack of clarity in customs relating to the *laudatio* to the fact that mutually incompatible Roman and Germanic principles of land tenure had not, at this time, been effectively harmonized (*Le retrait lignager*, pp. 9–10). For a different view, see above, chap. 3.

6. When considering regions where both feudal and allodial holdings were common, it is important to bear in mind that although previous writers have concluded that *all alienations*, whatever the status of the alienated property, were governed by the *laudatio parentum* (see, for example, Laplanche, *La réserve coutumière*, p. 99), this finding does not rule out the possibility that the normative basis of the *laudatio* varied, depending upon the tenurial status of land alienated with the consent of kin. On Norman allods, see Tabuteau, "Transfers of Property," pp. 309–18.

7. The relationship between the *laudatio parentum* and the development of heritability of fiefs has been most fully discussed by Laplanche (*La réserve coutumière*, pp. 66–114, esp. pp. 71–73, 101–6).

8. On the question of whether cognatic kin groups can serve as enduring, property-holding corporations, see, for example, Keesing, *Kin Groups*, pp. 91–97; and Freeman, "On the Concept of the Kindred."

9. See, for example, Leacock, Introduction, pp. 18–20, where the question of whether hunting bands held land communally is discussed in relation to the question of whether all group members had general access to land. When dealing, at the level of theory, with the real rights of feudal tenants and their lords, at least during certain periods, it may be reasonable to follow Maitland in arguing that because "the tenant in demesne owns the land," while "his immediate lord owns a seignory," "we have not many ownerships of one thing, we have many things each with its owner" (Pollock and Maitland, *History*, 2:4). But when we confront the question of whether relatives of the tenant in demesne have any rights in the land held by the tenant and whether, together with him, they hold land communally, it is

hard to locate any evidence that will help us to resolve this problem definitively.

10. According to a more extreme form of the individualist theory, the *laudatio parentum* was nothing more than a practical precaution whose prevalence tells us nothing about laws or customs regulating the alienation of land. On this theory, see above, chap. 3.

11. See Laplanche, *La réserve coutumière*, pp. 102, 110. Compare Maitland's argument in Pollock and Maitland, *History* 2:13.

12. Laplanche, *La réserve coutumière*, pp. 104–6, 110. See also Pollock and Maitland, *History*, 2:13, 15, 250 ff., 308–13.

13. Laplanche, *La réserve coutumière*, p. 106; Pollock and Maitland, *History*, 2:310.

14. Falletti, *Le retrait lignager*, p. 47.

15. Laplanche, *La réserve coutumière*, pp. 104–6. This passage concerns the basis of the *laudatio* during the twelfth century, when the consent of the donor's heir was assuming more prominence.

16. Olivier-Martin, *Histoire du droit français*, pp. 271, 274.

17. Duby, *La société*, pp. 215–27; Ourliac and Malafosse, *Histoire du droit privé*, 2:423; Laplanche, *La réserve coutumière*, pp. 102–3, 110.

18. Ourliac and Malafosse, *Histoire du droit privé*, 3:61.

19. This theory is adapted from Thorne's argument about the reason for the heir's consent in England ("English Feudalism").

20. On this problem, which merits further study, see Gold, *The Lady and the Virgin*, pp. 116–44; and Hajdu, "The Position of Noblewomen."

21. See Olivier-Martin, *Histoire du droit français*, p. 273; and Falletti, *Le retrait lignager*, p. 37.

22. On the prevalence of this form of consent, see app., tables 3-2A to 3-2E.

23. Fontette, *Recherches*, pp. 70–74. Olivier-Martin (*Histoire du droit français*, p. 265) discusses only the consent of the donor's immediate lord.

24. On this practice, see Fontette, *Recherches*, p. 71; and above, n. 22.

25. Thorne, "English Feudalism."

26. On this practice in France, see Laplanche, *La réserve coutumière*, pp. 35, 73; and Olivier-Martin, *Histoire du droit français*, p. 263. For more elaborate discussions of the English practice of making feoffments to the tenant and his heirs, see Pollock and Maitland, *History*, 1:308, 2:13–14; and Thorne, "English Feudalism."

27. In addition to Thorne, "English Feudalism," see White, "Succession to Fiefs."

28. Thorne, "English Feudalism."

29. This elaboration on Thorne's argument is designed to deal with a practice that is not found, apparently, in England.

30. Pollock and Maitland, *History*, 2:248. It should be noted that Maitland rejected the argument that in England heirs or other relatives had "birth-rights" of this kind (ibid., 2:241–60).

31. On the question of whether acquisitions were freely alienable, see above, chap. 3, nn. 103–4 and accompanying text.

32. For examples of countergifts amounting to twelve *denarii* or less to consenting relatives, see, for example, V 51, 58, 72, 79, 121–22, 125, 126, 146, 158, 196, 203, 228, 241, 257, 290; MD 31, 166; MV 35, 177, 185; MB 25, 75.

33. See above, chap. 3, nn. 156–58 and accompanying text.

34. For examples of countergifts of ten *solidi* or more to consenting relatives, see V 104, 121–22, 139, 306; MD 54, 70, 91; MV 50, 177.

35. See, for example, MV 104, 116, 161; MB 28; MD 26, 117; V 701; A 252, 321.

36. See app., table 3-3.

37. See V 104, 158, 241, 287, 375; MV 50; MB 70.

38. Except in the cases cited above in n. 35, records of familial challenges do not indicate that challenges of this type postdated the deaths of the donors whose gifts were challenged.

39. See app., table 3-3.

40. In other words, they may have considered themselves to have the kind of birthrights to which Maitland alluded (see above, n. 30 and accompanying text).

41. See the examples cited above in n. 37. If theory 3 were universally valid, it would be hard to explain why, in numerous joint gifts, additional consenting relatives played less prominent roles than the codonors did.

42. See Keesing, *Kin Groups*, pp. 92–93.

43. It is particularly difficult to see how consenting groups that included affines could have maintained any enduring corporate identity.

44. See above, n. 37.

45. On the need to explain the *laudatio* in different ways in discussing different periods, see Laplanche, *La réserve coutumière*, pp. 103, 110.

46. Falletti, *Le retrait lignager*, pp. 28–33; Laplanche, *La réserve coutumière*, pp. 104, 110; Ourliac and Malafosse, *Histoire du droit privé*, 2:424. See also below, chap. 6.

47. Laplanche, *La réserve coutumière*, pp. 104, 110.

48. Laplanche, *La réserve coutumière*, pp. 104, 110.

49. Fulbert, *Letters*, no. 51 (pp. 90–93).

50. Ibid., no. 51 (pp. 90–91). On the sources that Fulbert may have used, see ibid., no. 51 n. 1 (pp. 90–91).

51. A 364 (c. 1090). According to the judges, Vivianus had no right to the vineyards because the person who had granted them to him had had no right to them. For a fuller discussion of the case, see White, "Claims to Inheritances."

52. *Raoul de Cambrai*, verse 33, lines 684–85.

53. Ibid., verse 33, lines 700–701.

54. See above, chap. 3, n. 202 and accompanying text.

55. See above, chap. 4 at n. 156.

56. *Glanvill*, VII.1 (p. 70). The text goes on to state that this norm does not cover deathbed gifts.
57. Arguments of the second kind, if not the first, seem to underlie many familial challenges initiated by the sons-in-law of donors, on which see above, chap. 3, nn. 159–62 and accompanying text and app., table 3-3.
58. See Falletti, *Le retrait lignager*, p. 43.
59. Fulbert, *Letters*, no. 51 (pp. 92–93).
60. For a fuller discussion of this kind of argument, see below, chap. 6.
61. *Glanvill*, VII.1 (p. 70).
62. Laplanche, *La réserve coutumière*, pp. 54–61.
63. See above, chap. 3, n. 200 and accompanying text.
64. It is worth considering the possibility that deathbed gifts were the subject of lay criticism, not only because they were made at a moment when donors were very susceptible to pressure from monks, but also because they were likely to be made only for the spiritual benefit of the donor.
65. For examples, see MV 41; A 213, 299, 309, 638.
66. The fact that familial challengers were often given spiritual privileges, such as "society and benefit," suggests that they had previously been excluded from the kin group whose members were accorded such benefits in return for the gift that the challengers contested. For examples of "society and benefit" being granted to familial challengers, see MV 8, 44, 49; MD 26, 33, 55, 127, 129, 132, 133.
67. The hypothesis that preambles, in particular, were sometimes chosen with some regard to the nature of the transactions subsequently recorded is supported by documents in which preambles concerning marriage (V 492), manumission (MB 127), or oblation (N 9) are followed by charters concerned with the same subject.
68. On many of the ideas discussed below, see, in addition to the works cited above in chap. 3, n. 54, Brown, *The Cult of the Saints*; Brown, "The Rise and Function of the Holy Man" and "Society and the Supernatural"; Geary, "Echanges et relations"; Leclerq et al., *The Spirituality of the Middle Ages*; Rosenwein and Little, "Social Meaning"; Rosenwein, "Feudal War and Monastic Peace"; Vauchez, *La spiritualité*; Vicaire, *L'imitation des apôtres*.
69. These ideas are articulated in various ways in A 2, 3, 318; MB 8, 55; N 30, 65; T 58; V 282, 630.
70. T 58.
71. T 58; V 292.
72. V 292.
73. On the need to follow such precepts, see A 21, 22.
74. For a charter in which six such passages are quoted or paraphrased, see MB 68. A 136 cites three different passages.
75. Luke 11:41. MB 68; A 287; N 3.
76. Ecclus. 3:33. V 16, 829; N 18; MB 55, 68.

77. Ecclus. 29:15. MB 68; A 136.
78. Dan. 4:24. MB 68.
79. Tob. 4:11. MB 68.
80. Prov. 13:8. MB 68; A 136.
81. Luke 6:38. MV app. 33; V 765.
82. Ecclus. 12:3. A 136.
83. N 120. From Ecclus. 7:10.
84. Prov. 3:9. N 3.
85. A 36, 136; MB 8, 13, 68; MV app. 11, 15; N 8, 21, 56, 655; V 12, 184, 532, 605. Luke 16:9.
86. See N 344.
87. N 139.
88. N 139.
89. See above, chap. 2, n. 3.
90. MB 68.
91. On monastic charity at La Trinité, see Johnson, *Prayer*, pp. 158–62.
92. See above, chap. 2.
93. On martyrologies and other documents of this general type, see works cited above, chap. 2, n. 54. For a charter preamble stating that records should be kept to ensure not only that gifts would be remembered, but also that benefactors would be prayed for, see MB 12.
94. See A 8, 270, 345; MD 78; N 323, 464; T 122.
95. On malediction clauses, see above, chap. 2, n. 143 and accompanying text.
96. N 344; T 35; A 318. The last of these charters stresses the duty to procure prayers for *parentes*.
97. MB 7; MV 13.
98. For references to charters emphasizing the sinfulness of monastic benefactors, see above, n. 69.
99. See above, nn. 70–71.
100. On punishment in hell as an inheritance, see V 186.
101. See above, chap. 2, n. 3. For a passage in which future monks are represented as the heirs of the present ones, see MB 69. For a reference to the *hereditas* of a monastic community, see A 78. For passages stating that unborn kin who supported a gift should get an "eternal inheritance," see V 180, 186.
102. See, for example, the case of Odo Donkey Neck, discussed above in chap. 3 at n. 31.
103. See McLaughlin, "Consorting with Saints," esp. chap. 4.
104. See Geary, *Furta Sacra*, p. 22.
105. Brown, *The Cult of the Saints*, pp. 69–85.
106. On the church as "an artificial kin group," see Brown, *The Cult of the Saints*, p. 31.
107. Although this temporal schema is not fully set forth in any single charter from the documentary collections considered here, the passages cited above in the text accompanying nn. 69–95 clearly indi-

cate that gifts to saints took on their full meaning only when located in this temporal context.

108. Radcliffe-Brown, Introduction, p. 52.

109. Ibid., p. 49.

110. See Gregory, *Gifts and Commodities*, esp. pp. 18–20, 43–45.

111. Sahlins, "On the Sociology of Primitive Exchange," p. 148.

112. Evans-Pritchard, Introduction, pp. vii–viii. See also Mauss, *The Gift*, p. 1.

113. Falletti, *Le retrait lignager*, pp. 41–42; and below, chap. 6.

114. Lanfranc, *Letters*, no. 22 (pp. 104–5). Another letter of Lanfranc's forms part of a similar transaction:

> Archbishop Lanfranc sends greetings and his blessing to his beloved son and friend, Abbot Adelelm.
>
> These monks have come to me as their own accusers, saying that they have gravely sinned against you and that they are to blame for having withdrawn from their monastery. For my part I expatiated to them at length on their folly, rebuking them in the harsh and bitter language that their condition merited. Then I asked them if they desired to amend their life in the future; they answered that they did and that they grieved deeply for what they had done. They entreated me to intercede with you on their behalf and to make their peace with the monastery which they had left. In these circumstances I entreat you as a brother (if my entreaties carry any weight with you) that out of love for God and for me you forgive them wholeheartedly whatever injury they have done you and whatever offence they have committed against their monastic profession, and that you receive them back into the positions that they held before their offence; show them from now on such fatherly love that God may show mercy to you (*Letters*, no. 28 [pp. 113–15]).

115. For gifts of serfs in return for prayers, see, for example, *Livre des serfs*, nos. 4, 8, 31; and the works cited above in chap. 2, n. 6.

116. On the emphasis given to notions of exchange and reciprocity in the political and social thought of this period, see Duby, *The Three Orders*, esp. p. 161.

117. For an analysis of a remarkably well documented death from a slightly later period, see Duby, *William Marshall*, pp. 3–21.

118. V 69.

119. V 164.

120. V 170.

121. V 176.

122. V 414. For other gifts to Saint Vincent by dying donors, see, for example, V 59, 105, 149, 155, 166, 204, 207, 216, 247, 261, 263, 275, 357,

377, 484, 496, 523, 526, 541, 544, 688, 721, 728, 735, 783, 791. For gifts to Saint Aubin by dying donors, see, for example, A 250, 311, 409, 410, 412, 759, 872, 896, 897, 929.

123. For gifts to Saint Vincent in return for which the donor acquired burial rights, see, for example, V 39 (donor's W as well as donor), 69, 75 (donor's W and S, as well as donor), 131, 164, 176, 204, 275, 313 (donor's W and Ss, as well as donor), 338 (donor's W, as well as donor), 340 (donor's W, as well as donor), 439 (donor's Ss and Ds, as well as donor), 458, 752, 784. For grants of burial rights to a donor's kin, see, in addition to several of the charters just cited, V 66 (M), 147 (Z), 267 (W), 350 (W), 368 (S), 550 (S). For other transactions in which burial rights were accorded to lay people, see MV 49, 52, 56, 70, 83, 86, 96, 102, 107, 118; MV app. 24, 64; T 374, 476, 526, 565.

124. V 66.

125. V 110.

126. V 147.

127. V 155.

128. V 267. For other examples, see V 288, 368, 516, 664, 823; A 309, 310, 841; MV 58.

129. For cases involving the donor's entrance into an abbey, see V 30, 39, 70, 74, 102, 129, 136, 137, 143, 193, 197, 200, 207, 275, 285, 291, 328, 346, 356, 358, 379, 382, 441, 464, 473, 474, 491, 508, 520, 526, 534, 554, 598, 614, 634, 635, 645, 721, 748, 759, 768, 777, 778, 799, 820, 841. In some of the cases just cited, the donor was about to die. For cases involving the entrance of the donor's relative into an abbey, see V 61 (nepos), 71 (filiolus), 140 (WF), 313 (S), 329 (B), 354 (S), 355 (S), 384 (infant S), 447 (S), 520 (S), 618 (B), 640 (B), 646 (S), 682 (S), 752 (B), 766 (S), 820 (S), 841 (S), 842 (S).

130. V 233, 375, 522.

131. See Goody, Death, Property and the Ancestors, esp. pp. 3–46; Huntington and Metcalf, Celebrations of Death, pp. 65–67.

132. In order to stress the symbolic or extraeconomic significance of participation in exchange ceremonies, it is not necessary to slight the economic importance of the items exchanged.

133. Mauss, The Gift, pp. 47, 48.

134. V 398.

135. On Old English wergeld payments, see, for example, Loyn, Anglo-Saxon England, p. 296.

136. See Evans-Pritchard, Kinship and Marriage, pp. 74–99; and the essays collected in Comaroff, The Meaning of Marriage Payments.

137. See Evans-Pritchard, The Nuer, p. 89; and Evans-Pritchard, Kinship and Marriage, p. 89.

138. See the charters cited above in n. 97.

139. Gurevic, "Représentations et attitudes," p. 529.

140. A 325.

141. Gurevic, "Représentations et attitudes," pp. 530–38.

142. See, for example, Duby, "Lineage, Nobility, and Knighthood,"
     pp. 60, 87; Duby, "The Structure of Kinship," p. 139.
143. Gurevic, "Représentations et attitudes," pp. 530–38.
144. Geary, "L'humiliation des saints."

CHAPTER 6

1. See above, chap. 3, n. 5.
2. See above, app., tables 3-1A to 3-1E.
3. Bloch, *Feudal Society*, pp. 133–43, esp. pp. 130–33, 139.
4. Ibid., pp. 130–31.
5. Ibid., p. 133. Not having undertaken a precise quantitative analysis,
   Bloch exaggerated the prevalence of the *laudatio*.
6. Ibid., p. 132.
7. Falletti, *Le retrait lignager*, pp. 44–61.
8. Ibid.
9. Bloch, *Feudal Society*, p. 133.
10. Ibid., p. 132.
11. Ibid., p. 132.
12. Ibid., pp. 138–39.
13. Ibid., p. 139.
14. Ibid., p. 139.
15. Ibid., p. 139.
16. Ibid., p. 139.
17. Ibid., pp. 130–33.
18. For Duby's most important comments on the *laudatio*, see *La société*,
    pp. 66, 221, 367; and "Lineage, Nobility, and Knighthood," pp. 69–
    71.
19. See below, text accompanying nn. 65–82.
20. Although Bloch did not clearly indicate when the *laudatio* first be-
    came common, authors on whom he relied, notably Laplanche (*La ré-
    serve coutumière*, p. 68) had already argued that it became prevalent
    only in the tenth century.
21. Duby, *La société*, p. 221 and p. 66 n. 85.
22. Ibid., p. 221 and n. 14.
23. Ibid., pp. 366–67.
24. Ibid., p. 367 and n. 24.
25. Ibid., pp. 65, 219–20, 367.
26. Ibid., p. 66 n. 85 and p. 221. Duby also noted that a donor's kin
    rarely witnessed his gifts in this period (ibid., p. 66 n. 84) and that
    familial challenges were rarely successful (ibid., p. 66 and n. 87).
27. Ibid., pp. 65–66.
28. Ibid., p. 221.
29. Ibid., p. 221.
30. Ibid., p. 221 n. 14.

31. Ibid., pp. 221–22.
32. Ibid., pp. 219–20.
33. Ibid., p. 221.
34. Ibid., p. 367.
35. For an outline of this argument of Duby's about the history of the medieval family, see Thirsk, "The Family."
36. Duby, *La société*, p. 122.
37. Ibid., p. 122; see also pp. 64–66, 215.
38. Ibid., pp. 215–24.
39. Ibid., pp. 215–24.
40. Ibid., p. 367.
41. Poly and Bournazel, *La mutation féodale*, p. 187.
42. Bloch had noted, however, that "governmental authorities, through their activities as guardians of the peace, had weakened the kinship bond" (*Feudal Society*, p. 139).
43. Duby, *La société*, p. 122.
44. Ibid., p. 215.
45. Ibid., p. 122.
46. Ibid., p. 217.
47. Ibid., pp. 122, 367.
48. See below, text accompanying nn. 65–82.
49. Fossier, *La terre*, 1:262–73.
50. Ibid., 266.
51. Ibid., 266–69.
52. Ibid., 263–65. Eliminated from this sample were alienations by secular and ecclesiastical magnates (ibid., 263 n. 63).
53. Ibid., 266.
54. Ibid., 266.
55. Ibid., 266 and the graphs on 264, 265.
56. Ibid., 267.
57. Ibid., 267–69.
58. Ibid., 269–70.
59. Ibid., 269–70.
60. Ibid., 270.
61. Ibid., 270.
62. Ibid., 270–77.
63. Ibid., 272.
64. Ibid., 273.
65. Duby, "Lineage, Nobility, and Knighthood," pp. 69–71.
66. In "Lineage, Nobility, and Knighthood," Duby dealt with various topics not previously discussed in *La société* and also drew on his previous analyses of noble genealogies in "The Structure of Kinship and Nobility" and "French Genealogical Literature." In *The Three Orders* and *The Knight*, he broadened the scope of his inquiries even further so as to focus, respectively, on political ideology and marriage.
67. "Lineage, Nobility, and Knighthood," p. 69.

68. Ibid., p. 69.
69. Ibid., p. 71.
70. Ibid., p. 72.
71. Ibid., p. 75.
72. Duby, *The Knight*, pp. 93–94.
73. Ibid., p. 94.
74. Duby's discussion of marriage and kinship in *The Knight*, esp. pp. 87–106, where the *laudatio* is not directly treated, should be read in conjunction with the argument in "Lineage, Nobility, and Knighthood."
75. This association is made in "Lineage, Nobility, and Knighthood," esp. pp. 79–80 and, in a different way, in *The Three Orders*, pp. 147–66.
76. "Lineage, Nobility, and Knighthood," pp. 68–69. See also "The Structure of Kinship," p. 147.
77. "The Structure of Kinship," p. 147.
78. Ibid., p. 147. The contrast made by Duby between families organized horizontally and families organized vertically is similar to the distinction made by Claude Meillassoux between "two distinct modes of social organization": "adhesion" and "kinship" (*Maidens, Meal and Money*, p. 21). "In the band," where "adhesion" predominates,

> an individual's position depends on voluntary, unstable and reversible relationships in which he is involved for the limited period during which he actively participates fully in common activities. Kinship relations, on the other hand, are imposed by birth; they are lifelong, statutory and intangible, and it is on their basis that the individual's position in productive and reproductive relations are defined at the different stages of his life. In the former case society is constantly being reconstructed around the free movement of individuals between different bands; in the latter, individuals are subject to established norms of social reproduction within the limits of the lineage into which they are born. In the one, social membership is an individual affair, in the other it is transmitted from one generation to the next (ibid., p. 18).

Both Meillassoux's distinction and Duby's are associated with the notion that different kinds of kin groups are associated with different modes of production.
79. See above, n. 43. Fossier employed the same image (see above, n. 56).
80. Duby, "Lineage, Nobility, and Knighthood," p. 79.
81. See, for example, *The Three Orders*, p. 151, where Duby refers to "the head of the household's utter dominion [over] all his kin by blood, by marriage, or by rites of adoption—everyone he 'fed,' as it were, his servants, dependents, and slaves."
82. See Duby, *The Three Orders*, esp. pp. 147–66.
83. See Herlihy, "Land, Family, and Women"; Wemple, *Women in Frankish Society*, pp. 106–23; Gold, *The Lady and the Virgin*, pp. 116–44.

84. Hajdu, "Family and Feudal Ties" and "The Position of Noblewomen."
85. Hajdu, "The Position of Noblewomen," p. 127.
86. Ibid., pp. 125–26.
87. Hajdu, "Family and Feudal Ties," p. 121.
88. Ibid., p. 122.
89. Ibid., pp. 125–26.
90. Ibid., p. 126.
91. Ibid., p. 126.
92. See "Lineage, Nobility, and Knighthood."
93. Hajdu, "Family and Feudal Ties," p. 127.
94. Ibid., p. 127.
95. Fossier, La terre, 1:263.
96. See, for example, the work of Laplanche, whose generalizations about the long-term history of the laudatio are unsupported by statistics (La réserve coutumière, pp. 66–114).
97. See above, n. 58.
98. Bloch, Feudal Society, p. 133; Fontette, Recherches, esp. pp. 28–29.
99. Southern, Western Society and the Church, pp. 240–72.
100. Southern, Western Society and the Church, p. 263.
101. See McLaughlin, "Consorting with Saints," pp. 329–412.
102. Lynch, Simoniacal Entry, pp. 36–50.
103. McLaughlin, "Consorting with Saints," pp. 349–78.
104. Ibid., pp. 329–411.
105. Ibid., pp. 349–78.
106. Ibid., pp. 386–411.
107. Ibid., pp. 378–86.
108. Ibid., pp. 413–65.
109. On incidental references in charters to the retrait lignager, see Falletti, Le retrait lignager, pp. 67–102 passim.
110. On incidental references in charters to the réserve coutumière, see Laplanche, La réserve coutumière, pp. 161–247 passim.
111. Falletti, Le retrait lignager, p. 7.
112. Laplanche, La réserve coutumière, p. 1.
113. Ibid., pp. 115–16.
114. Alienors: MD 211, 215, 216, 217, 218, 225, 226, 229, 232; lords: MD 212, 219, 220, 224; bishops: MD 208, 214, 223; deacons: MD 231, 245; officiales: MD 254, 255, 267, 276. These charters date from the period 1200 to 1274.
115. For examples of the newer type of record, see the charters cited above in chap. 3, n. 208.
116. On these methods of stabilizing transactions, see Tabuteau, "Transfers of Property," chap. 5.
117. See the documents cited above in n. 114, almost all of which were authenticated by seals and list no witnesses.
118. On warranty see Fontette, Recherches, pp. 91–101; Olivier-Martin, Histoire de la coutume, 1:25–36; Ourliac and Malafosse, Histoire du droit privé, 1:286; Floren, La vente immobilière, pp. 71–73; Tabuteau,

"Transfers of Property," pp. 803–26. Only during the course of the thirteenth century, according to Fontette, were the details of the later law of warranty fully worked out (*Recherches*, p. 97). Falletti makes it clear that during the period when the *laudatio parentum* was commonly practiced, a relative who gave it had no obligation to warrant the transaction he approved (*Le retrait lignager*, pp. 41–42).

119. T 688 (1233), 699 (1239), 717 (1259).

120. MB 302 (1264), 330 (1273); MD 246 (1232), 247 (1242), 249 (1244), 254 (1255), 265 (1262), 267 (1264), 271 (1269), 275 (1271), 278 (1288).

121. Of the charters cited in n. 120, see MD 249, 265, 267, 275.

122. See Thorne, "English Feudalism."

123. See below, text accompanying nn. 153–55.

124. See Falletti, *Le retrait lignager*, pp. 28–33; Laplanche, *La réserve coutumière*, pp. 81, 104–6.

125. Laplanche, *La réserve coutumière*, pp. 104–6. According to another view, members of consenting kin groups had always been acting in their capacities as heirs or potential heirs (Falletti, *Le retrait lignager*, p. 45).

126. The change discussed by Laplanche (*La réserve coutumière*, pp. 104–6), for example, cannot be clearly represented in the kinds of indices that writers on the quantitative history of the *laudatio* have generally employed. Fossier's procedure, which involves counting gifts approved only by eldest sons as individual gifts (*La terre*, 1:263), does not fully deal with this problem.

127. The date at which scribal conventions changed probably varied considerably from monastery to monastery and area to area.

128. For examples of the *laudatio* in thirteenth-century transactions involving Marmoutier, see MD 216 (1208), 220 (1210), 225 (1215), 226 (1216), 229 (1218), 231 (1222), 233 (1222), 234 (1222), 242 (1231), 249 (1244), 280 (1298–1300). This list suggests that the *laudatio* may have become less prevalent in the Dunois after the middle of the thirteenth century.

129. See Poly and Bournazel, *La mutation féodale*, p. 187.

130. See above, nn. 71–72.

131. See below, pp. 204–7.

132. See above, chap. 3, text accompanying nn. 207–11.

133. See Olivier-Martin, *Histoire du droit français*, p. 271.

134. See Fontette, *Recherches*, pp. 28–29. During the eleventh and early twelfth century, according to Fontette, the distinction between sale and gift was not clearly understood (ibid., pp. 19–20). See also Chevrier, "Remarques sur la distinction" and "Evolution de la notion de donation."

135. Laplanche, *La réserve coutumière*, pp. 137–40.

136. Falletti, *Le retrait lignager*, pp. 81–82.

137. Ibid., pp. 62–93.

138. See Falletti, *Le retrait lignager*; and Laplanche, *La réserve coutumière*.

139. Duby, "Lineage, Nobility, and Knighthood," pp. 68, 71.
140. On the importance of specifying the precise context in which particular methods of kinship reckoning are used, see, for example, Goody, *The Development of the Family and Marriage*, pp. 222–27.
141. See above, esp. pp. 124–29.
142. This is one corollary of Goody's argument in *The Development of the Family and Marriage*, pp. 222–27.
143. Poly and Bournazel make the same point about tenth-century land transfers (*La mutation féodale*, pp. 187–88).
144. See above, n. 72.
145. This is one of the implications of Falletti's contention that "le *laudator* n'est point constitué, de par son approbation, garant de l'acte vis-à-vis des tiers; à cet effet, un engagement spécial de fidejussion demeure nécessaire" (*Le retrait lignager*, p. 42). If the obligation to warrant or serve as a *fidejussor* had to be voluntarily assumed, then a monastic benefactor could not be sure that after he died, a relative of his would assume this duty.
146. See Falletti, *Le retrait lignager*; and Laplanche, *La réserve coutumière*.
147. See above, n. 9.
148. See Thorne, "English Feudalism."
149. On the differences between English and French law during the thirteenth century, see Bloch, *Feudal Society*, p. 133, where he notes that in England the *retrait lignager* was found only in certain municipal customs. Previously, Maitland had noted that if asked to comment on English law, Beaumanoir would have been struck by the fact that in England, "There is no *retrait lignager*; the landowner can sell or give without the consent of his heir" (Pollock and Maitland, *History*, 2:446).
150. T 667.
151. T 745.
152. See above, chap. 3, n. 201 and accompanying text.
153. Although the fact that quitclaims by familial challengers were sometimes approved by relatives of theirs suggests that certain challenges of this kind were not made solely on behalf of individuals, our finding that the *laudatio* was given less often in the case of quitclaims than it was in the case of gifts suggests that in a significant number of cases, familial challengers were not supported by any kin. See app., tables 3-1A, 3-1B, 3-1C, 3-1D, and 3-1E.
154. See above, n. 40.
155. On the history of warranty in England, see the works cited above in chap. 3 at n. 9.
156. See Herlihy, *Medieval Households*, pp. 82–83.
157. MB 8 (1032–47).
158. MD 267 (1264).
159. MB 8. This familiar biblical passage is from Luke 16:9.
160. MD 267.

161. MB 8. The biblical passage is from Matt. 25:34.
162. MD 267.
163. MB 8.
164. MD 267.
165. On other ties linking Salomon and his kin to Marmoutier, see above, chap. 3, nn. 111–15 and accompanying text.

Bibliography

PRIMARY SOURCES

Cartularies and Collections of Charters

Cartulaire d'Azé et du Géneteil. Edited by du Broussay. In vol. 3 of Archives historiques du Maine, pp. 49–146. Le Mans, 1903.

Cartulaire de l'abbaye cardinale de la Trinité de Vendôme. 5 vols. Edited by Charles Métais. Paris, 1893–1904.

Cartulaire de l'abbaye de Noyers. Edited by C. Chevalier. Mémoires de la Société archéologique de Touraine, vol. 22. Tours, 1872.

Cartulaire de l'abbaye de Saint-Aubin d'Angers. 3 vols. Edited by Bertrand de Broussillon. Paris, 1903.

Cartulaire de l'abbaye de Saint-Martin de Pontoise. 2 vols. Edited by J. Depoin. Pontoise, 1895–1904.

Cartulaire de l'abbaye de Saint-Vincent du Mans. Edited by R. Charles and Menjot d'Elbenne. Mamers, 1886–1913.

Cartulaire de Marmoutier pour le Dunois. Edited by Emile Mabille. Châteaudun, 1874.

Cartulaire de Marmoutier pour le Perche. Edited by Philibert Barret. Mortagne, 1894.

Cartulaire de Marmoutier pour le Vendômois. Edited by A. de Trémault. Vendôme, 1893.

Cartulaire manceau de Marmoutier. 2 vols. Edited by E. Laurain. Laval, 1911–40.

Liber Controversiarum Sancti Vincentii Cenomannensis, ou Second cartulaire de l'abbaye de Saint-Vincent du Mans. Edited by A. Chédeville. Paris, 1968.

Livre Blanc de Saint-Florent de Saumur. Archives départementales du Maine-et-Loire, H 3713.

Livre des serfs de Marmoutier. . . . Edited by A. Salmon. Paris, 1845.

Marmoutier: Cartulaire blésois. Edited by Charles Métais. Blois, 1889–91.

Other Primary Sources

Anselm of Canterbury. *The Prayers and Meditations of St Anselm.* Translated by Benedicta Ward. Harmondsworth, England, 1973.

Dhuoda. *Manuel pour mon fils.* Edited and translated by Pierre Riché, Bernard de Vregille, and Claude Mondesert. Sources Chrétiennes, vol. 225. Paris, 1975.

Fulbert of Chartres. *The Letters and Poems of Fulbert of Chartres.* Edited and translated by Fredrick Behrends. Oxford Medieval Texts. Oxford, 1976.

Garin le Loherain. Translated by A. Paulin Paris. Paris, 1862.

Guibert of Nogent. *Self and Society in Medieval France: The Memoirs of Abbot Guibert of Nogent (1064?–c. 1125)*. Edited and translated by John F. Benton. New York, 1970.

Helgaud of Fleury. *Vie de Robert le Pieux: Epitoma Vitae Regis Rotberti Pii*. Edited and translated by Robert-Henri Bautier and Gillette Labory. Sources d'histoire médiévale, vol. 1. Paris, 1965.

John of Salisbury. *The Statesman's Book of John of Salisbury* [books IV, V, VI and selections from books VII and VIII of the Policraticus]. Translated by John Dickinson. New York, 1963.

Lanfranc of Canterbury. *The Letters of Lanfranc, Archbishop of Canterbury*. Edited and translated by Helen Clover and Margaret Gibson. Oxford Medieval Texts. Oxford, 1979.

Raoul de Cambrai: Chanson de geste. Edited by P. Meyer and A. Longnon. Société des anciens textes français. Paris, 1882.

Thomas Aquinas. *The Political Ideas of St. Thomas Aquinas: Representative Selections*. Edited by Dino Bigongiari. New York, 1953.

The Treatise on the Laws and Customs of the Realm of England Commonly Called Glanvill. Edited and translated by G. D. G. Hall. London, 1965.

Le très ancien coutumier de Normandie. In vol. 1 of *Coutumiers de Normandie*. Edited by Ernest-Joseph Tardif. Paris, 1881.

SECONDARY SOURCES

Ariès, Philippe. *The Hour of Our Death*. Translated by Helen Weaver. New York, 1980.

Auffroy, Henri. *Evolution du testament en France des origines au XIIIe siècle*. Paris, 1899.

Baldwin, John W. "The Intellectual Preparation for the Canon of 1215 against Ordeals." *Speculum* 36 (1961): 613–36.

Barnard, Alan, and Anthony Good. *Research Practices in the Study of Kinship*. ASA Research Methods in Social Anthropology, vol. 2. London, 1984.

Bartlett, Robert. *Trial by Fire and Water: The Medieval Judicial Ordeal*. Oxford, 1986.

Becker, Marvin. *Medieval Italy: Constraints and Creativity*. Bloomington, Indiana, 1981.

Beer, Max. "Communism." In vol. 4 of the *Encyclopedia of the Social Sciences*, edited by R. A. Seligman, pp. 81–86. New York, 1931.

Beitscher, Jane K. " 'As the Twig is Bent . . .': Children and Their Parents in an Aristocratic Society." *Journal of Medieval History* 2 (1976): 181–92.

Berlière, Ursmer. "Les confraternités monastiques au moyen âge." *Revue liturgique et monastique* 11 (1926): 134–42.

————. "Les confréries bénédictines au moyen âge." *Revue liturgique et monastique* 12 (1927): 135–45.

Biebuyck, Daniel P. "Land Tenure." In vol. 4 of the *International Encyclope-*

dia of the Social Sciences, edited by R. A. Seligman, pp. 562–66. New York, 1931.

Bloch, Marc. *Feudal Society*. Translated by L. A. Manyon. Chicago, 1961.

Boinet, Amédée. "L'illustration du cartulaire du Mont-Saint-Michel." *Bibliothèque de l'Ecole des Chartes* 70 (1909): 335–43.

Boissevain, Jeremy. *Friends of Friends: Networks, Manipulators, and Coalitions*. 1974. Reprint. London, 1978.

Bongert, Yvonne. *Recherches sur les cours laïques du Xe au XIIIe siècle*. Paris, 1944.

Bouchard, Constance B. "The Structure of a Twelfth-Century Family: The Lords of Seignelay." *Viator* 10 (1979): 39–56.

Bourdieu, Pierre. *Outline of a Theory of Practice*. Translated by Richard Nice. Cambridge Studies in Social Anthropology, edited by Jack Goody, no. 16. Cambridge, England, 1977.

Boussard, Jacques. *Le comté d'Anjou sous Henri Plantagenêt et ses fils (1151–1204)*. Paris, 1938.

———. "L'origine des familles seigneuriales dans la région de la Loire moyenne." *Cahiers de civilization médiévale*, 5 (1962): 303–32.

———. "La vie dans le comté d'Anjou aux XIe et XIIe siècles." *Le Moyen Age*, 56 (1950): 29–68.

Brissaud, Jean. *A History of French Private Law*. Translated from the 2d French ed. by Rapelje Howell. Continental Legal History Series, vol. 4. Boston, 1912.

Brown, Peter. *The Cult of the Saints: Its Rise and Function in Latin Christianity*. Haskell Lectures on History of Religions, n.s. 2. Chicago, 1981.

———. "The Rise and Function of the Holy Man in Late Antiquity." In Peter Brown, *Society and the Holy in Late Antiquity*, pp. 103–52. London, 1982.

———. "Society and the Supernatural: A Medieval Change." In Peter Brown, *Society and the Holy in Late Antiquity*, pp. 302–32. London, 1982.

Bullough, D. A. "Early Medieval Social Groupings: The Terminology of Kinship." *Past and Present* 45 (1981): 3–18.

Bur, Michel. *La formation du comté de Champagne v.950–v.1150*. Nancy, 1977.

Bynum, Caroline Walker. "The Body of Christ in the Later Middle Ages: A Reply to Leo Steinberg." *Renaissance Quarterly* 39 (1986): 399–439.

———. *Holy Feast and Holy Fast: The Religious Significance of Food to Medieval Women*. Berkeley, 1987.

———. *Jesus as Mother: Studies in the Spirituality of the High Middle Ages*. Publications of the Center for Medieval and Renaissance Studies, UCLA, vol. 16. Berkeley, 1982.

Cailteaux, L. "Note sur le délai d'exercice de l'action en retrait lignager dans le droit coutumier rémois." *Revue historique de droit français et étranger* 29 (1951): 93–96.

———. "La solidarité familiale dans la région rémoise au XIVe siècle." *Revue historique de droit français et étranger* 42 (1964): 283–89.

Calisse, Carlo. *A History of Italian Law*. Translated by Layton B. Register. Continental Legal History Series, vol. 8. 1928. Reprint. New York, 1969.

Charles-Edwards, T. M. "Kinship, Status and the Origins of the Hide." *Past and Present* 56 (1972): 3–33.

Chartrou, J. *Anjou de 1109–1151: Foulque de Jerusalem et Geoffroi Plantagenêt*. Paris, 1928.

Chédeville, André. "Avant-Propos." In *Liber Controversiarum*, edited by A. Chédeville, pp. 9–14. Paris, 1968.

———. *Chartres et ses campagnes, XIe–XIIIe siècles*. Paris, 1973.

———. "Etude de la mise en valeur et du peuplement du Maine aux XIe siècle, d'après les documents de l'abbaye de Saint-Vincent du Mans." *Annales de Bretagne* 67 (1960): 209–25.

———. "Notice historique: Le domaine de l'abbaye de Saint-Vincent: Sa formation; ses aspects." In *Liber Controversiarum*, edited by A. Chédeville, pp. 35–70. Paris, 1968.

———. "Les restitutions d'églises en faveur de l'abbaye de Saint-Vincent du Mans." *Cahiers de civilizations médiévales* 3 (1960): 209–17.

Chénon, E. *Histoire générale du droit français public et privé*. 2 vols. Paris, 1926–29.

Chevalier, C. *Histoire de l'abbaye de Noyers au XIe et au XIIe siècles d'après les chartes*. Mémoires de la Société archéologique de Touraine, vol. 23. Tours, 1873.

Chevrier, G. "Evolution de la notion de donation dans les chartes de Cluny du IXe à la fin du XIIe siècle." In *A Cluny: Congrès scientifique*, pp. 203–9. Dijon, 1950.

———. "Remarques sur la distinction de l'acte à titre gratuit d'après les chartes du Rouergue au XIIe siècle." In *Etudes d'histoire du droit dediées à M. Auguste Dumas*, Annales de la Faculté de Droit d'Aix, no. 43, pp. 67–78. Aix-en-Provence, 1950.

Cheyette, Fredric L. "Custom, Case Law and Medieval Constitutionalism: A Reexamination." *Political Science Quarterly* 78 (1963): 362–90.

———. "The Invention of the State." In *Essays in Medieval Civilization: The Walter Prescott Webb Memorial Lectures*, edited by Bede Karl Lackner and Kenneth Roy Phillip, pp. 143–76. Austin, Tex., 1979.

———. "Suum Cuique Tribuere." *French Historical Studies* 6 (1970): 287–99.

Clanchy, M. T. *From Memory to Written Record: England, 1066–1307*. London, 1979.

Colman, Rebecca V. "Reason and Unreason in Early Medieval Law." *Journal of Interdisciplinary History* 4 (1974): 571–96.

Collet, Peter, ed. *Social Rules and Social Behaviour*. Totowa, N.J., 1977.

Comaroff, J. L., ed. *The Meaning of Marriage Payments*. Studies in Anthropology. London, 1980.

Comaroff, J. L., and Simon Roberts. "The Invocation of Norms in Dispute Settlement: The Tswana Case." In *Social Anthropology and Law*, edited by Ian Hamnett, pp. 77–112. London, 1977.

————. *Rules and Processes: The Cultural Logic of Dispute in an African Context*. Chicago, 1981.

Constable, Giles. "The *Liber Memorialis* of Remiremont." *Speculum* 47 (1972): 261–77.

————. *Medieval Monasticism: A Select Bibliography*. Toronto Medieval Bibliographies, no. 6. Toronto, 1976.

————. *Monastic Tithes from Their Origins to the Twelfth Century*. Cambridge, England, 1964.

Cowdrey, H. E. J. *The Cluniacs and the Gregorian Reform*. Oxford, 1970.

————. "Unions and Confraternity with Cluny." *Journal of Ecclesiastical History* 16 (1965): 152–62.

Dawson, John P. *Gifts and Promises: Continental and American Law Compared*. New Haven, Conn., 1980.

Depoin, J. *Les relations de famille au moyen âge: Recherches préliminaires*. Pontoise, 1914.

Donahue, Jr., Charles. "What Causes Fundamental Legal Ideas? Marital Property in England and France in the Thirteenth Century." *Michigan Law Review* 78 (1979): 59–88.

Dopsch, Alfons. *The Economic and Social Foundations of European Civilization*. London, 1937.

Duby, Georges. *The Age of the Cathedrals: Art and Society, 980–1420*. Translated by E. Levieux and B. Thompson. Chicago, 1981.

————. *The Chivalrous Society*. Translated by Cynthia Postan. 1977. Reprint. Berkeley, 1980.

————. *The Early Growth of the European Economy: Warriors and Peasants from the Seventh to the Twelfth Century*. Translated by Howard B. Clark. Ithaca, N.Y., 1974.

————. "The Evolution of Judicial Institutions." In Georges Duby, *The Chivalrous Society*, pp. 15–58. Berkeley, 1980.

————. "French Genealogical Literature." In Georges Duby, *The Chivalrous Society*, pp. 149–57. Berkeley, 1980.

————. *The Knight, the Lady and the Priest*. Translated by Barbara Bray. New York, 1984.

————. "Lineage, Nobility and Knighthood." In Georges Duby, *The Chivalrous Society*, pp. 59–80. Berkeley, 1980.

————. *Medieval Marriage: Two Models from Twelfth-Century France*. Translated by E. Forster. Baltimore, 1978.

————. "The Middle Ages." In Georges Duby and Robert Mandrou, *A History of French Civilization*, translated by James Blakely Atkinson, pp. 3–196. New York, 1964.

————. *Saint Bernard et l'art cistercien*. 1976. Reprint. Paris, 1979.

————. *La société au XIᵉ et XIIᵉ siècles dans la région mâconnaise*. 1953. Reprint. Paris, 1971.

————. "The Structure of Kinship and Nobility." In Georges Duby, *The Chivalrous Society*, pp. 134–48. Berkeley, 1980.

————. "Structures familiales aristocratiques en France du Xe siècle en rapport avec les structures de l'état." In *L'Europe aux IXe–XIe siècles: Aux origines des états nationaux*, edited by T. Manteuffel and A. Gieysztor, pp. 57–62. Warsaw, 1968.

————. *The Three Orders: Feudal Society Imagined*. Translated by Arthur Goldhammer. Chicago, 1980.

————. *William Marshall: The Flower of Chivalry*. Translated by Richard Howard. New York, 1985.

Duby, Georges, and Guy Lardreau. *Dialogues*. Paris, 1980.

Dunbabin, Jean. *France in the Making, 843–1180*. Oxford, 1985.

D'Espinay, Georges. *Les cartulaires angévins: Etude sur le droit de l'Anjou*. Angers, 1864.

Evans-Pritchard, E. E. Introduction to *The Gift: Forms and Functions of Exchange*, by Marcel Mauss. Translated by Ian Cunnison, London, 1970.

————. *The Nuer: A Description of the Modes of Livelihood and Political Institutions of a Nilotic People*. 1940. Reprint. New York, 1971.

————. *Kinship and Marriage among the Nuer*. Oxford, 1951.

Falletti, Louis. *Le retrait lignager en droit coutumier français*. Paris, 1923.

Floren, R. *La vente immobilière en Provence au moyen âge et sous l'ancien régime*. Aix-en-Provence, 1956.

De Fontette, F. *Recherches sur la pratique de la vente immobiliere (X^e–XIVe siècles)*. Paris, 1957.

Fossier, Robert. *Enfance de l'Europe: Aspects économiques et sociaux*. 2 vols. Paris, 1982.

————. *Histoire sociale de l'Occident médiéval*. Paris, 1970.

————. "Les structures de la famille en occident au moyen âge." In vol. 2 of the *XVe Congrès international des sciences historiques*, pp. 225–35. Bucarest, 1980.

————. *La terre et les hommes en Picardie jusqu'à la fin du XIIIe siècle*. 2 vols. Paris, 1968.

Fox, Robin. *Kinship and Marriage: An Anthropological Perspective*. 2d ed. Cambridge, England, 1983.

Freeman, J. D. "On the Concept of the Kindred." *Journal of the Royal Anthropological Institute* 91 (1961): 192–220.

Gantier, Odile. "Recherches sur les possessions et les prieurés de l'abbaye de Marmoutier du Xe au XIIIe siècles." *Revue Mabillon* 53 (1963): 93–110, 161–64; 54 (1964): 15–24, 56–67, 125–35; 55 (1965): 32–44, 65–79.

Geary, Patrick J. "Echanges et relations entre les vivants et les morts dans la société du Haut Moyen Age." *Droit et Cultures*. Forthcoming.

————. *Furta Sacra*. Princeton, N.J., 1978.

————. "L'humiliation des saints." *Annales E. S. C.* 34 (1978): 27–42.

————. "Vivre en conflit dans une France sans état: typologie des mécanismes de règlement des conflits (1050–1200)." *Annales E. S. C.* 42 (1986): 1107–33.

Geertz, Clifford. *The Interpretation of Cultures: Selected Essays.* New York, 1973.

——. "Religion as a Cultural System." In Clifford Geertz, *The Interpretation of Cultures,* pp. 87–125. New York, 1973.

——. "Thick Description: Toward an Interpretative Theory of Culture." In Clifford Geertz, *The Interpretation of Cultures,* pp. 3–30. New York, 1973.

Geertz, Hildred, and Clifford Geertz. *Kinship in Bali.* Chicago, 1975.

Geiger, George Raymond. *The Theory of the Land Question.* New York, 1936.

Génestal, Robert. "Le retrait lignager en droit normand." In *Travaux de la semaine d'histoire du droit normand tenue à Jersey. . ., 1923,* pp. 191–236. Caen, 1925.

Génicot, L. *Les généalogies.* Fasc. 15 of Typologie des sources du moyen âge occidental, edited by L. Génicot. Turnhout, 1975.

Giddens, Anthony. *Capitalism and Modern Social Theory: An Analysis of the Writings of Marx, Durkheim and Max Weber.* Cambridge, England, 1971.

Gold, Penny Schine. *The Lady and the Virgin: Image, Attitude, and Experience in Twelfth-Century France.* Chicago, 1985.

Goody, Jack. *Death, Property, and the Ancestors: A Study of the Mortuary Customs of the Lodagaa of West Africa.* London, 1962.

——. *The Development of the Family and Marriage in Europe.* Cambridge, England, 1983.

——, ed. *The Developmental Cycle in Domestic Groups.* Cambridge, England, 1971.

Gregory, C. A. *Gifts and Commodities.* London, 1982.

Guillot, Olivier. *Le comte d'Anjou et son entourage au XIe siècle.* 2 vols. Paris, 1972.

Gurevic, A. [Aaron J. Gourevitch]. *Les catégories de la culture médiévale.* Translated by Helene Courtin and Nina Godneff. Paris, 1983.

——. "Représentations et attitudes à l'égard de la propriété pendant le haut moyen âge." *Annales E. S. C.* 27 (1972): 523–47.

——. "Wealth and Gift-Bestowal among the Ancient Scandinavians." *Scandinavica* 7 (1968): 126–38.

Hajdu, Robert. "Family and Feudal Ties in Poitou, 1100–1300." *Journal of Interdisciplinary History* 8 (1977): 117–28.

——. "The Position of Noblewomen in the Pays des Coutumes, 1100–1300." *Journal of Family History* 5 (1980): 122–44.

Hallam, Elizabeth M. *Capetian France, 987–1328.* 1980. Reprint. London, 1983.

Halphen, Louis. *Le comté d'Anjou au XIe siècle.* Paris, 1906.

Harris, Marvin. *The Rise of Anthropological Theory: A History of Theories of Culture.* New York, 1968.

Herlihy, David. "Church Property on the European Continent, 701–1200." In David Herlihy, *The Social History of Italy*, Chapter 5. London, 1978.

———. "Family Solidarity in Medieval Italian History." In David Herlihy, *The Social History of Italy*, Chapter 7. London, 1978.

———. "Land, Family and Women in Continental Europe, 701–1200." In David Herlihy, *The Social History of Italy*, Chapter 6. New York, 1978.

———. "Mapping Households in Medieval Italy." *Catholic Historical Review* 58 (1972): 1–23.

———. *Medieval Households*. Cambridge, Mass., 1985.

———. "Numerical and Formal Analysis in European History." In *The New History: The 1980s and Beyond*, edited by Theodore K. Rabb and Robert I. Rotberg, pp. 115–36. Princeton, 1982.

———. *The Social History of Italy and Western Europe, 700–1500: Collected Studies*. London, 1978.

Humphreys, Sally. "Law as Discourse." In *The Discourse of Law*, edited by Sally Humphreys. *History and Anthropology* 1 (1985): 241–64.

Huntington, Richard, and Peter Metcalf. *Celebrations of Death: The Anthropology of Mortuary Ritual*. Cambridge, England, 1979.

Huyghebaert, N. *Les documents nécrologiques*. Fasc. 4 of Typologie des sources du moyen âge occidental, edited by L. Génicot. Turnhout, 1972.

Hyams, Paul. "The Common Law and the French Connection." In vol. 4 of *Proceedings of the Battle Conference on Anglo-Norman Studies*, edited by R. Allen Brown, pp. 77–92, 196–202. London, 1981.

———. "Henry II and Ganelon." *Syracuse Scholar* 4 (1983): 22–35.

———. "Trial by Ordeal: The Key to Proof in the Early Common Law." In *On the Laws and Customs of England: Essays in Honor of Samuel E. Thorne*, edited by Morris S. Arnold et al., pp. 90–126. Chapel Hill, N.C., 1981.

———. "Warranty and Good Lordship in Twelfth-Century England." California Institute of Technology Humanities Working Paper, no. 116. Pasadena, 1986. Reprint with modifications. *Law and History Review*. Forthcoming.

Johnson, Penelope D. *Prayer, Patronage and Power. The Abbey of La Trinité de Vendôme, 1032–1187*. New York, 1981.

Keesing, Roger M. *Kin Groups and Social Structure*. New York, 1975.

Kronman, Anthony T. *Max Weber*. Stanford, 1983.

Lancaster, Lorraine. "Kinship in Anglo-Saxon Society." *British Journal of Sociology* 9 (1958): 234–48 and 359–77.

De Laplanche, J. *La réserve coutumière dans l'ancien droit français*. Paris, 1925.

Laslett, Peter. *Introduction to Household and Family in Past Time*, edited by Peter Laslett, pp. 1–89. Cambridge, England, 1972.

Latouche, Robert. "Fustel de Coulanges, Numa Denis." In vol. 6 of the

International Encyclopedia of the Social Sciences, edited by R. A. Seligman, pp. 43–44. New York, 1931.

———. *Histoire du comté du Maine pendant le Xe et le XIe siècles*. Paris, 1910.

Lawrence, C. H. *Medieval Monasticism: Forms of Religious Life in Western Europe in the Middle Ages*. London, 1984.

Leacock, Eleanor Burke. Introduction to *The Origin of the Family, Private Property, and the State. . .* , by Frederick Engels. New York, 1972.

Leclerq, Jean, F. Vandenbrouke, and L. Bouyer. *The Spirituality of the Middle Ages*. Translated by the Benedictines of Holmes Eden Abbey, Carlisle. Vol. 2 of *A History of Christian Spirituality*. London, 1968.

Le Goff, Jacques. *The Birth of Purgatory*. Translated by Arthur Goldhammer. London, 1984.

———. "Le rituel symbolique de la vassalité." In Jacques Le Goff, *Pour un autre moyen âge: Temps, travail et culture en occident: 18 essais*, pp. 349–420. Paris, 1977.

Lemarignier, Jean-François. *La France médiévale: Institutions et société*. Paris, 1970.

———. "La dislocation du 'pagus' et le problème des 'consuetudines' (X^e-XIe siècles)." In *Mélanges . . . Louis Halphen*, pp. 401–10. Paris, 1951.

———. "Les institutions ecclésiastiques en France de la fin du XIe au milieu du XIIe siècle." In Jean-François Lemarignier, Jean Gaudemet, and Guillaume Mollat, *Les institutions ecclésiastiques*, pp. 3–139. Vol. 3 of *Histoire des institutions françaises au moyen âge*, edited by Ferdinand Lot and Robert Fawtier. Paris, 1962.

Lesne, Emile. *Les églises et les monastères: Centres d'acceuil, d'exploitation et du peuplement*. Vol. 6 of *Histoire de la propriété ecclésiastique en France*. Lille, 1943.

Lewis, I. M. *Social Anthropology in Perspective: The Relevance of Social Anthropology*. Harmondsworth, England, 1976.

Leyser, Karl. "Maternal Kin in Early Medieval Germany." *Past and Present* 49 (1970): 126–34.

Little, Lester. "La morphologie des malédictions monastiques." *Annales E. S. C.* 34 (1978): 43–60.

———. *Religious Poverty and the Profit Economy in Medieval Europe*. Ithaca, N.Y., 1978.

Loyn, H. R. *Anglo-Saxon England and the Norman Conquest*. London, 1962.

———. "Kinship in Anglo-Saxon England." In vol. 3 of *Anglo-Saxon England*, edited by Peter Clemoes, pp. 197–209. Cambridge, England, 1974.

Lukes, Steven. *Individualism*. Oxford, 1973.

Lynch, Joseph. *Simoniacal Entry into Religious Life from 1000 to 1260: A Social and Economic Study*. Columbus, Ohio, 1976.

Macfarlane, Alan. *The Origins of English Individualism*. Oxford, 1978.

McLaughlin, Molly Megan. "Consorting with Saints: Prayers for the Dead in Early Medieval French Society." Ph.D. diss., Stanford University, 1985.

Magnou-Noirtier, Elisabeth. "Les mauvaises coutumes en Auvergne, Bourgogne méridionale, Languedoc et Provence au XIe siècle." In *Structures féodale et féodalisme dans l'occident méditerranéen (X^e–XIIIe siècles): Bilan et perspectives de recherches.* Vol. 44 of Collection de l'Ecole Française de Rome, pp. 135–72. Rome, 1980.

Maines, Clark. "Good Works, Social Ties, and the Hope for Salvation: Abbot Suger and Saint Denis." In *Abbot Suger and Saint Denis: A Symposium,* edited by Paula Lieber Gerson, pp. 77–94. New York, 1986.

Martène, Edmond. *Histoire de Marmoutier.* Mémoires de la Société archéologique de Touraine, vol. 24. Tours, 1874.

Martindale, Janet. "The French Aristocracy in the Early Middle Ages: A Reappraisal." *Past and Present* 75 (1977): 4–45.

Mascard-Hermann, Nicole. *Les reliques des saints: Formation coutumière d'un droit.* Paris, 1975.

Mauss, Marcel. *The Gift: Forms and Functions of Exchange in Archaic Societies.* Translated by Ian Cunnison. London, 1970.

Meillassoux, Claude. *Maidens, Meal and Money: Capitalism and the Domestic Community.* Cambridge, England, 1981.

Meinhard, H. M. "The Patrilineal Principle in Early Teutonic Kinship." In *Studies in Social Anthropology: Essays in Memory of E. E. Evans-Pritchard,* edited by J. H. M. Beattie and R. G. Lienhardt, pp. 1–29. Oxford, 1975.

Milsom, S. F. C. *Historical Foundations of the English Common Law.* 2d ed. Toronto, 1981.

———. "Law and Fact in Legal Development." *University of Toronto Law Journal* 17 (1967): 1–19.

———. *The Legal Framework of English Feudalism.* Cambridge, England, 1976.

Mollat, Michel. "Les moines et les pauvres, XIe–XIIe siècles." In *Il monachesimo e la riforma ecclesiastica (1049–1122).* Settimana internazionale di studio, 4th. Passo della Mendola, 1968. Vol. 6 of Miscellanea del Centro di studio medioevali, pp. 193–215. Milan, 1971.

Morris, Colin. "*Judicium Dei*: The Social and Political Significance of the Ordeal in the Eleventh Century." In *Church, Society and Politics,* edited by Derek Baker. Vol. 12 of Studies in Church History, pp. 95–111. Oxford, 1975.

Olivier-Martin, F. *Histoire de la coutume de la prévoté et victomté de Paris.* 3 vols. Paris, 1922–30.

———. *Histoire du droit français des origines à la révolution.* 1948. Reprint. Paris, 1984.

Ourliac, Paul. "Le retrait lignager dans la coutume de Bordeaux." *Revue juridique et économique du Sud-ouest* 37 (1961): 3–44, 117–51.

Ourliac, Paul, and Jean-Louis Gazzaniga. *Histoire du droit privé français de l'an mil au code civil.* Paris, 1985.

Ourliac, Paul, and J. de Malafosse. *Histoire du droit privé.* 3 vols. Vol. 1, *Les obligations.* 2d ed., Paris, 1969. Vol. 2, *Les biens.* 2d ed., Paris, 1971. Vol. 3, *Le droit familiale.* Paris, 1968.

Oury, G. "La reconstruction monastique dans l'Ouest. . . ." *Revue Mabillon* 54 (1964): 69–124.

Palmer, Robert C. "The Origins of Property in England." *Law and History Review* 3 (1985): 1–50.

Partsch, Gottfried. *Das Mitwirkungsrecht der Familiengemeinschaft im älteren Walliser Recht (Laudatio Parentum et Hospicium).* Geneva, 1955.

Poirier-Coutansais, Françoise, and Cécile Souchon. *Guide des archives de Maine-et-Loire.* Angers, 1978.

Pollock, Sir Frederick, and Frederic William Maitland. *The History of English Law before the Time of Edward I.* 2d ed. of 1898. Reprint. Cambridge, England, 1968.

Poly, Jean-Pierre, and Eric Bournazel. *La mutation féodale (X^e–XIIe siècles).* Paris, 1981.

Radcliffe-Brown, A. R. *Introduction to African Systems of Kinship and Marriage,* edited by A. R. Radcliffe-Brown and Daryll Forde, pp. 1–85. London, 1950.

Radding, Charles M. "Superstition to Science: Nature, Fortune and the Passing of the Medieval Ordeal." *American Historical Review* 84 (1979): 945–69.

Reynolds, Susan. *Kingdoms and Communities in Western Europe, 900–1300.* Oxford, 1984.

_____. "Law and Communities in Western Christendom, c. 900–1140." *American Journal of Legal History* 25 (1981): 205–224.

Roberts, Simon. *Order and Dispute: An Introduction to Legal Anthropology.* Harmondsworth, England, 1979.

Rosenthal, Joel T. *The Purchase of Paradise: Gift Giving and the Aristocracy, 1307–1485.* London, 1972.

Rosenwein, Barbara H. "Feudal War and Monastic Peace: Cluniac Liturgy as Ritual Aggression." *Viator* 2 (1971): 129–57.

_____. *Rhinoceros Bound: Cluny in the Tenth Century.* Philadelphia, 1982.

Rosenwein, Barbara H., and Lester K. Little. "Social Meaning in the Monastic and Mendicant Spiritualities." *Past and Present* 63 (1974): 4–32.

Sahlins, Marshall D. "On the Sociology of Primitive Exchange." In *The Relevance of Models for Social Anthropology,* edited by Michael Banton, pp. 139–236. London, 1965.

Schlatter, Richard. *Private Property: The History of an Idea.* New Brunswick, N.J., 1951.

Schneider, David M. *A Critique of the Study of Kinship.* Ann Arbor, Mich., 1984.

Schmid, Karl, and Joachim Wollasch. "Die Gemeinschaft der Lebenden und Verstorbenen in Zeugnissen des Mittelalters." *Frühmittelalterliche Studien* 1 (1967): 265–405.

Southern, R. W. *Western Society and the Church in the Middle Ages.* Vol. 2 of the *Pelican History of the Church*. Harmondsworth, England, 1970.

Stenton, Sir Frank. *The First Century of English Feudalism, 1066–1166*. 2d ed. Oxford, 1961.

Tabuteau, Emily. "Transfers of Property in Eleventh-Century Norman Law." Ph.D. diss., Harvard University, 1975.

Thirsk, Joan. "The Family." *Past and Present* 27 (1964): 116–22.

Thorne, S. E. "English Feudalism and Estates in Land." *Cambridge Law Journal* n.s. 6 (1959): 193–209.

Ungar, Roberto Mangebeira. *Law in Modern Society: Toward a Critique of Social Theory*. New York, 1976.

Vauchez, André. *La spiritualité du moyen âge occidental, viiie–xiie siècles*. Paris, 1975.

Vicaire, M. H. *L'imitation des apôtres: Moines, chanoines, mendiants, ive–xiiie siècles*. Paris, 1963.

Vigneron, B. "La vente dans le mâconnais du XIe au XIIIe siècle." *Revue historique de droit français et étranger* 5th ser. 39 (1959): 17–47.

Vodola, Elisabeth. *Excommunication in the Middle Ages*. Berkeley, 1986.

Weinberger, Stephen. "Les conflits entre clercs et laïcs dans la Provence du XIe siècle." *Annales du Midi* 92 (1980): 269–79.

Wemple, Suzanne. *Women in Frankish Society: Marriage and the Cloister, 500–900*. Philadelphia, 1981.

Wheaton, Robert. "Family and Kinship in Western Europe: The Problem of the Joint Family Household." *Journal of Interdisciplinary History* 5 (1975): 601–28.

White, Stephen D. "Claims to Inheritances and Legal Argument in Western France, ca. 1050–ca. 1150." *Traditio*. Forthcoming.

———. "Feuding and Peace-Making in the Touraine around the Year 1100." *Traditio*. Forthcoming.

———. "'Pactum . . . Legem Vincit et Amor Judicium': The Settlement of Disputes by Compromise in Eleventh-Century Western France." *American Journal of Legal History* 22 (1978): 281–308.

———. "Succession to Fiefs in Early Medieval England." *Past and Present* 65 (1974): 118–27.

White, Stephen D., and Richard T. Vann. "The Invention of English Individualism: Alan Macfarlane and the Modernization of Pre-modern England." *Social History* 8 (1983): 345–63.

Wollasch, Joachim. "Les obituaires, témoins de la vie clunisienne." *Cahiers de civilization médiévale* 22 (1979): 139–71.

Yver, Jean. "Les caractères originaux du groupe de coutumes de l'ouest de la France." *Revue historique de droit français et étranger* 4th ser. 29 (1952): 18–79.

———. *Egalité entre héritiers et exclusion des enfants dotés: Essai de géographie coutumière*. Paris, 1966.

Index

DATE DUE

APR 03 1997 MAR 2 6 1997		
MAY 1 – 2004		
JUL 2 3 2004 APR 1 4 2016		

DEMCO 38-297